A Free Trade Association

Prepared under the Auspices of
The Centre for International Studies, New York University

A Free Trade Association

Edited by Thomas M. Franck and Edward Weisband

Thomas M. Franck
Jacob K. Javits
Edward Weisband
Robert G. Hawkins
Maxwell Stamp
Harry Cowie
H. Edward English
Harry G. Johnson

London: University of London Press Limited
New York: New York University Press

SBN 340 09865 1

Published by University of London Press Ltd 1970
First published in the U.S.A. by New York University Press 1968

University of London Press Ltd
St Paul's House, Warwick Lane, London EC4

Printed in Great Britain by
Clarke, Doble & Brendon Ltd, Plymouth

Foreword

These essays offer together one of the few really serious and constructive contributions to the study of world economic and trade policy published in recent years. They are all the more interesting, because they have been written by British American and Canadian authors, all acknowledged experts on these issues in their own countries; and the book follows a lively discussion at New York University in the spring of 1968.

The main thesis of this book will, I believe, gain steadily growing acceptance by informed opinion everywhere, as its implications are understood. The objective set out is indeed as ambitious as any properly conceived grand design must be. But in this case it is practicable, because it accords with economic and political realities. It is proposed by the authors that the world should follow up the successes of the post-war Marshall Aid Plan, and of the Kennedy Round, and the aspirations of UNCTAD, by the launching of a world-wide Free Trade Association, open for all to join, without distinction of continent, race or internal politics, but with far-reaching non-reciprocal privileges for the trade of the developing countries. Such an association, like EFTA, would have the blessing of GATT; and the success of EFTA, as an industrial free trade area without supranational or other restrictive barriers, proves that it is practicable.

There is no doubt, in my judgment, that this liberal conception, whatever the precise details, is at once the logical next step after the GATT, Dillon and Kennedy Rounds, the most feasible way of achieving a rapid expansion of world trade and employment, and far the most effective method of speeding up economic development and a rise in living standards in the grievously poor countries outside Western Europe and North America. If you could at once establish at least industrial free trade among the advanced countries, including North America and Japan, thereby rapidly increasing their demand for imports, and throw open their markets to the less developed nations, you would transform the economic prospect before the poorer countries. You would also be pursuing a trade and economic policy which fitted admirably into the expansion of IMF facilities by means of Special Drawing Rights which is now going forward.

You would also open up for the U.K. a future far brighter and more promising than any other broad strategy can offer. For the U.K. would retain the right, vital for its economic and political vigour, to import food and materials at economic prices from those countries able to produce them most efficiently; and at the same time would enjoy far wider tariff-free markets for its industrial exports than any single continent – America or Europe – can ever supply. We should not be bound to burden our cost of living or balance of payments with the crippling load which would follow our joining the European Economic Community in its present form; nor should we lose the present precious free entry rights enjoyed by our exports within the Commonwealth, developed and undeveloped. It would of course be open for the EEC itself to join such an enterprise; and it would be elementary wisdom for it to do so, though if it refused at first, the world-wide association could go forward without it.

I have little doubt that if the U.S. and U.K. adopted this broad policy as their aim, it would soon gather the political momentum in the Atlantic world achieved by the Marshall Plan and the Kennedy Round. Compared with such immense possibilities, a policy by the U.K. of merely joining the EEC Six would be narrow, inward-looking, insular and parochial. I hope this book will spread an even wider understanding of the far-reaching prospect; which would be opened up by a world-wide initiative of this kind, and of the lasting credit which would rightly accrue to those nations which first took the lead.

Douglas Jay

The Free Trade Association Project

A group of businessmen, writers, political and trade union leaders, economists, and lawyers from Canada, Great Britain, and the United States has met for two days, February 17–18, at the Center for International Studies of New York University. It has worked with five draft studies prepared by the N.Y.U. Center for publication in October, 1968, and has held discussions with economists who have recently published "Atlantic Trade Studies" in Britain and the Montreal-based research series "Canada in the Atlantic Economy." The group has reached the following consensus:

1. The conclusion of the Kennedy Round of Tariff negotiations and the rejection of Britain's application and those of other countries to join the European Community create the need for new initiatives towards multilateral trade liberalization and the promotion of economic growth on a worldwide scale.

2. The discussions held at the N.Y.U. University Seminar and the draft studies here considered indicate that such a new initiative might well take the form of a free trade association in industrial products of the United States, Canada, Great Britain, and other EFTA countries, to their mutual economic and political benefit.

3. A free trade association of the kind examined should be outward-looking and open to others to join. To this end further research is to be undertaken into the implications of including other industrial nations and groupings such as those of the European Free Trade Association, the European Community, Japan, Ireland, Australia, and New Zealand, as well as of special beneficial relationships with the developing nations.

4. The conclusions of these discussions set out in the preceding paragraphs should be given the most earnest attention and consideration by governments, leaders of opinion, and the public in the countries represented at this seminar.

THE STATEMENT OF THE FTA–NYU CONFERENCE HAS BEEN ENDORSED BY:

Hon. Theodore C. Achilles
James Baechle, Esq.
Mr. Peter Bessel, M.P.
Congressman Jonathan B. Bingham
Professor Gordon C. Bjork
Sir George Bolton
Mr. Fraser W. Bruce
Sir Arthur Bryant
Lord Caccia
Professor George E. G. Catlin
Hon. J. V. Clyne
Professor Richard N. Cooper
Rt. Hon. Frank Cousins
Mr. Harry Cowie
Professor Stanley A. de Smith
Professor H. Edward English
Professor Thomas M. Franck
Rt. Hon. Hugh Fraser, M.P.
Sir Roy Harrod
Professor Robert G. Hawkins
Mr. Andrew Hay
Mr. John W. Holmes
Senator Jacob K. Javits
Rt. Hon. Douglas Jay, M.P.
Professor Harry G. Johnson
Professor Peter B. Kenen
Hon. Eric Kierans, M.L.A.
The Hon. Marcel Lambert, P.C., M.P.
Mr. Sperry Lea
Professor James Edward Meade
Mr. Alfred Morris, M.P.
Mr. Justice N. T. Nemetz
Professor Andre Raynauld
Professor Arthur Schlesinger
Mr. Kenneth Spang
Hon. Maxwell Stamp
Mr. Ralph I. Straus
Viscount Watkinson, P.C., C.H.
Professor Edward Weisband
Commander Edward Whitehead, C.B.E.

Contents

Foreword to Peaceful Change Studies
Thomas M. Franck v

Statement of the Conference on a Free Trade Association, New York University, February 17-18, 1968 vii

Introduction
Jacob K. Javits xi

A Study of the Political Implications of a Free Trade Association
Thomas M. Franck and *Edward Weisband* 3

I. Purpose of This Study 3

II. What is the Free Trade Association 4

III. The Political Case for American Participation in a Free Trade Association 8

IV. Current Alternatives for Britain 23

V. The Political Case for British Participation in a Free Trade Association 29

VI. The Political Case for Canadian Participation in a Free Trade Association 43

VII. The Choice for the Future 47

The Economic Impact on the United States of a U.K.-Canada-U.S. Free Trade Association
Robert G. Hawkins 53

I. Introduction 53

II. A Preliminary View of a Canadian-U.K.-U.S. Free Trade Association (FTA) 57

III. The Direct Effects on U.S. Trade and Economic Welfare 67

IV. Import Competition and Domestic Adjustment 81
V. Indirect Production Effects 92
VI. U.S. Foreign Investment and an FTA 100
VII. Adjustment Burdens of FTA Membership 109
VIII. Additional FTA Members and the Impact on the U.S. 113
IX. Summary 117
Appendix 120

The Economic Consequences for Britain of a Free Trade Association
Harry T. Cowie and *Maxwell Stamp* 151
I. The Multilateral Alternative 151
II. The Free Trade Association Option 162

Canada's Economic Interests in Trade Liberalization
H. Edward English 191
I. Canada and World Trade 192
II. Short-Run Influences on Canadian Trade Patterns 199
III. Longer-Run Trade Determinants 201
IV. Implications of Free Trade for the Canadian Economy 206
V. Locational Forces: A Summary 212
VI. The Relative Merits for Canada of the Traditional GATT Approach and the Free Trade Association Approach 220

The Monetary Implications of a Free Trade Association
Harry G. Johnson 225
I. Introduction 225
II. The International Monetary System 228
III. Possibilities of International Monetary Cooperation in an FTA 235

INTRODUCTION

Changes in World Economics and Political Balance Demand Study of a Free Trade Association

by Jacob K. Javits

As a trustee and member of the President's Council of New York University's Center for International Studies, I extend a warm welcome to the distinguished participants of this conference. As a United States citizen and Senator, I want to extend our heartfelt gratitude to the many distinguished political, academic, and business leaders from the United Kingdom and Canada who have journeyed so far to participate in this conference which could have such a historic role in the future of our country and of the free world.

We are here to consider a free trade association to include our three countries and such other industrialized and trading nations as choose to join. We meet under the auspices of a great university and draw upon the wisdom of academic experts. The issue, however, is of practical importance in consideration of urgent international economics and political questions—it is not academic at all.

When in 1965 I first addressed myself to the possibility of such a Free Trade Association, I was dealing with a theory. But time and events have caught up with us and changes in the structure of world economics and political power demand that we begin to test our theories against present realities and that we find answers to our problems before they overwhelm us.

Now what are the realities:

—The nations of western Europe tend to believe that the United States has become preoccupied in Asia, and has been diverted from the maintenance of its European ties;
—President de Gaulle continues to insist on French domination of the European Common Market, and shows no signs of wavering in his determination to keep Britain out of the EEC;
—The pound sterling has been devalued and Britain has taken austerity measures which reduce the effectiveness of the pound as international reserve currency.

The harshest reality of all, as far as the Western community of nations is concerned, is the present situation of Britain. How will its future role be affected as a leading factor in international security, diplomacy, and finance? It is clear that unless some decisive steps are taken there is a real possibility of further drift and deterioration of Britain's overall economic position.

Well nigh stripped of empire, drained by two world wars, excluded from the European Economic Community, the United Kingdom cannot carry on a world role from a position of economic isolation. Because the United States, Canada, and the entire Western world need the strength, the wisdom, and the leadership of the United Kingdom, we must work to overcome that enforced economic isolation. In my judgment, the Free Trade Association proposal is a practical and reasonable way to do it. It would not only throw the United Kingdom a lifeline in its time of distress but provide the United Kingdom government and people with a means of getting out of economic danger through their own efforts.

The FTA concept is important for other reasons too, beyond the present plight of the United Kingdom. To me and to many others, the concept of a Free Trade Association represents the next step in the continuing effort to liberalize world trade.

Obviously, there is a great feeling of brotherhood and common heritage between the peoples of the United States,

Canada, and Britain. But we cannot—or should not—proceed on this basis. What we are talking about here is not philanthropy; it is reality. The Western world needs Britain as much as Britain needs the Western world. This is an exercise in enlightened self-interest for all concerned.

I wish to emphasize that I favored—and continue to favor—the admission of the United Kingdom into the EEC, and that the Free Trade Association idea was proposed by myself and others only as an alternative. With Britain facing no immediate prospect of EEC membership, however, I feel that the alternative of the FTA must be considered now in more practical terms. Basic decisions designed to restore the economic health of Britain and the Western world simply might be too long deferred if we await solution to the question of British membership in the EEC, or even associate membership.

Let us take the lead here today, so that it can be said in years to come that we saw an impending economic crisis in Europe and worked as valiantly as we could to head it off before it was too late. I, for one, consider it my duty to bring these studies to the attention of the highest authorities in my government and I respectfully urge those of you in a similar position to do likewise.

In assessing the situation that now confronts us, it is essential to bear in mind the fact that the postwar arrangements in Europe depend on Britain being a major power there. Should economic factors compel Britain to withdraw from its military and political commitments in Germany and Berlin, the most unsettling and dangerous consequences would ensue. Present arrangements, while providing at least some stability, could rapidly come undone and bring on a volatile and potentially explosive situation in central Europe.

This prospect is certainly one that should give pause to the leaders of France—on whom it seems to be making no impression—and to the leaders of all western European nations. A sober realization that nothing less than the stability of Europe is involved in Britain's well-being and financial situation should be the common platform from which the Atlantic community of nations—the entire Western community of nations in fact—proceeds. Nor can central Europe and the U.S.S.R. be unconcerned: dislocation of the *status quo* in the Federal Republic of Germany and Western Berlin abruptly and in response to financial stringency could create grave problems and tensions for them, too.

It would be altogether too tempting a target for opponents to resist. If they took advantage of it because of the inviting target, it would involve a crisis far greater than any which now faces the United States and its Western allies.

Therefore, the concept of a Free Trade Association composed initially of Canada, Britain, and the United States could be of vital importance.

What gives the FTA concept relevance and importance? The five papers that will be discussed today and tomorrow examine this question in great detail but I would like to give you my beliefs, which were the basis originally for my proposal, and the reasons why, in my judgment, FTA is worthy of serious consideration.

1. FTA could provide the economic base to support the capacity of the United Kingdom to continue to perform a significant economic and political role in the world.

2. FTA could result in the harmonization of national economic policies of its members without encroaching upon essential national political sovereignty.

3. FTA could meet this need described in Prof. Franck's paper "... Britain needs an association with other states which will preserve her freedom of initiative in the Afro-Asian part of the Commonwealth, while relating the British home market and defense establishment to much larger units to effect economies of scale and provide a growing home market for her industrial production."

4. FTA could also be looked upon as a means to strengthen sterling and the U.S. dollar as international reserve currencies. Britain's membership in a large and viable industrial and trading community would strengthen world confidence in the viability of the sterling and take the pressure off the U.S. dollar.

5. FTA could well represent the next practical step after the Kennedy round to liberalize world trade. We are now facing a situation where regional trade groupings will be a fact of

life and where the unconditional most-favored nation principle will become applicable as between trading communities or associations rather than nations. The paper submitted by Theodore Geiger and Sperry Lea to the U.S. Congressional Joint Economic Committee's hearings on future U.S. trade policy last year conclude that the Free Trade Association concept promises to be relevant for the United States in any eventuality. If the next attempt at trade negotiations by the traditional multilateral approach fails—or, even possibly, is insufficiently promising to be attempted—then we would shift to the only other approach that is sanctioned by GATT, establishing a free trade area among willing countries as the first move toward a more generalized agreement. On the other hand, if another round of multilateral negotiations succeeds, then we would find ourselves so close to free trade that the GATT countries could commit themselves to full free trade at a fixed date and undertake other commitments as if they were in a formal Free Trade Association.

6. The FTA idea is also very relevant to the United States in its future relations to continental western Europe, which even after de Gaulle could very well be unwilling to accept our long cherished concept of an Atlantic Community unified economically and politically. FTA could then be an excellent parallel grouping to the EEC, pursuing parallel goals.

I would be the last to deny that it would be easy to bring FTA into being in view of prevailing opinion in the three countries involved or that it does not involve costs. You will find, however, that the three country studies show that the costs are acceptable, especially in view of the benefits to be shared, and in fact, preferable to those involved in permitting Britain to continue its drift and isolation.

I congratulate the participants of this conference for investing their time and energy in this exercise. I am confident that you will debate the studies presented to us in the most considered and practical terms. I hope you will be convinced as I am that the FTA proposal deserves the same kind of consideration in Washington, Whitehall, and Ottawa.

A Free Trade Association

A Study of the Political Implications of a Free Trade Association

by Thomas M. Franck
Edward Weisband

I. PURPOSE OF THIS STUDY

The purpose of this study is to examine the political and economic possibilities of a proposal, to advocate its acceptance but, at the same time, to question its feasibility.

The proposal is to establish a Free Trade Association for the purpose of creating, first, a free flow of goods, capital, and men; and, second, a more refined process of economic consultation among governments.

Because of limited time and resources this study has considered *the implications of a Free Trade Association for only three countries, which could serve as its core: Great Britain, Canada, and the United States.*

What are the exigencies which occasioned this study?

A group of economists, political leaders, industrialists, and professors in Britain, Canada, and the U.S. joined in November, 1966, to think about a *fall-back position* should Britain again fail to gain entry into the EEC during the then current round of discussions.

And indeed, even if such negotiations were still underway, this study could have been helpful to the negotiators in providing a fuller assessment of Britain's bargaining position and options.

Events have not conformed to the more optimistic expectations, and our study has been completed not, as originally intended, while negotiations between Britain and Europe were joined, but with the negotiators' massed flotillas lying becalmed in their harbors.

These developments placed the purpose of this study in new perspective. Reality has changed and we have no choice but to try to conform to its new requirements. Thus the reader is requested to confront the issues raised and the evidence presented here with a different set of questions from those which would have concerned him were Britain and the EEC now negotiating over terms of membership.

First, it is no longer profitable to compare other proposals with the formula that had Britain and other EFTA states join, strengthen, and liberalize the EEC. For the forseeable future, the merits of this formula have been rendered hypothetical. Second, there have arisen several other alternatives which are relevant in the new circumstances of today. They are:

1. a period of British *association* with the EEC during which it might play an economic but not a political role within the framework of the Treaty of Rome; and

2. an indefinite period prolonging the present situation, during which Britain could try to *"go it alone,"* aided by bilateral and multilateral trade agreements, as well as by traditional invisible bonds which constitute her special relationships to friendly countries and to communities such as NATO, WEU, and the Commonwealth.

These have become the *real* alternatives to which the proposal for a Free Trade Association should be compared.

II. WHAT IS THE FREE TRADE ASSOCIATION?

Senator Jacob K. Javits, one of the earliest advocates of a "fall-back" position for Britain should her EEC application fail, described his idea for a Free Trade Association on November 8, 1965, as a "treaty of free trade and economic co-operation with the UK, other EEC and EFTA (European Free Trade Area) nations, Canada, New Zealand and Australia, and other industrialized countries of the OECD (Organization for Economic Co-operation and Development) which agree to adhere to the new rules of trade of the free trade area."

Similar proposals have come from eminent economists in the United States,[1] Britain,[2] and Canada,[3] several of whom subsequently participated in the committee sponsoring this study.

The three principles of such a free trade area are: (1) a gradual phasing out, perhaps over a ten to fifteen year period, of all internal tariffs and other discriminatory restrictions on the movement of industrial products, capital goods, raw materials and investment capital[4] among the members, but not including, at this stage, agricultural products and not requiring members to adopt a common external tariff; (2) an open-endedness, permitting membership by any industrial nation willing to adhere to the system, including members of regional trading systems; and (3) development by systematic negotiation rather than by supernational political authority.

To avoid misunderstanding two emphatic disavowals must be made:

1. The proposal envisages no political federation or union between members of the trading association.

2. Neither does it argue for a club of white, Anglo-Saxon, or capitalist states pursuing a policy of exclusiveness.

Although Britain, Canada, and the United States have, by reason of practical necessity, been used as its focus, this study considers a trading association that is open to participation by any country that fits within its loose, pragmatic guidelines. Members of the European Free Trade Area might wish to join, as well as such industrially advanced nations as Japan, Australia, New Zealand, and possibly Latin American states. The rapid industrialization of countries like South Korea, Malaysia, and Kenya suggests that these, too, might soon be in a position to benefit from free trade.

Members of regional communities such as EEC and

COMECON might also wish to join the Free Trade Association by adhering to its reciprocal free trade rules. These communities might also join FTA as entities.

The FTA proposal clearly does not contemplate the establishment of a union of rich nations indifferent to the rest. Less-industrialized countries would require special tariff arrangements to protect their infant industries and clearly would not benefit by exposure to full membership in a Free Trade Association. However, they could benefit from transitional nonreciprocal arrangements for free access to the markets of the richer members of FTA. Some forms of special "associate" membership might also be worked out for developing countries nearing the "take off" phase. Such arrangements might soon be appropriate, for example, for Kenya and Malaysia.

The growth of the Free Trade Association to include as many states as are willing to go over to phased, reciprocal free trade on specific items is thus a key feature distinguishing the FTA proposal from the more restrictive regional blocs. Whereas the blocs perhaps tend to exclude, and thus set up rival supernationalisms, FTA would aim at an outward-looking, growing system of free trade that could one day include all nations and blocs of nations.

Indeed, the broadening of the base of the Free Trade Association to include nations other than the United Kingdom, U.S., and Canada is an important political, as well as economic, consideration. Whatever the economic findings indicate, there will be psychological problems inherent in any partnership between 200 million Americans, 25 million Canadians, and 55 million British. In the words of former Foreign Minister George Brown, Britain, in a trading area with Canada and the U.S. might be "a small country in a group which inevitably would be dominated by its one super-power member."[5] This widely shared suspicion would be alleviated if the Association were to extend itself to other states such as Japan, Australia, and New Zealand.

Fear of overwhelming U.S. predominance should be relieved further by basing FTA's decision-making machinery on the EFTA, rather than the EEC model—which is to say that decisions are negotiated by unanimous agreement of the representatives of sovereign members, rather than by majority vote of national representatives upon the recommendation of a supernational Commission.

One need not look beyond the political realities of Canada, the United States, and Great Britain to see that a supernational solution is not likely to be acceptable.

On the contrary, it is an essential part of the FTA proposal that it should provide the economic base to support, not limit the capacity of each member to pursue its independent inclinations in the world community.

That these inclinations—at least in the case of Canada, the United States, and Britain—rest on so many common interests and firm, institution-based assumptions—parliamentary democracy, independence of the judiciary, a stable system of political parties—should not obscure the existence of, and need for diversity. It should, on the contrary, enable diversity to flourish without endangering the element of unity necessary to the discharge of the trading area's economic functions.

If continuing diversity with broad common objectives is the fundamental political consideration of the Free Trade Association idea, it is essential also to its economic structure.

Article 9 of the EEC's Treaty of Rome provides that "The Community shall be based upon a customs union . . . *and the adoption of a common customs tariffs as against third countries*" (italics added). It adds that free movement of goods within the EEC shall extend not only to "products originating in the Member States" but also "to products coming from third countries which have entered the Common Market through any one of the Members."

It is this which most clearly distinguishes a Common Market from the Free Trade Association considered here.

Unlike a common market or federation, a Free Trade Association—while abolishing tariffs, for example, on products manufactured by Member States in trade between Members—would not impose a common external tariff but would permit each Member to retain for itself certain favorable relations with states outside the association.

Thus, a nation wishing to pursue its own special external

interest, the United States with Latin America, Britain with the Commonwealth, would be able to continue existing tariff concessions within the latitude provided by the GATT Agreement without all other FTA members having to make the same concessions. Problems that may result could be solved by an administrative system of control, including the use of certificates of origin to prevent one member with lower external tariffs leaking its imports to all the rest, as is done in EFTA under article 4 and Annex B of the Convention.

In summary: the viability of a Free Trade Association of the kind examined here must be judged (1) by its capacity to benefit economically each of the participants; (2) by the extent to which it is able to harmonize national economies and economic policies without encroaching upon essential national political sovereignty; and (3) by the degree to which it can lend support to the political pursuits, interests, and roles which the perspective members might choose to follow in the future.

These considerations are given further attention below in respect of each of the three countries studied.

III. THE POLITICAL CASE FOR AMERICAN PARTICIPATION IN A FREE TRADE ASSOCIATION

The Need for a New Economic-Political Initiative

The flow of international events rushes quickly even for great powers. How different the world is from the days when, only five years ago, the Trade Expansion Act of 1962 was passed. Then, as now, the arguments enlisted in the name of freer trade linked economic prosperity to the security of nations.

With this in view, Congress bestowed unprecedented powers upon the President permitting him to reduce tariffs on all but a few items by 50 per cent. Freer trade would lead to the domestic prosperity of the western European states which, in turn, would become full partners to the United States, so the argument ran. The Grand Strategy urged Britain and the EFTA countries into the EEC. Britain, especially, so close to the United States, so near to Europe, would serve as a link, as the crossbeam between the "twin pillars" of the Atlantic community.

Events have not flowed along the expected channels but have spilled rapidly in other directions. The Atlantic edifice is not about to be built. An inward looking EEC revolving about a Franco-German axis increasingly protected by a customs union, a little England with a devalued pound and no role east of Suez, and a fractured NATO, such is America's reality facing Europe.

In 1962, with the Trade Expansion Act, Congress tried to ward off the effects of an exclusivist EEC by enhancing the bargaining position of a U.S. Executive anxious to try an imaginative initiative. But other policies were less imaginative, and tended to work against the initiative. In the opinion of Professor H. Edward English, of Carleton University in Canada, "The end product of failure to push the industrial free trade area and of pushing too hard for British entry into the EEC appears to have been to weaken the U.S. bargaining position."[6]

The FTA proposal seeks to reestablish the American initiative in pursuit of trade liberalization by taking into account the changed circumstances of American foreign policy options and the U.S. national interest at the end of the 1960's.

The Need for a Balanced Two-Oceans Policy

The U.S., today as before, must pursue its policies on two fronts: one being the Atlantic Community, and the other Asia. The balance between these two has altered radically in the past five years. Today it can no longer be taken for granted that the U.S. can preserve its role as a two-ocean power, can maintain its traditional influence in western Europe and across the Pacific, without having the policies in these two areas cancel one another out, either through conflicts of purpose or as a result of an attrition of overextended resources.

It is notable that our pursuit of Asian priorities, and our growing involvement in Asia has been concurrent with a radical decline of U.S. influence in western Europe: that at the very time when we speak of a Marshall Plan for Asia we are seeing the erosion of the U.S. role in western Europe which the original Marshall Plan so successfully established.

To redress the balance of our two-oceans commitment is a prime political objective of the recommendations being made in this paper. The Free Trade Association proposal seeks to reenforce U.S. involvement in the North Atlantic, while retaining, rationalizing, and reenforcing the role of our Atlantic partners in ensuring the peace and developing the prosperity, in partnership with us, of the Pacific region.

There are two traps that a Free Trade Association approach will help avoid. The first is globalism, the second is isolationism. These are the maximalist and the minimalist approaches to world politics.

By globalism we mean the attempt to apply what is best for our country to the whole world, to do so in accordance with an image which closely approximates an idealization of our own society.

The knowledge that this cannot succeed may tempt some of us to the conclusion that because we cannot control all events everywhere we cannot influence any events at all.

Isolationism, therefore, like globalism, is an idealistic solution, in contrast to a pragmatic one. It is, in essence, a negative globalism. Like globalists, the isolationists refuse to attempt to work within pragmatic political parameters for the attainment of limited objectives which fall in the middle range between an ultimate ideal and certain unalterable present predicaments.

If a Free Trade Association succeeds in strengthening the British and Canadian economies to the point where British and Canadian initiatives in Europe and Asia substantially supplement and complement our own, and if this can be achieved at no economic cost to the United States, we will have secured the political viability of a limited two-oceans role without falling into either the globalist or isolationist traps. We will have built a policy which, while avoiding the impossible, makes maximum use of the possible. That these political advantages can be achieved through FTA without economic cost—a rare and happy eventuality in our foreign policy—is the conclusion of the economic studies that have been conducted by Professor Robert Hawkins and others at New York University's Center for International Studies.

British-United States Partnership in Global Responsibility

In evaluating American interests, therefore, it should be remembered that important advantages could accrue to the United States if Britain, economically bolstered in its present role by a Free Trade Association, were to continue to shoulder responsibility for the pursuit of diplomatic objectives which one might reasonably expect to be similar to those of the United States.

The point is that at no economic cost and with moderate economic gains, the United States could reduce its two-oceans dilemma. By crossing the Atlantic, by reviving the British economy, by providing the basis for a "Big England," the United States would be reaching across to the other side of the globe. Through a British surrogate east of Suez, the U.S. can promote stability in Asia without having to play the role of solitary global policeman.

The fact that it is desired by the nations of southeast Asia that Britain share in this peace-keeping task was made unequivocably clear by the Prime Minister of Singapore, Lee Kuan Yew, in late January, 1968. When Prime Minister Wilson announced his government's decision to withdraw British troops from southeast Asia by 1970, three to five years earlier than originally expected due to its trade deficit problem, Mr. Yew traveled to England to inform the British people that this was disastrous and to implore the British government to remain for the period of the original commitment. A precipitous British withdrawal would lead to Communist infiltration and a revolutionary situation throughout Malaysia, he indicated. Yet an American presence was not welcome as an alternative. Mr. Yew specifically wanted the British and only the British. It is to our interest to have the British play the role in Asia that their history and culture has taught them and which, by virtue of today's international circumstances, only they can play.

It should also be noted that the British military contingent in southeast Asia numbered approximately 48,000 men. Should the United States have to replace these forces, the costs would be more than double those to the British.[7]

But does Britain still have the will to play such a role, in view of its new interest in entering Europe? The answer appears to be that it does.

Mr. Heath, the most vociferous leader of the move to enter Europe, in a speech before the House of Commons stated, "I have not worked in my way as much as I could to achieve a wide European unity in order to take a lot of little Englanders into a mini-Europe . . . that has not been our conception." He strongly urged Britain to remain in southeast Asia and in the Persian Gulf for as long as she was wanted and needed.[8] An American could not have made a stronger plea.

If, through FTA the United States were to help create the economic conditions for a continuing British presence east of Suez, what gain would there be to the United States? We have already noted that it is unrealistic to suppose that the U.S. can play the role of policeman, counsellor, and friend to everyone, everywhere, simultaneously. Given this limitation, Britain (together with Canada) is undoubtedly America's best surrogate.

This is not a matter of domination. There is clear recognition in both nations of the identity between American and British interests. The history of relations between the two countries has not always been one of perfect harmony, to be sure. Professor Bruce Russett of Yale, in his study of Anglo-American relations, *Community and Contention: Britain and America in the Twentieth Century,* indicates that there has been as much contention as community between the two countries.[9] Yet "each remains the other's favorite foreign country among the populace,"[10] says Russett. He notes that there is a balance of cultural flows between the countries. Furthermore, at a time when many new countries with alien cultures are emerging, Russett notes that the common heritage of the two countries creates a contrast between them and the others, what Russett calls "the contrast effect."[11] He notes that elite approval of the other country has run very high throughout most of this century and that both elites view each other with a high

degree of "mutual predictability,"[12] Suez and Vietnam notwithstanding. The United States and Britain, therefore, already represent a "pluralistic security community"[13] that has had no expectations of war in this century. In fact, the American Joint Chiefs of Staff was originally established because there was no agency in the American government that corresponded to the British Joint Chiefs and therefore no American officer could speak with his British counterpart as a peer.

This identity of interests between Britain, Canada, and the United States is important in the greater Asian context despite strains over Vietnam; it is equally significant in the European context. And, it has become more important than ever in the light of the emerging political realities of present-day Europe.

A Continuing United States Responsibility in Europe

There are those who would attribute the new, inward-looking style of European politics wholly to President de Gaulle. It would follow from this that, after a time, France will return to the NATO fold along with the rest of Europe including Britain. It would be dangerous, however, to base U.S. policy wholly on this expectation. If it proves to be wrong, America should have ready a "fall back" position of its own. And it may well prove wrong to expect a return to the *status quo ante* after de Gaulle. A noted European diplomat and scholar, Professor E. H. van der Beugel, himself a close friend of the United States, has warned Americans against this kind of simplification. To blame Europe's growing separation from the United States solely on de Gaulle or even France, he says, is to

> . . . give France and French policy more importance than it really deserves. The changing character of the cold war, the reluctance toward a continued dependence of Europe on the United States, the changing circumstances of economic and monetary strength on both sides of the ocean, the preoccupation of the United States with its Pacific problems, all this would have arisen even without the destructive activities of our French allies.[14]

A Free Trade Association with the United States and Britain as two of its core members, seems to confirm the emerging political realities of the 1970's and provides the necessary economic foundation for them to work in our favor. But it does not represent a break with the Continental Six nor an attempt to divide irrevocably the Atlantic Community. The Free Trade Association would welcome the participation of the EEC, and, for so long as this cannot be realized, would serve as a lever for the U.S. and Britain in reducing further barriers to trade with the Common Market and in harmonizing the policies of the EEC and non-EEC nations.

For reasons discussed in earlier portions of this paper and adumbrated by Professor van der Beugel, it is necessary to envision a future in which the continental nations of western Europe come to rely increasingly upon each other and less upon the United States for maintaining their regional security for defining their economic interests, for determining their world policy. Further evidence to this effect was recently provided by Chancellor Kiesinger. In an editorial entitled "Gaullism, Bonn Version,"[15] *The New York Times,* itself an advocate of British entry into the EEC, stated, "Dr. Kiesinger even sounded like General de Gaulle when he said that in spite of ties to the Atlantic alliance and the United States, 'we should not seek our own future and . . . that of a united Western Europe within the fixed framework of a North Atlantic imperium.' Instead he envisioned 'an independent Europe, linked in friendship with America. . . .' This is pure Gaullism." *The New York Times* went on to say, "It moves the Federal Republic away from the Jean Monnet concept of a united Western Europe linked indissolubly to the United States and Canada." *The New York Times* also took cognizance of the fact that although Kiesinger wanted Britain to enter the Common Market, he would take no "meaningful stand" against France.

A study entitled *France, Germany and the Western Alliance: A Study of Elite Attitudes on European Integration and World Politics,*[16] by Karl W. Deutsch and others indicates that in the summer of 1964, 72 per cent of the elite tested in West Germany identified Germany's "long-term common interest" with the United States, whereas only 35 per cent identified such interests with EEC countries and only 28 per cent with France. This goes to show how quickly circumstances have changed. Such growing support for Gaullism, inside France and in other parts of western Europe at least militates against relying too heavily on the likelihood that these are transitory phenomena.

It should also be noted in this context, that a day later, March 14, *The New York Times*[17] published the results of a survey by SOFRES, a private French poll, showing that 61 per cent of people interviewed in France agreed with de Gaulle's foreign policy with only 13 per cent in disagreement.

We are here postulating a Europe that is not as we would prefer it, but as reality would have it. And reality requires us to reevaluate a policy no longer responsive to it.

For the past decade the United States has favored a British role in Europe in part because it was clearly in Europe's own interest, but also in part because it would serve American objectives. As President Johnson said on October 7, 1966, the "outlines of the new Europe are clearly discernible. It is a stronger, increasingly united but open Europe—with Great Britain a part of it— and with close ties to America."[18]

New York's prestigious Council on Foreign Relations has reported, in a 1963 study of the views of "leading citizens in thirty-two cities" of the United States that some felt that "disadvantages of British entry (into EEC) from the U.S. point of view would be non-existent" because of "the assurance of closer and more sympathetic response to U.S. views, which would result from Britain's having a major stake in the Market" and because of "the politics, traditions and temperament of the British which would weigh against any tendency of the Six to conceive their role in the narrow and inward way."[19]

More important, even those who saw disadvantages for the U.S. in the short-run resulting from British entry into the European Communities, felt sure that "Britain's entry will ultimately lead . . . to a much closer tie between the United States and the Common Market countries."[20]

More recently, the British economist, Hon. Maxwell

Stamp, has written, "Many English people, and even more Scots, even if they are shy of saying so, believe that if we were in Europe our views would predominate."[21]

But it is at least an open question whether, if Britain had been able to enter Europe in 1967 even in the company of other EFTA states, she would have succeeded in reorienting western European patterns of concern from their eastward and inward preoccupation and back toward the North Atlantic. One leading Cabinet Minister in the present Labor Government told the authors in a recent conversation, that the idea of the United States using Britain as a Trojan horse in Europe "was always a lot of waffle."

It has long been doubtful whether getting Britain into Europe would, in fact, achieve the expected reorientation of Europe back to the Atlantic concept. It was doubtful when British entry seemed probable and when Britain was approaching a fledgling European Community from a position of strength; it is much more doubtful now.

If Britain's entry into the European Communities were to mean, on balance, that not European but British foreign policy would have to be redirected, if the Atlantic Community were not to regain a continent but to lose an island kingdom, then it could no longer be an objective which the United States should welcome.

On the contrary, there would be no good reason for the United States to welcome, instead, the opportunity for the continuation of a close relationship with its principal European ally. However, it cannot be expected that the value of this relationship can be retained and enhanced unless it is given an economic basis sufficient to nourish its political potential. That political potential, to return to our opening proposition, certainly includes the mutually supportive roles Britain and the United States can play in their "home" region of the North Atlantic. But since both nations have a strong concern for, experience in, and commitment to the entire free world, the political potential is of worldwide significance.

The world is a round place as we long ago discovered. To go in one direction is to go in the other. So can it be in the world of politics, so must it be for the United States. The Free

Trade Association strengthens our Atlantic and Pacific ties, at no cost but with profit, at no risk but with increased security, without our becoming either globalist or isolationist, without our having to place Europe before Asia, Asia before Europe, and without a loss to either our national identity or political sovereignty.

Canadian-United States Partnership in Global Responsibility

Canada also fits into this picture. In this period of detente and diversity, it is useful for the West to speak to the varied peoples of the world with more than one voice, in different nuances, and through flexible initiatives—all in the service of essentially compatible goals. Canada's role in the postwar period as a leading middle power, especially in relation to the nonaligned and Communist nations, hardly needs elaboration. Although Canada, like Britain, pursues its foreign policy objectives in its own style and in accordance with its own precepts, these goals are almost invariably also America's. Insofar as there are disagreements as to means, these are insignificant compared to the broad areas of commonality. And the differences at times permit the West to try to achieve a common objective by experimenting with more than one strategy.

Canadian-American similarities in world perspective, like those between America and Britain, rest on a strong tradition of common values, as well as a history of effective cooperation in defense and economies. This latter point was recently illustrated in a speech by the Minister of Finance, Hon. Mitchell Sharp, before the Canadian House of Commons. Mr. Sharp noted that during the Canadian dollar crisis he had been in direct and personal contact with the United States' Secretary of the Treasury who had issued a "clarifying statement" which eased the pressure of speculation against Canadian currency by giving "reassurance that the new U.S.A. balance of payments program does not call for, nor is it intended to have the effect of causing, abnormal transfers of earnings or withdrawals of capital by U.S.A. companies having investments in Canada."[22] Again the argument can be made that a Free Trade

Association will provide the economic basis for a still more imaginative Canadian role in international politics.

This was illustrated by the Honorable Eric Kierans, M.P., President of the Quebec Liberal Federation and a former Finance Minister of Quebec, when he stated, at the New York University Center for International Studies' Seminar on the Free Trade Association that the French speaking segment of Canada's population would welcome a Free Trade Association, even though it linked three English-speaking countries together, if FTA permitted a close association with the French-speaking lesser-developed nations. Given the open-ended nature of the Free Trade Association proposed here this would certainly be possible.

It is clearly in America's interest to help Canada develop her latent "special relationship" with the Francophonic nations of Africa and the Caribbean, something Canada could expect to do much more effectively if she were acting on behalf of a large grouping of industrial nations—including the U.S.—able to offer important trade-expanding opportunities to less-developed countries.

This leads to the question of other countries joining the FTA. Australia with its central position in Oceania, with its strategic position in relation to the Far East, its close connections to the United States and Britain, and its heavy reliance upon trade is a logical candidate for membership. The same holds true for Japan. Neither of these two important industrial powers can be expected to develop its full potential unless it can trade freely in a wider market than its home economy. To the United States the political advantage of being joined with them in an FTA is obvious: it strengthens our circle of relations in an area where such strengthening is necessary, and it encourages these nations to act as leaders in regions where they are particularly able to encourage political stability and economic development.

In this context, it should be noted that Japan's role as America's ally in east Asia is not immune to the winds of trade. Japan sustained a $1.2 billion trade deficit last year despite its $300 million favorable trade balance with the U.S. and could not afford losses in this its most profitable relationship. Such was the position, reported on March 23, 1968, in *The New York Times* of a trade delegation headed by Akio Morita, an officer of the Sony Corporation. Mr. Morita "left no doubt that any unilateral import restrictions in the United States would force his country to look for more markets elsewhere, particularly the Eastern bloc."[23] Morita also made the following points:

(1) "a slowdown in Japan's export sales to the U.S. would have a particularly harmful effect on small and medium Japanese enterprises."

(2) Japan would "help the U.S. to improve its balance of payments by accelerating the schedules of tariff reductions negotiated in the Kennedy Round if major European Trading partners did the same."

American-Japanese trade relations are clearly of the most serious political consequence. The FTA idea might provide the necessary machinery for consultation and adjustment needed to keep the Japanese-American alliance viable.

Also in this context, the recent declaration by Leopold Senghor, the President of Senegal,[24] should be duly appreciated. Africa, warned Senghor, is now being abandoned by both the Soviet Union and the United States and may have to adopt "a solution of despair." This, he said, would involve Africa's turning to Communist China. Senghor declared:

> The result is gradual paralysis of world trade and our poverty. And it is not in the interest of the rich to see us become poorer. Because, politically, we would have only one solution: the Chinese solution.

This on the part of a man who admitted his "fear" of Red China due to its "awesome messianic spirit."

An analysis, therefore, of the political implications for the United States of a Free Trade Association would not be complete unless it indicated how the scheme of free trade could work in relation to lesser-developed countries. The foreign exchange positions of these countries have been in relation to the developed states during the past few years in large measure worsening because of their inability to compete in world markets dominated by the developed countries. World trade patterns reflect a growing division between rich and poor. The share of total trade between countries of the developed area rose from 63 per cent in 1953 to 71 per cent in 1965, which is only one of many indicators revealing that the disparities are increasing.

Although there are purely economic reasons for this, certain commercial policies of the developed countries are an aggravating factor. These include protection of developed agriculture, discriminatory trading systems, the broadening of restrictions on imports of manufactures and semi-manufactured items from lesser-developed countries, especially of labor-intensive industrial products, and tariff, quota, subsidy, and other systems for encouraging the production in developed countries of synthetics in competition wih primary products of developing nations.

Added to this is the fact that little relief seems to be forthcoming under the GATT. A report to the Economic and Social Council of the United Nations stated,

> By the very nature of its philosophy . . . GATT inevitably shows a marked lack of understanding of the interests of the under-developed and developing countries in the matter of bargaining power.[25]

David Wall, in his analysis of the economic implications of an FTA for developing countries (written under the auspices of The Atlantic Trade Study Committee) lists a number of ways in which operations through the GATT "ensure that negotiations will be dominated by industrial nations."[26] The bargaining strength of the rich nations has meant that most of the discussions under GATT, deal with manufactured goods of export interest to the developed societies alone, and that the reciprocity principle works to the disadvantage of the countries least able to make significant concessions.

For these reasons, two United Nations Conferences on

Trade and Development were convened under the able Chairmanship of Raul Prebisch. The specific proposals that came out of UNCTAD I and II raise economic questions and will not be reviewed here.

The underdeveloped nations acting through UNCTAD are asking for preferential treatment for their exports, particularly manufactured goods, in the markets of the industrialized nations. FTA could serve as a general preference area for specific underdeveloped countries. Wall lists the four general forms which such a scheme might take:

> (a) a completely non-discriminatory form in which all NAFTA members extended preferences to all participating less developed countries which chose to participate in the system;
>
> (b) a discriminatory form in which NAFTA members would extend preferences to all participating lesser developed countries but the degree of preference given to each developing nation would vary according to its stage of development;
>
> (c) either (a) or (b) with only those less developed countries which are prepared to accord reciprocal preferential benefits to FTA members—from the outset or
>
> (d) either (a) or (b) with only those less developed countries which are prepared to accord reciprocal preferential benefits to FTA members—from the outset or after a fixed period—allowed to participate.[27]

Whichever system or combination is most suitable, it is clear that such methods of nonreciprocal trading with developing countries has political advantages for the United States. FTA could be a means for shifting the emphasis from direct grants-in-aid to preferential trade as the principal method of promoting national development. This would be a more dignified and perhaps more constructive method of aiding economic growth. It has the further advantage, for the United States, of distributing the aid burden more broadly and equitably among developed nations.

THE NEXT STEP

FTA can therefore be regarded as an act of high political self-interest on the part of the United States. On the basis of the following New York University studies, the benefits for Britain and Canada appear to be primarily economic, mainly political. That this is so is not, however, by itself sufficient to ensure domestic political support for FTA. A major question, therefore, is whether strong executive pressure will be brought to the difficult task of winning congressional support. Without it, FTA stands little chance of implementation. However, the Trade Expansion Act has proven that Congress can respond boldly to the efforts of an energetic administration.

Geiger and Lea[28] point out that the success of the Kennedy round brings free trade within reach as an eventual objective for the United States, and that a Free Trade Association is likely to emerge as a relevant choice regardless of what happens next in U.S. trade policy. As they see it, another attempt may be made with the traditional multilateral approach used in the Kennedy round. However, like a wartime convoy, such negotiations are committed to the pace of their slowest member and may thus bog down due to the unwillingness or inability of certain states to reciprocate desired concessions. In this event, the United States and other willing countries might opt to preserve their momentum toward trade liberalization by moving ahead as a group to establish an "advance base" in the form of a Free Trade Association under GATT rules. But if, the authors continue, the next multilateral GATT round did succeed, its participants would find themselves on "the threshold of free trade, at which point they could be expected to commit themselves to that goal by a fixed date and to ensure its meaningfulness and permanence by firm agreements that, taken together, would resemble a Free Trade Area in all essential respects."

The economies of the United States, Britain, and Canada share common problems vis-à-vis the world economy and numerous frictions vis-à-vis each other. In this, they are little different from all others. Uniquely, however, there already exists among these states a tradition of consultation, cooperation, and harmonization in political matters. It should be relatively easy to translate this tradition into a system of economic cooperation. Such a system would, in the words of Sir Roy Harrod at the N.Y.U. seminar, provide "an opportunity through consultation to minimize mutual problems and maximize economic growth." One could reasonably expect that these states, with firm traditions of mutual trust and cooperation, form a promising core for the proposed Free Trade Association.

IV. CURRENT ALTERNATIVES FOR BRITAIN

It has already been noted that, whatever the intrinsic merit of an FTA, its feasibility *at this moment* is intimately related to the position of Britain. Whatever happens, the decision to proceed with negotiations toward FTA or to do something else, or to do nothing at all, will affect Britain more than the U.S. and probably more than Canada. Britain's future is now most in the balance, most in doubt, most in need of a defining purpose.

Even with entry to the EEC blocked, Britain has several alternatives besides the FTA which warrant consideration:

Associate Status in the EEC

The Treaty of Rome provides, in art. 238, that

> The Community may conclude with a third country, a union of States or an international organization, agreements creating an association embodying reciprocal rights and obligations, joint actions and special procedures.

As with applications for membership itself, nations seeking association with the EEC must secure the unanimous agreement of all member states. Various agreements of association have been signed with Greece, Turkey, and certain African countries including Nigeria and the parties to the Yaounde Convention (mostly former French territories).

The form of these associations varies both as to their terms and purpose—the Greek and Turkish arrangements being transitional to full membership, those with African states being designed to extend beneficial markets that do not violate the General Agreement on Tariffs and Trade (GATT).

It has been suggested, by some British and European leaders, that the United Kingdom might enter into an appropriate form of association with EEC.

Arguments on behalf of Associate Status for Britain are dampened at the outset by a number of considerations.

First among these is the unqualified declaration by Prime Minister Wilson on November 29, 1957, that "association is out."[29]

The reason for this opposition is the expectation that associate status would deny Britain participation in the supernational political organs of the Communities, in particular the Council, the Commission, the Court, and the Assembly. The vision of participations in a great new political adventure called Europe is perhaps more important to Britain even than the economic advantages of EEC membership.

This political goal, set out in the preamble to the Treaty of Rome—"to establish the foundations of an ever closer union among the European peoples"—has drawn Britain toward the European Communities.

Moreover, while French objections to British full membership appear to be insuperable because they are theoretical, those to association are more practical but perhaps almost as difficult to overcome.

There is, for example, little reason to hope that agreement could be reached on a fixed timetable or standard for converting associate status into full membership. Nor is there much indication that the Inner Six of Europe could be brought to share with the Outer Seven a common market and external tariff that included industrial goods but excluded agricultural and primary products. There is certainly much to be said for such an arrangement between EFTA and the EEC.[30]

It recalls a British proposal, held to be technically feasible by a working party of the Organization for European Economic Cooperation in January, 1957, which would have created an outer free trade area embracing all the OEEC European countries and an inner Common Market of the Six. The attractiveness of this plan is increased by the prospect that such an arrangement might adequately safeguard the most vital interests of Commonwealth primary producers, while leaving open the possibility of industrial states such as Canada, the United States, Ireland, Japan, Australia, and New Zealand later entering the outer perimeter.

But it must be admitted that there may be little advantage to the EEC in such a bargain, politically or economically; and, in any event, the EEC has made no such offer to Britain.

On the contrary, there is every reason to believe that the only form of British association acceptable to France at the present time is one subjecting British agricultural and primary imports, as well as industrial products, to full Common Market regulations, but leaving Britain without any formal role in the formulation of these policies.

While the possibility thus should not be excluded, even those who have been the most ardent advocates of British entry into the EEC tend to see association as a third best, a new fall-back position.

Former British Foreign Secretary George Brown has said that "such a solution would mean that we would be joining a group in the development and organization of which we should have no influence. We would be passengers on the train, but the driving would be done by someone else, and we should not even be able to decide where we wanted to go."[31]

"Going It Alone"

"Going it alone," on the other hand, is a real alternative, at least for the next decade.

Some economists believe that the tariff reductions effected by the Kennedy and Dillon rounds are sufficient, combined with certain advantages Britain derives from the Commonwealth and the European Free Trade Area, to permit a reasonable rate of growth in the British economy.

Nevertheless, economic indicators do not warrant unbridled optimism if western Europe is to divide permanently into two blocs. For example, EFTA exports to EEC countries declined by 4.2 per cent in the first quarter of 1967 as compared to the same period in 1966, a decline attributable in part to deteriorating business conditions within the EEC, but probably also in part to the latter's increasingly effective operation of its customs union and common external tariff.[32]

The prospects for Britain "going it alone" involve risks which Britain can only reasonably be expected to take if there is likelihood of a payoff in the forseeable future.

EFTA and the Commonwealth, it must be recalled, are not necessarily the repositories of the best future trading prospects for Britain. The total EFTA market outside the United Kingdom is relatively small and scattered around the periphery of the high-density EEC, which exerts a strong pull on such small individual EFTA members as Austria, Switzerland, and Denmark. This pull may, in time, become irresistible, particularly to those countries which are looking for an expanding agricultural market in the EEC. A regional political context also may seem more natural to a younger generation born to the idealistic continental vision of building Europe, a generation which no longer harbors the grudges of earlier wrongs done to small states by the big continental powers.

It must also be expected that, as the EEC edges toward a "third force" posture between the West and the East, neutral countries like Sweden, Switzerland, Finland, and Austria will feel less inhibited about membership in that system.

Commonwealth countries, too—both developed and underdeveloped—are diversifying their trade and the sources of investment capital.

Since 1958, British exports to EEC countries have doubled, as have those to EFTA nations, while trade with the Commonwealth rose hardly at all.[33]

The possibility of a form of association between the EEC and African Commonwealth countries being worked out along lines like those of the Lagos Agreement with Nigeria suggest that, if Britain continues to "go it alone," this trend might continue.[34]

It must not be taken for granted that, in the long run, EFTA and the Commonwealth will provide Britain with a sufficiently expanding export market, market for investment capital, opportunities for British venture capital, pool of trained, mobile industrial labor, and the less-tangible psychological prerequisites for economies of scale to maintain a rate of growth comparable to that of the EEC and the United States.

In the words of the British Foreign Minister Michael Stewart, "If we do not get into the Common Market, as the years go by the difficulties which we shall face in trying to sell in world markets in competition with industries that can reap the economies of scale will grow. . . ."[35] This is why Britain must weigh very carefully the cost of "going it alone."

Realizing this, a policy of "going it alone" is not ordinarily advocated as an end in itself but only as a stopgap that preserves Britain's free hand to resume negotiations for entry into the Common Market as soon as possible.

Even if one were to agree that entry into the Common Market would have been the best possible solution for Britain today, one need not accept that, having failed again to be admitted, Britain's rightful place is to sit and wait on Europe's chilly doorstep.

Waiting may be expensive. To do nothing is not necessarily to preserve the *status quo*, for an expectation of drift tends to be self-fulfilling. Uncertainty about the future can cause—and some say already has caused—industry, both British and foreign investors, to delay plans for expansion and construction in Britain[36] until the future becomes more predictable. Britain's EFTA partners, too, are unlikely to have much confidence, or retain binding loyalty to, a partnership which the principal participant regards as merely a temporary convenience.

Although EFTA states have "welcomed" Britain's two bids to enter the EEC, they were less enthusiastic about the British government's refusal, in the most recent bid, to make entry of other EFTA countries a precondition of her own acceptance of the Treaty of Rome. Moreover, the unilateral U.K. surcharge imposed in the autumn of 1964 without adequate consultation with her EFTA partners had already shaken the faith of the Seven in their bloc.

It came as no surprise, therefore, that a Nordic summit meeting comprised of officials from Denmark, Norway, Sweden, Finland, and Iceland met in Copenhagen on April 22 and 23, 1968, for the purpose of discussing greater economic cooperation, perhaps, even a Nordic Five Free Trade Area.[37] This too must have an important effect on British calculations.

Prime Minister Wilson, therefore, has called for a speedy end to the inevitably harmful state of being betwixt and between, declaring: "We must—all of us—know before many months are up exactly where we stand. . . ."[38]

Waiting out in the cold when all around you others are warming themselves by their hearths creates not only uncertainty, but also discouragement. In choosing to apply to the EEC, Prime Minister Wilson emphasized that integration with the European Market "would, I believe, create an elan of its own, just as the original formation of the Market created an elan within the Six. But don't ask me for figures or estimates. You can't quantify an elan."

So, too, you can't quantify the cost of an elan lost to a nation's pride and thus to its momentum. This is perhaps the principal argument, again unquantifiable, against waiting and for pursuing what other challenging opportunity there may be.

The FTA opportunity is different from the EEC opportunity—it does not offer the same political elan, for an FTA could not and would not be a supernational start toward a great political unification.

But FTA does offer a kind of lower-keyed elan—a functional or piecemeal way of dealing with the questions of a meaningful British role in world politics and trade, while waiting and going it alone offers little in this regard.

In summary, there may be valid arguments for awaiting another opportunity for Britain to apply to the EEC but the cost of waiting, like the costs of other possible courses of action, must be carefully calculated.

Such calculations, while necessary, are also difficult because they involve a gamble. Whether the cost of "going it alone" for a while is reasonable or not depends on one's guess as to whether Britain will, in fact, succeed "in a while" where it has three times failed in the past—and, also, on how long one supposes "a while" to be. An informed guess—no less, no more—can be made only after a reexamination of the changing roles of the western European Communities and the North Atlantic Community in the emerging new political style of global alignments.

One further point.

In assessing whether Britain should and could, eventually, enter Europe it remains necessary to ask whether, even if the answer is affirmative, Britain must await that day "out in the cold." Senator Jacob Javits has suggested that Britain could "leapfrog" the waiting stage "by helping to form, and then joining an Atlantic Free Trade Area. Eventually, the European Economic Community will come along and accept Britain into membership or join such an Atlantic Free Trade Area itself."[39] There would seem to be nothing inherently inimical about the Free Trade Association proposal and a later entry of Britain into the EEC, should there be a change of direction in the European Communities.

Present trends do not, however, make such a change appear certain.

V. THE POLITICAL CASE FOR BRITISH PARTICIPATION IN A FREE TRADE ASSOCIATION

Failure of the Initiative Toward Europe

The theory that Britain is separated from its goal of membership in the EEC by the whim of one man, the aging President of France, encourages the conclusion that the goal is only a breath away, and that it is therefore plainly worth the waiting.

Worth waiting for it may be, but it may be unrealistic and misleading to personify all obstacles to British membership in the European Community in this way. As we have already noted, these obstacles could include fundamental geopolitical trends of probably greater longevity than the President of France. Just as Americans may be making a very serious error if they expect the end of the de Gaulle era to bring a revival of French loyalty to the Atlantic Alliance, so the British may be deluding themselves, to their cost, if they expect post-Gaullist France to welcome Britain as its rival for leadership of the European Communities.

Nor are French attitudes likely to be modified by pressures from Bonn. Speaking in London on September 15, 1967, the British Minister of State for Foreign Affairs in charge of negotiations with the EEC reported to the Foreign Press Association that during a recent visit to Germany he had been told "over and over again that the German people—perhaps somewhat in distinction from the German political establishment, the German Government—were not convinced of Britain's sincerity and determination in the approach to Europe."[40] The tendency apears to be for Germany to ratify rather than to modify French views on Britain. Recent joint declarations by President de Gaulle and Chancellor Keisinger tend to rebut the notion of a "friendly five" of secret anglophiles within the EEC capable of smuggling Britain into Europe through a back door.

German popular opinion in this matter seems to give some support to the views of President de Gaulle. So, too, does the French public. A poll taken in December, 1967, by the French Institute of Public Opinion indicates that 41 per cent of those polled expressed agreement with their president's opposition to British entry into the EEC and 37 per cent were indifferent or had no opinion. Only 27 per cent expressed disagreement with the policy,[41] scarcely a result to reassure those who expect a speedy reversal of Gaullist opposition to Britain after de Gaulle.

That the French president's views, far from being idiosyncratic may be responsive to profound political trends has perhaps been stated most dispassionately by a British spokesman, Sir Arthur Bryant, who wrote recently of de Gaulle's mission:

> His twin objectives have been to restore, after a period of national eclipse and defeatism, the faith and vitality of the French people—something which a statesman has still to do for Britain—and to create a union of western, or Roman, Europe based on the values of French civilization

> which, whatever an Anglo-Saxon may think, a Frenchman may be forgiven for regarding as the finest and most civilizing of all. To create that union out of six historic nations speaking at least four different languages must seem to him quite difficult enough without the entry of another whose language, traditions, and maritime and commercial interests instinctively link her with the United States and the English-speaking ocean-nations of the old and new Commonwealth.
>
> The truth is that the Europe we envisage—an outward-looking commercial one with close ties with America—is a fundamentally different ideal to de Gaulle's. That we, or many of us, think it a better one is no reason why we should belittle him. What matters to him about the European Economic Community is that it should succeed, not that we should be in it.[42]

Whatever changes may occur in French and western European policies after the end of the de Gaulle era, it is far from certain that these changes will reverse widely shared and deeply felt attitudes toward the challenges of the 1970's.

The political and economic community of the EEC is a genuinely felt response of many Europeans to three new circumstances of historical importance. The first of these is the *detente between Russia and the U.S.*, the second is the *end of the colonial era,* and the third is the *new industrial revolution.*

These three circumstances have combined to shape a western European Community that strives to emancipate itself economically from the dominant competitive position of United States industry and politically seeks "a strong and united voice in the affairs of the world."[43]

Since these developments are an important aspect of the new political realities to which FTA is responsive, they require some further analysis:

The Style of Detente

The wartime years conditioned the world, psychologically, politically, and militarily, to an international system of strategic and ideological absolutes counterposed in simple policy alternatives. Thus, Hitler affords one of history's few examples of undifferentiated evil and Nazi Germany became the model for simplistic classification. Given such an absolute evil, the conflict against Germany and its axis was waged as *total* war. And the objective was the enemy's *total* unconditional surrender.

In the years following the Second World War, this gestalt continued to dominate our thinking about international relations.

Joseph Stalin slipped readily and naturally into the role vacated by Hitler. Germany's *drang nach osten,* in Russian hands, simply reversed geographic direction, becoming, for that, the more menacing to the Atlantic powers. Neutral Czechoslovakia fell before Communist manifest destiny much as Austria was once subject to *putsch* and *anschluss*. Eastern Europe became a Soviet fiefdom as it had just previously been Germany's.

The object of the Soviet Union, like Germany a decade earlier, was to enlarge that fiefdom to encompass the entire world. The Atlantic Alliance, which had been the effective response to Nazi Germany, became NATO, the effective response to Stalinist Russia.

There are Western political historians such as Professors George Kennan and Marshall Shulman,[44] who doubt that these analogies were ever valid. There can be no doubt, however, that they dictated the style of the fifteen years of international confrontation following World War II.

In the 1960's, that style began to change.

The nuclear stalemate precluded war as a means by which the Soviet Union could hope to expand the empire of communism; and since de-Stalinization, and certainly since the Cuban missile crisis, it has also become ideologically unorthodox for Russians to see the unrelenting struggle against capitalism and social democracy in traditional military terms.

This is not to say that situations of military confrontation between the two super-powers do not exist and will not continue to arise. But where rival political maneuverings lead to a confrontation, as in Vietnam, the war, to invert Clauswitz, becomes the conduct of politics by other means. This inversion of objectives totally alters the traditional means for their attainment not only in imposing limits on the scope, intensity, and objectives of struggle, but in two other respects.

First, the style of confrontation in this period allows Russia and the United States to continue to cooperate elsewhere, while backing opposite sides in the Vietnam conflict. We note such current phenomena as the increase of Russian-American contact and agreement on matters of air transport, consular relations, the regime of outer space, nuclear nonproliferation, nonstrategic trade, and cultural exchange.

Second, neither Russia nor the United States has used the Vietnam confrontation to draw tight its lines of alliance, lines which, in the spirit of detente, have tended to slacken.

Since total war has given way to political maneuvering as the accepted means to expand the national interest, and since a pragmatic plurality of objectives has replaced the simplistic formulae of unrelenting, universal struggle as the style of international relations, it is natural that the coalitions and blocs formed in an earlier wartime and postwar period of simple bipolarity should yield to a greater diversity of policy and motive not only between but *within* global alliances.

Today, French, British, and American interests; or on the other hand, Russian, Roumanian, and East German interests may, at least in the short-run and in specific instances, be unidentical and even appear to conflict.

This development within NATO and, to some extent, within the group of the Warsaw Pact is, probably, at once an inevitable and even a desirable response to the current realities of global policies.

The result is a new, looser, more creative style in international relations which, in the case of the reborn nations of Europe as well as the new nations of Africa and Asia, has led to thoughts about regional unity, facilitating economic and political self-determination—free of, although not necessarily opposed to the hitherto predominant interests of Russia or the United States.

The Style of Decolonization

The opportunities for diversity in international relations created by the detente between the United States and Russia has occurred at approximately the same historic period as the dissolution of European empire in Asia and Africa. These two coincidental tendencies have undoubtedly been the dominant motifs of the 1960's.

That Holland, Belgium, France, Italy, and Britain have effectively ceased to have direct ownership of vast lands overseas has undoubtedly prepared the ground for a new way in which the peoples perceive their role in the world.

Nations who frequently pursued their interests in terms of territorial expansion abroad and who tended to regard their European neighbors primarily as rivals for foreign dominion, now define their first priority as industrial expansion at home and see their neighbors as collaborators in industrial development.

The former British Foreign Secretary, George Brown, recently said of these developments, "To a great extent, of course, this has come about because of a sense of our changed position in the world. The development of the world means that there is no longer a place for imperial powers. But we, a European country, still have a crucial and influential role to play in the world."[45]

That Britain has wanted to share in Europe's new role seems natural, viewed in this way. For, Britain, like other western European countries, has lost an empire and must find a context.

The Style of the Second Industrial Revolution

The new emphasis on industrial development in Europe followed the Marshall Plan, postwar reconstruction and the end of imperial opportunities for protected, profitable ventures abroad. It also coincided with technological innovations of revolutionary proportions.

This technological revolution has thrown up new industries producing the jet engine, nuclear power, computers, plastics, electronic equipment, chemicals, automobiles, as well as more humble products and processes. It has devoured huge quantities of money and scientific research, and it has been highly competitive.

Divided, Europe could only look forward to falling behind in this race, or to running it in tandem with the United States' or Russia's industrial complexes. To provide the capital, sustain the research establishment, and ensure the economies of scale that alone could absorb the benefits of the new industrial revolution, European states had either to seek unity among themselves or to establish a workable economic relationship with one or other of the super powers.

It is only just coming to be understood outside western Europe that the European Communities represent an attempt to do the former; that is, to create a bloc pursuing its own political and economic interests, bolstered by an economy of scale and a protected market, an independent research and defense establishment, and a foreign policy using the room for maneuver created by the detente.

Western Europe today has adopted policy priorities which entail expansion of East-West trade, protection of the western European economy against American encroachment, a detente between western and eastern Europe sufficient to permit at least some functional reunification of the Germanies, and an independent role in world affairs.

Britain's Self-Interest and the Choice of Roles

These European priorities may prove to be reconcilable to United States, British, or Canadian policy in this era of detente and diversity. But are they likely to become *Britain's* genuine, felt priorities? Some British leaders would answer this question in the affirmative.[46]

But British world policy, even as conceived by ardent British supporters of entry into the EEC, still seems to differ notably from that of the European continental powers. And that difference frequently seems to be emphasized by the very words with which British leaders seek to establish their credentials as Good Europeans. Thus Prime Minister Harold Wilson announced his country's decision to apply for membership in the European Community with the assurance that "the Government's purpose derives above all from our recognition that Europe is now faced with the opportunity of a great move forward in political unity and that we can—and indeed must—play our full part in it." But in his very next sentence Wilson added: "We do not see European unity as something narrow or inward looking. Britain has her own vital links through the Commonwealth and in other ways with other continents."[47]

Britain's reluctance to narrow its perspectives is equally evident in its continued championing of an American presence in Europe. President de Gaulle will not warm to the reminder by Rt. Hon. Edward Heath, leader of the opposition in the House of Commons and the most pro-European of British statesmen, that "What is essential is that the U.S. presence remains in Europe. Nothing must be done to damage that."[48]

If this is Britain's view, it would appear to be different at least in important shading and nuance from that emerging in the European Community.

Nor is this difference merely old fashioned or sentimental. Hard-headed arguments can be adduced in its favor.

It is not always fully realized that Britain continues to have commitments and interests outside Europe that are of an order quite different from those of any other western European nation. To put matters into proportion it must be recalled that, in 1966, the Common Market supplied Britain with only 18.6 per cent of her imports and took only 19.9 per cent of her exports. By contrast, the rest of the Sterling Area, North America and the EFTA nations, supplied 63.4 per cent of Britain's imports and took 62.2 per cent of her exports. Similarly, 66 per cent of British "invisible" earnings from overseas came from the Sterling Area, EFTA, and North America, as against only 14 per cent from the EEC.[49]

It has, however, been noted that Britain's traditional trading patterns may already be subject to erosion.

If, for example, most EFTA nations were to prefer association with the EEC to the present somewhat clouded *status quo,* the consequences for British trade might be even more onerous than the running down of the Commonwealth preference system.

This warning can, however, suggest two possible courses of action: either Britain must create new patterns—as by entering into the European Common Market—or it must shore up existing patterns wherever possible.

A Free Trade Association in industrial goods, uniting Britain, Canada, and the United States, and open-ended to include EFTA countries, Australia, New Zealand, Japan, and other industrial nations which might wish to join, and affording continued free access to the British market of tropical primary products and some other products covered by Conmonwealth preference, could help to rejuvenate these existing patterns.

The economic implications of a Free Trade Association are discussed in separate chapters of this study, and are mentioned here only to indicate that Britain's political role outside Europe is not yet an eccentric relic of a past best forgotten, but still reflects quite accurately a persisting pattern of far-flung economic interests.

The political role, however, warrants closer examination.

Britain has devoted an extraordinarily large part of its wealth to investment in the less-developed nations of the world. More than any industrial nation except Japan, it depends on a worldwide market of primary products to supply its needed raw materials and foodstuffs. More than any other nation it earns a large proportion of its national income by handling worldwide commercial transactions, acting as broker and banker to the international community.

To develop this role: to safeguard its overseas investments, protect access to its sources of supply, defend its trade routes, and maintain confidence in its financial integrity, Britain has played an active worldwide part in international politics. There may be much to be said for abandoning this gregarious role in favor of a compact continental one. The past decade's comparatively greater rate of trade and industrial expansion in the developed nations of the northern hemisphere, as against, for example, the Britain-related tropical Commonwealth nations, seems to argue for such a switch.

If, however, the role is not to be discarded—either because Britain as a matter of political responsibility thinks it best to retain it, or because it has no choice of other viable roles for the forseeable future—then at least the role must be made more responsive to current political and economic realities.

A rejuvenated Britain, energetically pursuing world (as against strictly regional or continental) interests, is an objective Britain cannot expect to reach without help.

It has already become apparent that an economy of fifty-odd million persons cannot, in comparative isolation, sustain a role as banker, policeman, and entrepreneur to the world.

If Britain is to maintain and develop its worldwide commercial interests, if she is to modernize her industry, if she is to continue to finance world trade through the sterling currency system, and if she is to support her weaker but important friends and relations throughout the world with a credible, mobile, and effective military force, she must do so in a context that lets her pursue her economic and political interests from a much broader economic base.

FTA's Responsiveness to British Self-Interest

Ideally, Britain needs an association with other states which will preserve her freedom of initiative in the Afro-Asian part of the Commonwealth, while relating the British home market and defense establishment to much larger units to effect economies of scale and provide a growing market for her industrial production.

Fortunately, there are other nations: Japan, Canada, Australia, New Zealand, the nations of EFTA and, of course, the United States, who also might find such an economic link with Britain to their advantage.

In the case of the United States, such a link might reasonably include cooperation in the development of military equipment, including transport, missiles, and nuclear weapons, and in the planning of joint international political initiatives. To some extent, such a link need not be invented but only rationalized and strengthened.

Although it has become fashionable of late, on both sides of the Atlantic, to debunk the so-called "special relationship" between the United States and the United Kingdom, the fact of the matter is that a degree of interdependence undoubtedly does already exist in fiscal matters, in defense, in diplomacy.

The gold crisis at the end of 1967 following upon the devaluation of the British pound demonstrated incontrovertibly that the dollar and sterling must swim together, at least until another and better unit of international liquidity can be devised by agreement among the principal trading states.

The monetary "special relationship" is not one of sentiment but of necessity. We have already discovered that a loss of confidence in sterling can have two effects—a transfer of sterling holdings into dollars or a transfer of both currencies into gold. Both effects are equally undesirable for the United States, which can no longer doubt that sterling is its first line of defense.

And the British government knows that its role as world banker cannot be divested. As with any reserve system, the liquid assets do not nearly equal the paper liabilities. Britain could not simply close down the bank even if it so desired.

As the Minister of State for Commonwealth Relations said recently, "We have made it clear in our discussions with the Six that sterling is bound to continue as an important international currency."[50]

It is generally agreed by the British government and the British financial community that the world role of sterling continues to be important and needs not liquidation but strengthening. Such strengthening could come about by British entry into a larger industrial and trading community which would see its interests served by continuing the role of sterling. This is true of a community including the United States and Canada. It is not presently true of the European Communities.

If it is to Britain's interest to maintain a world role for sterling it is equally so to maintain a scale of military preparedness equivalent to its worldwide economic interests.

It must, of course, be recognized that an independent British military nuclear capability is no longer financially feasible.

However, according to a former U.S. diplomat specializing in military strategy, Dr. Andrew Pierre, the "British military still retains a world-wide peace-keeping role and a nuclear force which is integrated with the U.S. military deterrent and which Britain seeks to internationalize by way of greater western strategy integration and with hope of diminishing proliferation and the development of more independent national deterrents."[51]

And it should be seriously considered whether British strategic and diplomatic interests are not served better by having an integrated, key part in a credible Anglo-American *deterrent* than a mere first-strike *capability* maintained independently at excessive cost or in partnership with western Europe.

This does not assume that Britain's role in world affairs will cease, but rather the contrary. In the era of detente, the style of international politics not only encourages more states or blocs of states to play *different* roles, but also to play *similar* roles *differently.*

It is this subtle difference that presently distinguishes relations between Britain and the U.S. on the one hand, and, for example, the U.S. and France on the other.

While the difference between method and objectives cannot be defined exactly and may be one of degree, it can still be said with expectation of being understood that Britain and the United States often play their roles in world politics with different methods but very rarely in pursuit of incompatible objectives. This has been so not as a matter of necessity but of choice and self-interest and will continue only as long as the reasons remain compelling to both nations.

Because this is widely realized, a basis of U.S.-U.K. cooperation has already been laid which extends beyond military planning into the broader political context.

The Tradition of U.K.-U.S. Cooperation as a Foundation on which to Build FTA

Consultations between the United States and the United Kingdom have been unique in peacetime diplomacy.

In the period immediately following the Suez invasion, and at present because of current U.S. action in Vietnam, consultation has tended to diminish. Even so, the two countries continue to share nuclear secrets, and plan joint military and political policies. The U.S. and Britain operate staging bases jointly in the Indian Ocean. At present, an ultra-modern radar system designed to peer around the curvature of the earth is being constructed by both countries in Oxfordness, England. British and American officials regularly meet each year a month before the opening of the United Nations General Assembly to negotiate and develop agreed positions on matters likely to be on the agenda.[52] And the United States has seen it in its interest to leave much responsibility for Western policy to Britain in such important areas of the world as East Africa, Malaysia and Singapore, and the Anglophonic Caribbean.

In its relations with the United States and in its relations with the Commonwealth, Britain has forged a network of functional contacts at various levels—between judges of a common system of laws, between the professions and the arts, which are, in the words of John Holmes, former Canadian Deputy Undersecretary of State for External Affairs, "of a different order of confidentiality" than those freely and spontaneously formed between other states.

BRITAIN AND THE COMMONWEALTH

In the Commonwealth, too, as in the related role of sterling, Britain has a function of global importance which could be reexamined and perhaps rejuvenated.

Although the Commonwealth no longer is an intimate club of overseas Britishers (if it ever was), it has become, through its very diversity, a unique link between black, brown, and white nations, rich and poor, northern hemisphere and southern. That there should be violent disagreements in this final stage of decolonization is inevitable because the final stage involves all those hardcore, intractable problems: Rhodesia, Aden, Swaziland. But this phase, too, will pass. And if the Commonwealth were to survive, it could be a bridge between parts of a chasmically divided world.

If it were to end, nothing so loose, so unstructured, so inexplicable yet functional could ever be invented. Yet Britain, alone, could probably not hold the Commonwealth together indefinitely. A Britain economically strengthened by partnership in the FTA would stand a much better chance of so doing.

It seems increasingly unlikely that Britain will be able to

have it both ways: that she will be able to share in the building of a western European bloc, with its own role—regional in its economic interests, operating politically in the new diplomatic terrain between Russia and America opened by the detente; and that she will at the same time be able to continue her close economic and political ties to the United States and the Commonwealth as well as her worldwide diplomatic and financial role.

New Opportunities for Britain

Exclusion from Europe, by blackball or even by choice, affords new opportunities for Britain.

Whatever reason there has been for pursuing entry into Europe, the alternative for Britain is not, as seems sometimes almost to be suggested, to sink slowly and obscurely into a northern sea.

Prime Minister Wilson, in launching the recent campaign to enter the Common Market, said prophetically,

> I shall not say to you . . . that there was no other choice for Britain. We are faced with a series of choices, each of them challenging, each of them difficult, each capable of being supported or attacked with powerful arguments. . . . And if we do take the decision and then do not succeed—through the decision of others, not of ourselves—we shall not whine about it. Rather will we harden our resolve to succeed within the parameters that such a decision will force upon us. We ask no favours, we crook no knee. . . . If the decision is to apply to join the Community we shall not put it forward on the basis that this is the only choice for Britain. We shall put it forward on the basis that other alternatives are possible, but in our judgment would be second best.[53]

Debating whether these opportunities be best, or only second best is now perhaps less productive than a study of their implications, and their chances of implementation.

If the "other alternative" to which Prime Minister Wilson refers, is to be feasible for Britain, the task of rejuvenating her present world role will require careful planning, management, and cooperation by the United States.

It is, for example, clear that Britain can no longer afford to produce the complete range of armaments necessary to a world strategic role. If, as now seems probable, she fails in her efforts to develop such expensive items as the variable geometry aircraft in joint ventures with France, she must turn even more to the United States.

But a growing "tie-in" to American defense industry must be carefully managed if it is not to have the opposite of the intended effect on Britain by draining away the money and brains necessary to a continuing, independent global-strategic role. Thus the United States must be prepared to assign to Britain a fair share[54] of the benefits of an increasingly integrated (and potentially more economical) defense industry.

This equitable sharing must apply not only to design and production, but also to the crucial nonmilitary benefits of defense research. In the past, Congress and U.S. defense industries, as well as the British Cabinet, have tended to take a short-range view of their interests which would require thorough reassessment if these proposals were to be implemented.

Rejuvenation of the Commonwealth as part of Britain's global role would again require the cooperation of the United States as well as the rest of the FTA.

The EEC provides us with an adaptable precedent. Just as, in the Yaounde Convention, the French government gained from its European partners special trading concessions for its overseas spheres of influence, so, too, perhaps the developing nations of the Commonwealth ought to be encouraged to regard the Commonwealth link as the way to an advantageous association with a Free Trade Association of Britain, Canada, and the United States.

VI. THE POLITICAL CASE FOR CANADIAN PARTICIPATION IN A FREE TRADE ASSOCIATION

Concerns about U.S. Predominance

Finally, one must examine some of the principal political considerations of the FTA idea for Canada.

Professor Douglas Gibson of York University, Toronto, has pointed out that Canada and Britain share some of the same political reasons both for favoring and for being suspicious of a Free Trade Association proposal.

Canada, like Britain (as well as most EFTA states, Japan, Australia, and New Zealand), is concerned about being left out of the major trading blocs now being organized on regional bases. To this extent, the Free Trade Association has appeal.

At the same time, both countries have political and psychological difficulty seeing themselves in balance with the disproportionate power of the United States.

In the case of Canada, however, there are already studies underway which appear to favor a bilateral free trade area with the United States.[55] The governing Liberal Party has gone on record favoring the pursuit of a North American Free Trade arrangement.[56] Professor Gibson points out that a proposal including the United Kingdom and, perhaps, other industrial nations like Australia, the EFTA states and Japan would probably be more politically acceptable than the bilateral proposal: "If the British and others were to come into a Free Trade Area agreement as well as the Americans, Canadians would, I think, be less concerned, though the question of American dominance would not disappear."[57]

Canada and the United States also share certain political considerations bearing on the Free Trade Association proposal.

Neither one is much interested in new supernational political formulations to replace the existing pattern of loose associations of sovereign states such as the North Atlantic Treaty Organization, the Organization of American States, the Commonwealth of Nations, and the United Nations. These pragmatic instruments of relations between nations have served, historically, to dampen crises and to encourage diversity, experimentation, dialogue, and sometimes concensus. Being functional associations, they tend to respond to the Great Challenges and then to lapse back into routine quiescence. They generally operate by sovereign agreement rather than supernationally.

Canada, particularly, could not contemplate a form of

association that tied it politically to the United States or to a supernational organization in which the United States was the majority shareholder.

To both Canada and the United States, for different reasons, it is important not always to have to act alone in international affairs; but it is equally important to retain the power to initiate action alone if necessary. Agreements within the FTA or among the Atlantic partners, whether over trade, defense, or diplomacy would thus continue to be consensual and not institutionally imposed.

In the words of Professor Edward English of Carleton University, Ottawa,

> The self-conscious discomfort Canadians sometimes feel and express concerning the similarities between Canadian and U.S. foreign policies arises in part out of a feeling that our national identity requires more distinctive Canadian policy positions. It also arises, however, from real differences between Canadian and U.S. attitudes and interests. For the most part, these are small and subtle, while the parallel concerns are large and obvious, but this does not mean that they are unimportant. Often they concern methods and pace, but method can make a difference between war and peace."[58]

The nature of the Canadian dilemma is stated by two distinguished Canadians. John Holmes recently wrote: "Canadians, ... while recognizing the inevitability of closer continental, economic integration, plan to retain their identity in world affairs."[59]

On the other hand, Professor English points out the dangers of "going it alone" for Canada, which is "the only industrially advanced country in the North Atlantic region, and except for Australia the only one in the world, which cannot now anticipate free access to a market of 100 million or more."[60] In this sense, Canada's need for a trading community engendering selective economies of scale may be even more urgent than that of Great Britain.

FTA and Canada's Two Cultures

To these Canadian political considerations must be added the special "problem" of the two cultures.

Quebec, conscious of the difficulties of preserving a heritage in a nation where those of Anglophonic culture outnumber the Francophonic three to one, is bound to be much more sensitive to any suggestion of an English-speaking Union in which the French-English ratio would be fifty-three to one. Yet, as we have seen, this could be mitigated by bringing certain other English to French countries into association with FTA. Moreover, French Canada, and specifically the province of Quebec is urgently in need of development capital for the exploitation of its extraordinarily rich resources. It has traditionally been a hospitable recipient of U.S. investment. Quebec leaders of all shades of political opinion concede that French cultural parity in Canada can come only with developing economic parity.

Thus the political attraction of FTA for Canada will depend on its success in steering a narrow path between the nation's economic needs and her fears of being dominated politically, economically, and culturally. This underscores the political necessity of devising what is clearly a community of sovereign states and not a supernational organization or incipient federation.

To say this, however, is to give only half of the picture.

It is inevitable that a working system of free trade implies some surrender of sovereignty and, particularly, a high degree of joint planning and mutual consultation. It must, however, be understood by the participating states that the sovereignty of a country with a faltering economy is no sovereignty at all. This the British Government learned when it saw the terms which international financial institutions sought to impose in November, 1967, as their price for rescuing the pound. Since there are very few, if any, states that can any longer afford to "go it alone" in the face of developing regional markets, the issue is not one of independence versus association but of how much independence small and medium powers can gain through association with others.

VII. THE CHOICE FOR THE FUTURE

The FTA proposal seeks to offer nations a choice between the kind of economic association which proceeds toward supernational institution building, and one which promotes economic association between nations while safeguarding their separate political roles and identities.

It is logical that the latter kind of association, designed to preserve sovereign differences, should be initiated first among the three nations which probably have the fewest radical differences to preserve.

In Britain, the political drive for realistic reevaluation and reform has so far gone primarily into the effort to gain entry into the European Communities. The time is at hand for a new strategic initiative on Britain's part more in accordance with the political realities. There is a real danger of a policy void between the "ideal" policy which has failed (entry into Europe) and consequent tendency to retreat to isolation. Britain, like the United States, must search for realistic solutions in the fertile field between a maximal solution which cannot be attained and a minimal solution which solves nothing. The FTA proposal would offer such a realistic middleground alternative.

It must be recognized, however, that a new initiative in favor of the FTA proposal would require radical shifting of fixed official policies both in Britain and the United States. Neither government is anxious to make such a shift, however untenable the venerable policies of the past have become, if in doing so they risk another failure. In both Washington and London there appears something of the Alphonse/Gaston syndrome. Neither wishes to be the first to raise the free trade alternative with the others, although each is quietly engaged in studying it. In London there is a conviction that the proposal, whatever its merits, will not be given serious consideration so long as the United States is totally preoccupied by internal unrest and its Vietnam commitment. In Washington, there is a feeling that Britain has already irretrievably turned its back on the Atlantic. In London, the government is wary of launching the FTA alternative because, after two rebuffs from Europe, it is understandably reluctant to expose itself to a third from America. The United States government does not want to be seen as the sponsor of an idea which, if rejected by Britain, will appear as an effort to force a reluctant satellite into orbit. The British, on the other hand, feel the first move is up to the stronger power, and so on. Yet, on both political and economic grounds there is much support in government, business, and public opinion for the FTA idea.

This public stalemate, which may be no more than a temporary phenomenon attributable to the indirect predominance of the Vietnam factor in all policy reviews, creates a particular responsibility for private initiatives such as this one.

Also, given the politically powerful sectional interests which, in all three countries, would be concerned with the economic consequences of the Free Trade Association, most careful consideration must now be given to temporary measures that can alleviate the impact of short-term dislocation on certain vulnerable sectors of the economy of each FTA participant. In this respect, the experience of the EEC and especially of EFTA will require close study. Among the tools available to planners are gradual phasing and emergency suspension of the freeing of trade in certain products as well as compensatory payments to permit modernization or diversion of industries, and to aid the retraining of workers.

All this means that the time has come when old answers must be traded for new questions. It is a form of commerce upon which it is never easy to persuade people or nations to embark.

NOTES

1. Cf. Geiger and Lea, "The Free Trade Area Concept as Applied to the United States," submitted to Subcommittee on Foreign Economic Policy, Joint Economic Committee, U.S. Congress, July 28, 1967.

2. Cf. Maxwell Stamp Associates, "The Free Trade Area Option," Atlantic Trade Study (London, 1967).

3. Cf. "A Possible Plan for a Canada-U.S. Free Trade Area," Canadian-American Com-

mittee (Washington, D.C. and Montreal, 1965).

4. Emergency conditions might warrant temporary limitations on export of capital such as those announced by President Johnson in January, 1968. Such limitations, insofar as they affect other FTA countries, could presumably be taken only after multilateral consultation among the members in accordance with the agreement.

5. Rt. Hon. George Brown, House of Commons, May 10, 1967.

6. H. Edward English, *Canada in the Atlantic Economy,* Transatlantic Economic Community: Canadian Perspectives (Toronto: Private Planning Association of Canada, 1968), p. 31.

7. *British Record,* British Information Services, No. 4 (February 29, 1968), pp. 1–2.

8. Rt. Hon. Edward Heath, House of Commons, March 10, 1968.

9. Bruce M. Russett, *Community and Contention: Britain and America in the Twentieth Century* (Cambridge: M.I.T. Press, 1963).

10. Russett, *op. cit.,* Chapter 7, "Mass Communication and Attention," pp. 115–27.

11. *Ibid.,* Chapter 2, "The Basis of Political Community," pp. 26–48.

12. *Ibid.,* p. 220.

13. *Ibid.,* Chapter 12, "Notes on a Theory of Integration," pp. 208–21.

14. Professor E. H. van der Beugel, "Relations Between Europe and the United States," *The Atlantic Alliance, Current Views,* Prepared by the Subcommittee on National Security and International Operations of the Committee on Government Operations, U.S. Senate (Washington, D.C., 1967), p. 19.

15. *The New York Times,* March 13, 1968, p. 46.

16. Karl W. Deutsch, Lewis J. Edinger, Roy C. Macridis, Richard L. Merritt, *France, Germany and the Western Alliance: A Study of Elite Attitudes on European Integration and World Politics* (New York: Charles Scribner's Sons, 1967), p. 150.

17. *The New York Times,* March 14, 1968, p. 4.

18. President Lyndon Johnson, "Making Europe Whole: An Unfinished Task," address to the National Conference of Editorial Writers, New York, Oct. 7, 1966, in *The Atlantic Alliance: Current Views,* Prepared by the Subcommittee on National Security and International Operations of the Committee on Government Operations (Washington, D.C., 1967), p. 3.

19. Barber, Joseph, *Atlantic Unity and the American Interest* (New York: Council on Foreign Relations, 1963), pp. 1–10.

20. *Ibid.,* p. 10. (New York: Council on Foreign Relations, 1963.)

21. Maxwell Stamp, "The Atlantic Alternative to Europe," *The Director* (April, 1967).

22. *Canada,* Canadian Consulate-General Office of Press and Information (March, 1968).

23. *The New York Times,* March 23, 1968, pp. 41 and 50.

24. *The Evening Star* (Washington, D.C.), April 1, 1968, p. A.22.

25. "The Proceedings of the United Nations Conference on Trade and Development" (New York: United Nations, 1964), V, 409.

26. David Wall, *The Third World Challenge, Preferences for Development* (London: The Atlantic Trade Study, 1967), p. 16.

27. David Wall, *op. cit.*, p. 45.

28. See their article, "The Free Trade Area Concept as Applied to the United States," published in *Looking Ahead* (October, 1967), Vol. 15, No. 7.

29. Wilson, speech at Parliamentary Press Gallery lunch, House of Commons, November 29, 1967, B.I.S. Policy Statements, No. 149/67. See also remarks to the same effect by Lord Chalfont, the chief British negotiator, in a speech to the Foreign Press Association in London, September 15, 1967, B.I.S. Official Text, T. 39, pp. 2–3.

30. Cf. Rt. Hon. Douglas Jay, "The High Cost of Europe," *New Statesman*, (November 10, 1967), 625.

31. Rt. Hon. George Brown, House of Commons, May 10.

32. *EFTA Reporter*, June 26, 1967, No. 165, pp. 4, 5.

33. Rt. Hon. George Brown, House of Commons, May 10, 1967.

34. Cf. A. Rivkin, "After the Lagos Agreement" in *Africa Report* (March, 1967), p. 46.

35. Rt. Honorable Michael Stewart, House of Commons, May 10, 1967.

36. A recent British study refers to the "element of ambiguity, which has recently hampered British decision-making, both industrial and political." Stamp Associates, *The Free Trade Area Option* (1967), p. v.

37. *The New York Times*, April 7, 1968, p. 1F.

38. Wilson, Speech to Confederation of British Industry, May 17, 1967, *B.I.S. Policy Statements*, 65/67.

39. Hon. Jacob Javits, Address to The Pilgrims (London), June 27, 1967.

40. Lord Chalfont, Sept. 15, 1967, B.I.S. Official Text, T. 39, p. 1.

41. *The New York Times*, Dec. 17, 1967, p. 2.

42. *Times of London*, Aug. 16, 1967, Letter to the Editor.

43. Lord Chalfont, above, p. 9.

44. Cf. Professor Marshall D. Shulman, "Europe versus 'Detente?'" *Foreign Affairs* (April, 1967), p. 389.

45. Rt. Hon. George Brown, House of Commons, May 10, 1967.

46. Cf. Rt. Hon. Edwards Heath (Cambridge; Harvard University Press, 1969).

47. Rt. Hon. Harold Wilson, House of Commons, May 2, 1967.

48. Rt. Hon. Edward Heath, House of Commons, March 10, 1968.

49. Figures cited in Holloway, *The Case for an Atlantic Free Trade Area*, p. 7. The author cites Hansard, January 31, 1967.

50. Mr. George Thomas, Minister of State, Commonwealth Relations, in a speech to the Royal Commonwealth Society, London, June 1, 1967, B.I.S. Policy Statements, 72/67.

51. Dr. Andrew Pierre, Hudson Institute, comments prepared for this paper.

52. Cf. Report in the *Times of London*, August 10, 1967, p. 4.

53. Rt. Hon. Harold Wilson, House of Commons, April 27, 1967.

54. Cf. Proposal of Andrew Wilson, "Does Britain's Air Future Lie with America?" in the *Observer* (London), July 2, 1967, p. 7.

55. "A Possible Plan for a Canada-U.S. Free Trade Area," above.

56. Federal Liberal Party, Resolutions of the 1966 Convention on a North American Free Trade Area.

57. Comments by Professor Douglas Gibson prepared for this study, May 21, 1967.

58. Comments prepared by Professor English for this study, 1967.

59. Holmes, Los Angeles *Times*, January 22, 1967.

60. Comments prepared by English for this study, May, 1967.

The Economic Impact on the United States of a U.K.-Canada-U.S. Free Trade Association

by Robert G. Hawkins

I. INTRODUCTION

The success of the Kennedy round has left the United States in a kind of commercial policy vacuum, and without any major new trade initiative in the works. Such an environment, when coupled with the continuing balance of payments problem, is especially conducive for protectionist sentiment to be heard, and for a shift away from a liberal trade policy to occur.

A further movement toward free trade is, however, to the best interest of the U.S. economy. The economic advantages for the U.S. would, of course, be *relatively* small due to its large economic size and favorable endowment of resources, but nevertheless sizable in an absolute sense. In addition to the traditional advantage of using resources to produce exports which indirectly buy more imports than could have been produced with the same resources, a number of less tangible but no less significant advantages are possible. Freer trade may induce U.S industries to increase their rate of investment and modernization, to adopt more readily resource-saving techniques and innovations, and to improve management techniques. These types of gain, although difficult to measure, may make a sizable difference in real output even for a relatively closed economy such as the U.S.

In addition, foreign competition is a substitute for domestic competition and may partially offset tendencies toward monopolistic practices by U.S. firms and organized labor. And while the existing size of the U.S. market leaves little room for scale economies in production, a free market larger than the U.S. may permit research-and-development expenditures to be carried out on a more efficient scale.

These potential economic gains would, of course, not be forthcoming without costs. It is costly to reallocate resources, but the magnitude of that cost may vary greatly depending on the circumstances. All the same, to reap the benefits, some industries will lose sales and profits, and employees may be forced to switch jobs and industries. The income lost, and the moving and retraining expenses of displaced workers, as well as the resulting obsolescence of capital equipment are all explicit costs of reallocation. These costs, of course, fall on the previously protected firms and employees, and equity dictates that at least a part of these (nominal) costs be transferred to the public as a whole, which will benefit from the freer trade. In the long run, the benefits of freer trade established on a reciprocal basis must outweigh the costs to the U.S. and the world. And the alternative to freer trade may not be the *status quo,* but more restricted trade with its attendant losses for the nation as a whole.

Among the alternative approaches[1] toward more liberal trade available to the U.S. is that of promoting U.S. membership in a broadly based Free Trade Association (FTA).[2] Indeed, this may represent the most promising alternative to accomplish a major step toward freer trade among industrial countries.[3]

An FTA offers both flexibility and a fair probability of being adopted should the U.S. actively promote it. The flexibility advantage is important since any regional free trade arrangement requires complicated negotiations to safeguard vital national, regional, and industrial interests. A Free Trade Association, however, since it does not require common external tariffs, involves fewer complications and less policy coordination than customs unions or common markets and permits greater facility for widening membership.

In approaching a new trade policy, the U.S. could invite all major industrial countries to become a party to a Free Trade Association covering all major manufactured goods. Some countries or groups of countries might find this arrangement unfeasible in the foreseeable future. The EEC countries, committed to the integration of their economies and concentrating on the problems engendered by this integration, would likely find an additional broadly based arrangement unpalatable at the present time. However, a broad, open-ended FTA should be the goal of American policy in order to secure the maximum advantage of membership, to avoid a possible political reaction to a clubbish Anglo-Saxon arrangement, and to minimize the adverse effects of trade diversion on nonmembers. Such an open-ended arrangement, aside from the beneficial effects on the economies of the U.K., Canada, and other potential members, would also tend to enhance the collective bargaining power of the FTA with the EEC and thereby reduce the tendency of the EEC toward protectionist, inward-looking policies.

While the broadest possible membership in the proposed FTA should be encouraged, including advanced and possibly underdeveloped countries, and the expected membership would include the United States, Canada, the U.K., other EFTA countries, and perhaps Japan and Australia, the central portion of this study is based on the assumption that the United Kingdom, Canada, and the U.S. are the only members. This limitation was dictated by the available time and manpower and the notion that additional members, except for Japan, would alter the economic effects in the U.S. relatively little. Another consideration was the desire to avoid unnecessary duplication of research already done by others, and upon which our particular results depend heavily. The Atlantic Trade Project sponsored by the Council on Foreign Relations has examined the impact on the U.S. of free trade among all Western industrial countries.[4] The probable characteristics of a narrower Free Trade Association encompassing only Canada and the U.S. have been explored in depth by the Canadian-

American Committee and others,[5] and its impact on Canadian industry assessed by Wonnacott and Wonnacott.[6] No specific research on the impact of an FTA mid-way between the two, involving the three countries of concern here, has been undertaken.

Political considerations suggest that these countries would likely form the nucleus, or initial membership, of such an association with the intent that additional countries be added later. An FTA among these three countries would have the advantage of a common language and a broadly similar common approach to economic policy that would minimize the necessary coordination in such areas as labeling, packaging, and disclosure requirements.

Furthermore, the more closely knit the originating group of countries, the greater the chance for successfully concluding the negotiations and implementing an agreement. Canada, the U.K., and the U.S. would likely have greater success in establishing initially a new trade agreement among themselves than would be the case for a broader and more diverse group of countries, if for no other reason than that the number of interests to be reconciled is smaller. Once implementation has begun, arrangements with other countries could be introduced under a procedure for such negotiations.

The following section will make explicit the characteristics which it is assumed the FTA will have, the objectives which such an arrangement would further, and a preliminary look at the relative scope of its impact on U.S. trade. Section III presents estimates of the changes in U.S. exports and imports, on a commodity group basis, which would result directly from the elimination of tariffs. The change in the economic "welfare" of the U.S. associated with the tariff elimination is also estimated. Section IV discusses in more detail the adjustment to changed trade conditions required in selected U.S. import-competing industries which would probably suffer above average effects from new competition. Also, the domestic industries which would be expected to experience declining market shares, as predicted in other studies, are identified.

While the analyses in Sections III and IV deal with "direct" effects of tariff removal, much of the appeal of a Free

Trade Association resides in so-called positive effects arising from industries' response to changed prices and trade volume. These include scale economies, responses to increased competition, etc. A preliminary appraisal of these factors is given in Section V. Section VI attempts to indicate the direction of change in U.S. foreign investment resulting from an FTA, while Section VII is concerned with the nature and magnitude of the required adjustment to the FTA and possible financial arrangements for sharing these costs among the member countries. The question of additional members, and their effects on the findings of this study is taken up in Section VIII.

II. A PRELIMINARY VIEW OF A CANADIAN-U.K.-U.S. FREE TRADE ASSOCIATION (FTA)

CHARACTERISTICS OF THE FTA

A workable set of characteristics for an FTA has been outlined by the Canadian-American Committee, although for a narrower Canadian-U.S. Free Trade Association.[7] This plan provides for a "free trade association" under the articles of the GATT with free trade provisions providing the widest possible commodity coverage. The problem of trade deflection, arising because the existing tariffs would continue to apply to imports from nonmembers, would be met with appropriate origin rules and enforcing procedures patterned after those of the European Free Trade Association (EFTA).[8]

The agreement to eliminate tariffs and quotas would apply to all commodities except some agricultural products and a few other "special situation" commodities such as petroleum and petroleum products. Excepting some agricultural commodities from the general trade provisions is necessary due to national price support and subsidy programs of the member countries. Adjustment to free intra-FTA trade in agricultural commodities, although perhaps not so severe as sometimes imagined, would be sufficiently complicated to warrant exclusion of such commodities from the general free trade provisions. Separate provisions establishing limited free trade in agriculture and/or a program for the eventual integration of markets for agricultural commodities should be included but the form and economic effects of such provisions will not be considered in this study.

Petroleum is also subject to nonprice regulations of particularly complex, extensive, and subtle varieties. The multiplicity of political units that enter into the regulation procedure in the U.S. would make agreement in this area extremely difficult to reach in the early stages. In addition, the dominance of multinational oil companies, which are vertically integrated from exploration to retail outlet, makes the impact of quota and tariff elimination extremely difficult to predict, even if it were practicable. Special and, hopefully, more liberal trade arrangements should be expected from an FTA, but energy policies and their coordination, like agriculture, are better handled in special provisions.

This study also ignores the potentially fruitful free intercourse in services among the members. Eliminating restrictions on tourist expenditures in the member countries and eliminating discriminatory treatment of member shipping, freight, and insurance would undoubtedly have sizable impacts. Particularly important might be the impact on an unprotected, and presumably unsubsidized, American ocean shipping industry from free competition from British shipping. As with petroleum and agricultural commodities, however, the political and industrial ramifications of free trade in these types of services are extremely complex. As before, this does not suggest that special provisions relating to trade in these services should not be made.

Since the FTA should attempt to have the maximum possible commodity coverage, it is assumed that the cases mentioned above would constitute the only exceptions to the general provisions for complete tariff elimination on intra-FTA trade. To facilitate the adjustment to free trade in certain industries which might be particularily hard hit by foreign competition, a slower rate of tariff reduction on certain commodities by certain countries could be provided. This framing of the tariff-elimination timetable so as to avoid unusual hardship would be in addition to "adjustment assistance" for dislocated firms and employees. These will be discussed in later sections, but at this point, it is important to understand that such devices should be considered as the only available answer to adjustment problems. Only in this way will exceptions to the general tariff elimination provisions be minimized.

In order to reap the advantage of unrestricted trade and a widened market, a degree of consistency among the members in competitive practices and government tax-subsidy policy would be essential. The free trade agreement must, therefore, establish rules relating to competition, subsidies, direct taxes, and other national practices so as to reduce and eventually eliminate hidden nontariff and quota discrimination against partner countries' exports. Without effort in this area, tariff elimination may be empty of economic merit in many cases.

SPECIFIC U.S. OBJECTIVES

The most straightforward objective of the U.S. in such a scheme should be the economic gain associated with the creation of a tariff-free, multinational market. The elimination of tariffs (and quotas) on imports from members permits lower prices for the consumer, wider consumer choice among goods, improved allocation of resources, and hence, a net gain in the economic welfare of the member country.

The change in trade and capital flows which would result from a free trade area will have a net balance-of-payments effect in each country which may be positive or negative. It is, of course, possible and even likely that all three countries would experience a net improvement in their balances of payments due to displacement of nonmember country exports by those of the members. The broadening of the market may also have an impact on costs and competitiveness arising from such things as more competitive markets, productivity increasing responses to economic change, economies of scale, and increased rates of real investment. Significant gains in these areas are much more likely to acrue to the U.K. and Canada than to the U.S., simply because of the relative size of the individual national markets.

The proposed Free Trade Association may also provide a

favorable economic environment and the institutional framework for Great Britain and Canada to accomplish desired transformations in their economies. Canada, even though the second-highest income-per-capita country in the world, is still a relatively heavy producer of primary commodities and secondary manufactures. An oft-stated public goal of Canada is to become a full-fledged industrial society. Heretofore, the transformation to an industrial society has been partially blocked by a scarcity of capital, a small market, and a U.S. and Canadian tariff structure which provides an incentive for heavy manufacturing to locate south of the border. The elimination of tariffs between the two countries would, of course, eliminate the latter and provide Canadian industries unfettered access to the huge American market. Canadian firms could then produce on a scale which would permit lower costs.

The U.K. problem is of a different nature. Although highly industrialized, the past decade has seen relatively slow economic growth, periodic balance-of-payments problems, restrictions on foreign payments, controls over wages and prices, and finally a devaluation of the pound. The formula for ending British economic problems is unlikely to be found simply by associating with another economic grouping, although that would presumably have some economic advantages. To the extent that U.S. trade barriers have hindered the expansion of exports and output, the proposed FTA may be a useful stimulant. But the presumed gain from such intangibles as increased competition, the expectations of rapidly growing markets, and possible increased inflows of American capital and technology might well have more profound effects than those directly related to expansion of exports due to the elimination of tariffs.

Thus, the possible advantages to the U.S. of an FTA are both political and economic. The economic advantage, as will be seen below, is relatively small. Since the U.S. national interest is closely interrelated with the economic well-being of potential FTA members, the U.S. has also a considerable political stake in a successful FTA. Furthermore, since U.S. leadership toward an FTA may be the only feasible method of moving significantly toward free trade, and thus a means of avoiding the reversion to protection often accompanying inertia in trade policy, the U.S. stake is sizable indeed.

American Trade, Tariffs, and an FTA

The relative size of the foreign sector of the U.S. economy is relatively small as compared with the other countries. In 1965, U.S. merchandise exports equalled 3.8 per cent of GNP, while merchandise imports were 3.1 per cent of GNP. The comparable percentages for Canada were 17 per cent and 17 per cent respectively, and for the U.K., 15 per cent and 20 per cent. It is clear therefore that the U.S. economy is much less "open" than either of her potential partners. To the extent that this lack of openness has not been caused by American tariffs, an FTA would change American industrial structure very little and the gain would be small relative to total output. On the other hand, given the huge size of U.S. output vis-à-vis that of Canada or the U.K., the *absolute* amount of the gain to the U.S. may still be sizable.

American imports, reflecting relatively scarce and abundant resources in the U.S. economy, are concentrated in primary commodities and in commodities requiring relatively little manufacturing. Thus, food, crude materials, and "other" manufactured goods[9] were the leading import categories in 1966 (see Appendix, Table A-1). Engineering intensive commodities and chemicals account for relatively small shares of imports whereas the shares of commodities serving as inputs to the manufacturing process are relatively high.

Exports, on the other hand, are heavily concentrated in machinery and equipment and, to a lesser extent, agricultural commodities (Appendix, Table A-1). If the structure of U.S. trade reflects the structure of existing comparative advantage, a selective geographical elimiation of tariffs, assuming no great disparity in tariff levels for different commodities, should be expected to increase exports of sophisticated manufactured goods, and to increase imports of crude materials and those manufactured goods less intensive in capital, technology, and skilled labor.

The geographical structure of merchandise trade of the three potential partners—by broad commodity groups—is shown in Table 1. The total value of U.S. trade in virtually all commodity groups dwarfs that of Canada and the U.K. except for the greater U.K. imports of agricultural commodities. The close bilateral trade ties between Canada and the U.S. in all commodity types (except agricultural) emerges clearly from the table. About one-quarter of U.S. nonagricultural trade is with Canada. Exports to Canada are a particularly sizable share of U.S. manufactured goods exports (30 per cent), while Canada supplies the major portion of U.S. crude material imports (33 per cent). The U.S. trade concentration with the U.K. is the reverse, however, with the U.K. taking a larger share of U.S. exports of crude materials (9.3 per cent) than of other categories while supplying a relatively large share of U.S. manufactured imports (11.3 per cent).

U.K. transatlantic trade with the two partners is a significant proportion of total U.K. trade, in most categories, but not nearly so concentrated as U.S.-Canadian trade. U.K. exports to the potential members are concentrated in the manufacturing and semi-manufacturing categories while her imports are more heavily weighted in agricultural commodities and crude materials of which Canada and to a lesser extent the U.S. are significant suppliers.
The per cent of U.K. imports that the EEC supplies and the per cent of her exports that the EEC takes exceeds her trade with the proposed FTA members in manufacture goods, although the reverse is true for semi-manufactures.

Additional detail in the structure of U.S. trade with the proposed partner countries, and with other relevant regions, can be found in Appendix Tables A-2 and A-3. As was seen from Table 1, Canada is the major supplier in virtually every commodity group although the EEC dominates U.S. imports of "other manufactured goods," where Japan is also a significant supplier. In each of these instances, Canada also supplies a significant percentage of U.S. imports. The U.K. is already a significant supplier of machinery and transportation equipment, and other manufactured goods, but must compete in the

U.S. market in these categories with both the EEC and Canada.

The per cent of total U.S. exports going to Canada is 21.9 per cent and to the U.K. 5.7 per cent. Exports to both are heavily concentrated in the heavy manufacturing and engineering-intensive commodity groups. While Canada is by far the most important U.S. export market, the U.K. is less important than Latin America, Japan, and some individual continental European countries.

The major adjustment burden for the U.S. from the free trade provisions of an FTA would be the relative decline in the output of those import-competing industries which would suffer from increased foreign competition. This burden would, of course, be highly selective among industries. Adjustment to increased imports presumes the removal of a previously effective protective tariff. A significant percentage of U.S. imports already enter duty free, however (37 per cent in 1966), although this percentage has been declining in the postwar period (see Table A-4). Furthermore (Table A-6), only 42 per cent of imports from Canada were in the dutiable class. American inports from the U.K., on the other hand, were concentrated (77 per cent) in the dutiable category.

The level of tariffs and the stringency of other import restrictions in the partner countries after the Kennedy Round cuts have been implemented will partially determine the change in U.S. exports and imports due to the formation of an FTA. The tariffs to be eliminated on intra-FTA trade are only those which would not have been eliminated, or will still be remaining, after all other programs (the Kennedy Round) are implemented.

The estimated average (unweighted) tariff rates which will remain after all Kennedy Round cuts have been implemented are shown in Table 2 for the three countries and for the three commodity groups which would likely include all commodities covered by the tariff elimination provisions of an FTA. The average post-Kennedy Round rate will be relatively low (historically) in all categories. Further, for each country, the level of (nominal) tariff protection rises with the degree

Table 1

CONCENTRATION OF EXISTING TRADE AMONG PROPOSED FTA MEMBERS, 1966

	1966 Total Value in Thousands of U.S. Dollars	Per Cent with U.S.	Per Cent with Canada	Per Cent with U.K.	Per Cent with Proposed FTA Partners	Per Cent with EEC
United States:						
Exports	29,899,000		21.7	5.5	27.2	17.6
Agricultural Commodities	5,186,382		8.8	8.1	17.0	21.5
Crude Materials	4,049,747		16.2	9.3	25.6	21.2
Semi-Manufactures	4,760,883		19.0	6.6	25.6	20.4
Manufactures	14,746,000		29.6	5.1	34.6	14.0
Imports	25,550,000		24.0	7.0	31.0	16.1
Agricultural Commodities	4,589,191		10.5	7.0	16.4	5.7
Crude Materials	5,526,656		32.6	1.0	33.7	2.6
Semi-Manufactures	5,213,861		18.7	6.5	25.2	19.5
Manufactures	9,354,226		27.0	11.3	38.3	27.0
Canada:						
Exports	9,551,000	60.6		11.0	71.6	6.3
Agricultural Commodities	1,815,228	25.6		14.5	40.1	8.8
Crude Materials	2,848,546	63.3		11.1	74.5	9.1
Semi-Manufactures	1,688,153	31.4		36.1	67.6	16.6
Manufactures	3,318,006	73.9		4.1	78.0	2.5
Imports	9,127,000	72.4		6.5	78.9	5.7
Agricultural Commodities	722,745	51.3		5.4	56.8	5.5
Crude Materials	1,050,867	57.8		3.1	60.1	1.1
Semi-Manufactures	1,485,711	61.5		9.7	72.9	9.1
Manufactures	5,401,852	81.7		6.8	88.6	5.6

United Kingdom:					
Exports	14,118,000	12.4	4.3	16.7	18.9
Agricultural Commodities	916,145	24.0	3.9	28.0	19.9
Crude Materials	789,513	4.8	3.5	8.3	27.5
Semi-Manufactures	3,190,847	4.3	9.7	14.1	13.7
Manufactures	8,792,607	12.8	4.2	17.0	17.9
Imports	16,671,000	12.1	7.1	19.2	18.5
Agricultural Commodities	4,800,220	9.7	6.3	16.1	9.2
Crude Materials	4,551,706	4.1	7.4	11.4	9.3
Semi-Manufactures	3,094,444	13.3	11.5	24.8	21.9
Manufactures	4,001,289	21.8	4.1	25.8	32.6

Source: OECD, *Commodity Trade,* Series C *Exports* and *Imports* (1966).

Note: The broad commodity groupings shown here, and used elsewhere in this study are defined precisely as follows:

Agricultural Commodities: SITC Groups 0 and 1,
Crude Materials: SITC Groups 2 and 3,
Semi-Manufactures SITC Divisions 41–43, 51–54, 56–59, 61, 63, 65, 67–68
Manufactures: SITC Divisions 55, 62, 64, 66, 69, and Groups 7 and 8.

Table 2

TARIFF RATES FOR BROAD COMMODITY GROUPS UNWEIGHTED POST-KENNEDY ROUND AVERAGE RATES

	Crude Materials[1]	Semi-Manufactures	Manufactures
United States	2.6	8.8	11.1
Canada	2.1	6.6	11.5
United Kingdom (most-favored-nation rate)	3.8	7.3	12.4

[1] Excluding petroleum and petroleum products.

Source: See Table A-7.

of processing. Ranking average tariffs among the countries leads to no conclusive indication as to which countries' tariff rates are highest. The U.S. is lowest in manufactured goods but highest in semi-manufactures. The U.K. is highest in manufacture and crude materials, although the U.K. rate on the latter is the least defensible of any shown and is probably biased upwards in light of recent administrative changes in U.K. tariff procedures. Canada appears to represent an intermediate position in manufactures, but the lowest of the three in the other categories.

The "effective rate of protection" (of value added) is a more valid theoretical measure of relative protection among commodities and among countries than is the simple nominal tariff rates just described.[10] The "effective rate of protection" takes into account the effect of tariffs on imported inputs into the production process, and thus measures the per cent of value added by an industry as a result of tariffs on both inputs and imports competitive with output. No calculations of average "effective rates of protection" have been made on a post-Kennedy Round basis, but calculations using pre-Kennedy Round tariffs have indicated that effective rates of protection are generally higher than nominal rates in the industrial countries, including the U.S. and the U.K.[11] This is primarily a result of the structure of nominal tariffs, which gives more protection to highly processed goods and providing lower rates on imported inputs. This tends to provide an incentive for manufacturing industries to locate within the national border, or to offset such incentives offered by other countries. Even so, the ranking of countries by "effective" and "nominal" rates yields basically the same result. Tariff reductions in the Kennedy Round were more heavily weighted in the highly processed categories, implying that the "effective rates of protection" were reduced more than nominal rates.[12]

While "effective rates of protection" would be preferable to the nominal rates used in the following analysis, computational difficulties, lack of comparable date (especially an input-output matrix for Canada), and other problems militate against using the effective rates. Given the other shortcomings of the data and the method, it is doubtful that this omission adds significantly to the unreliability of the estimates.

The elimination of nontariff barriers will also affect the volume of trade flows in an FTA. It is virtually impossible, however, to identify all nontariff barriers or predict which ones would be removed, which ones left to remain upon the formation of an FTA. Leaving aside agricultural commodities and petroleum, the U.S. and Canada have no operative import quotas.[13] Great Britain imposes quotas on coal, and has imposed in the past temporary quota restrictions discriminatory to the dollar area for balance-of-payments reasons. The U.S., however, imposes purity and labeling requirements on imports which are more stringent than those in most any other country and tend to protect a part of the domestic market for domestic producers who normally produce the quality required by U.S. regulations. Because of the complexity of the matter, the estimates of this study do not explicitly consider the likely impact of changes in nontariff barriers.

III. THE DIRECT EFFECTS ON U.S. TRADE AND ECONOMIC WELFARE

The overall impact of an FTA on U.S. trade and production can best be viewed as consisting of two additive parts. The first is the *direct* result of the elimination of tariffs on intra-area trade on exports, imports, the trade balance, and economic welfare. Production techniques, tastes, and factor supplies are assumed to remain constant and only the results of the reallocation of existing resources at the same level of resource productivity are considered. A general indication of the magnitude of these effects by broad commodity group will be provided in the present section.

The second set of effects, which may be labeled *indirect* or induced effects, arise because of the tendencies for trade volume or output to change because of the direct effects.[14] These include economies of scale, more efficient management, and other results of increased competition and market size. Indications of the potential for these indirect effects and their results for the U.S. as an FTA member will be considered in Part IV.

The total advantage from both the direct and indirect effects of a Free Trade Association depends to a considerable extent on the structure of production among the members. The more competitive are the economies of the members—in the sense that a wide range of the same products are produced behind protective walls in each country—the greater the potential gain from the elimination of tariffs.[15] The scope for greater specialization and for the elimination of marginal and inefficient producers is one factor in determining the potential gain. Thus two countries with considerably different economic structures, i.e., complementary economies, would likely have less to gain from the formation of a free trade area than two countries with competitive economies.[16]

On the strength of this argument alone, it would be expected that the U.S. would receive relatively greater benefit from its membership in an FTA with the U.K., due to the more similar structure of output in those commodities covered by FTA, than with Canada with which the U.S. economic structure is more complementary. Put differently, the number of items produced in both the U.K. and the U.S. which would face new competition from the other country if tariffs were eliminated may be greater than is the case as between the U.S. and Canada (or between the U.K. and Canada).

There are obvious qualifications to this simple prediction.

First, it has been argued, with considerable truth, that the structure of Canada's existing output is partly the result of tariff protection in Canada and the U.S.[17] The implication is that an elimination in barriers and in both countries would lead to a changed economic structure in Canada so that it became more similar to and competitive with the U.S.

Second, the economic distance (transport costs) between the American market and the U.K. markets is, in general, much greater than between the U.S. and Canada. The result of this is that the range of effectively competitive products in the U.S. and U.K., even without tariffs, is greatly limited by transport costs. The latter are much less of a factor in limiting the range of potential competition between the U.S. and Canada. Whether this factor is sufficient to make the *effective* competitiveness between the U.S. and the U.K. less than that between the U.S. and Canada is impossible to evaluate in the present study. Furthermore, with changes in transportation technology, the importance of distance will be reduced, as indeed it has significantly in the postwar period, thus tending to increase the effective competitiveness between the U.K. and U.S. In any case, these factors will continue to be important. The quantitative methods utilized to estimate the effects on trade and welfare implicitly consider the competitiveness and transport factors only to the extent that they are reflected in the *existing* trade relationships among the countries. This, of course, limits the validity of the results but hopefully not greatly.

Estimating Procedure

These estimates presented in this section are based on highly restrictive assumptions and the results, therefore, are meant only to suggest rough orders of magnitude. The concern here is with the *direct* effects of the FTA; i.e., the reallocation of production and consumption due to the price changes, assuming that production techniques, tastes, and factor supplies are unchanged.

The removal of tariffs by the U.S. on imports from FTA members would tend to increase its imports because buyers would switch from competitive domestic products to the cheaper imports from the member countries. The switch from domestic producers to those in the partner countries would result in a net increase in imports (trade creation). In addition, imports from partner countries would be substituted for imports from nonmembers (trade diversion), but the latter would involve no net increase in U.S. imports; simply a switch in the country of origin.

The removal of barriers to the entry of U.S. goods in the other member countries, without removing barriers on imports from nonmembers, would tend to increase U.S. exports for two reasons. First, the lower price (without tariff) of American goods would induce switching from higher-priced domestic products to lower-priced U.S. exports (trade creation). Second, U.S. goods will be substituted for imports from nonmembers because of its tariff advantage (trade diversion). Both involve an increase in U.S. exports.

The estimates below attempt to quantify roughly these expected changes in the value of U.S. trade by broad commodity groups, and for overall trade. In this way, approximate estimates for the impact of an FTA on the U.S. balance of payments, on the volume of trade, on the volume of output in various industries, and the gain or loss in the U.S. real income are obtained.

The change in imports of any commodity (group) as a result of an FTA depends on (a) the height of the U.S. tariff to be eliminated: (b) the preexisting quantity of U.S. imports from Canada and Great Britain; (c) the proportion of the tariff by which the price in the U.S. will fall (determined by foreign supply conditions); and (d) the responsiveness of import volume to price changes (the price elasticity of demand for U.S. imports). The greater each of these factors, the greater the increase in the volume (and value) of imports.

Similar factors govern the change in U.S. exports as a direct result of the tariff elimination. First, the increase in the volume of U.S. exports due to trade creation depends on (a) the heights of the British and Canadian tariffs; (b) the existing volume of U.S. exports to each; (c) the proportion of the tariff by which the delivered price of U.S. goods falls; and (d) the responsiveness of U.S. exports to price changes in Britain and Canada (their price elasticity of demand for imports). Second, trade diversion—the substitution of U.S. for nonmember exports—depends on, in addition to the tariff rate and proportion of it by which price falls (a) the substitutability of U.S. goods for nonmember goods (the elasticity of substitution between U.S. and nonmember exports); and (b) the volume of Canadian and British imports from nonmembers competitive with U.S. exports. The sum of the increases in exports due to trade creation and trade diversion yields the total increase in U.S. exports in each commodity class.

The impact of an FTA on the value of U.S. imports and exports was estimated for forty commodity divisions of the Standard International Trade Classification (SITC).[18] For reasons given above, agricultural products (SITC Section 0) and petroleum and petroleum products (SITC Division 33) are excluded. Other exclusions include beverages and tobacco (Divisions 11 and 12), and coal, gas, and electric energy (Divisions 32–34).[19]

The U.S. currently exports and imports commodities within each of the forty broad commodity divisions used here. Thus, elimination of tariffs will tend to increase both exports and imports in each division. To estimate these increases, 1966 was chosen as a base year. This was the latest year for which complete trade data was available, and the most recent pattern of trade should be used as a basis for estimated changes.

Unweighted post-Kennedy Round tariff averages for each commodity division and for each country were used. Some distortion in the results are inevitable in any averaging procedure, and such is certainly the case here. The tariff data used, however, appear to be the most appropriate available.[20]

The estimates of the elasticities of demand (the per cent increase in quantity of imports due to a 1 per cent decline in domestic price) for imports in the U.S., Canada, and Great Britain were taken from various sources,[21] and in some cases, adjustments were made to make them more tenable for the purposes here. SITC commodity divisions were divided into three separate categories—crude materials, semi-manufacture goods.[22] Three separate elasticity estimates were used, one for each broad category. The same elasticity was applied to each SITC division in each category. This procedure, of course, overestimates the impact on U.S. trade for commodities with less than average substitutability, and underestimates the more homogeneous internationally traded goods. Hopefully, the degree of aggregation in each commodity division and the law of large numbers avoids any major systematic bias entering the estimates from this source. A similar procedure was applied in order to estimate the amount of substitution of U.S. exports for nonmember exports to the partner countries.[23]

On balance, the assumptions made in arriving at the following estimates have been purposely designed to yield a conservative estimate of the improvement in the U.S. trade balance and in the U.S. standard of living. Conservative choices have been made in estimating the increase in U.S. exports, while adjustments in elasticities and tariffs have been made to make the predicted increase in imports in the high range. Thus the estimates are purposely tilted to yield a conservative estimate of the balance of payments improvement from an FTA.

Results

Two sets of estimates of the direct impact on the value of U.S. trade were made. The first, labeled Assumption "A," is based on the assumption that both export and import supply prices (exclusive of tariff) remained constant after the tariff was eliminated. The second, Assumption "B," assumed that the supply price of U.S. exports remained constant while the price of U.S. imports (U.K. and Canadian export prices) rose by some proportion of the tariff which was eliminated.[24]

Some justification exists for both assumptions "A" and "B." To postulate a constant U.S. export price seems reasonable in view of the size of U.S. industry vis-à-vis exports to Canada and the U.K. The expansion of exports as a result of tariff elimination in these two countries may result in selective price increases in the U.S., but this is unpredictable and the mobility of U.S. resources suggests that such price pressure would not be general.

To assume that U.K. and Canadian export prices would not change ("A") would be valid only if appropriate policy control over aggregate demand could be used to keep prices from rising, and if the reduction in domestic demand fell on those industries supplying the increased U.S. import markets. There is some relevant evidence that elimination of tariffs in EFTA has not resulted in any significant increase in the supply price in most cases.[25] If that experience could be repeated in an FTA, our estimates under Assumption "A" would have even greater validity.

However, Assumption "B" may be the more realistic given the large size of the U.S. market relative to output in Canada or the U.K. The relative expansion of export industries in the latter may necessitate price increases in those industries, thus eroding a portion of stimulus derived from the removal of U.S. tariffs. Some evidence of this has recently been observed in connection with the pound sterling devaluation. Almost no export prices fell by the full amount of the devaluation, although the time elapsed is still too short for a definitive appraisal. The effect of a rise in export prices in the U.K. and Canada on U.S. payments for imports would depend on the responsiveness of U.S. quantity demanded to price changes. In cases where the elasticity of U.S. import demand is less than 1, U.S. payments would be higher while import volume would be lower than would have been the case had supply prices remained constant.

The results of the calculations are summarized in Tables 3 and 4, and are shown in detail (by SITC Division) in Appendix Table A-9. The value of exports is predicted to increase by $1.15 billion. Of this, $957 million (83 per cent) would represent an increase in manufactured goods exports, about $200 million (16 per cent) in semi-manufactures, and a negligible amount in crude materials. Furthermore, under the assumptions of the estimating procedure, the major portion (almost 75 per cent) of the export increase would be the result of trade creation, rather than trade diversion. In semi-manufactures, however, trade diversion would exceed trade creation.

Import value would increase by $1,100 million if foreign prices remained constant (Assumption "A") and by $800 million if foreign prices should rise according to the assumptions in the Appendix (Assumption "B"). As with exports, the major portion of the increase would occur in manufactured goods (84 per cent under "A," 79 per cent under "B"). Significant increases would likely occur in semi-manufacture imports, but the increase in imports of crude materials would be relatively small, although significant under Assumption "B."

The estimated net impact on the U.S. balance of trade is shown in the right columns of Table 3. Under Assumption "A," a slight improvement ($38 million) is predicted; under Assumption "B" a somewhat longer improvement of $347 million. In either case, the *direct* effect on the balance of payments would not be sizable, although the predicted change in total exports and imports would be significant. Among the broad commodity groups shown in Table 3, the net balance-of-payments impact in manufactures and semi-manufactures are both positive, while that in crude materials is negative but of minor magnitude. The major balance-of-payments difference resulting from the two assumptions regarding foreign price changes would arise through trade in manufactured goods, as the net effect under "A" is only a $21 million improvement while under "B" it is $318 million.

The *dollar value* estimates in Table 3 can at best be very rough indications of the magnitude of changes in export and import values to be expected from the formation of an FTA. Aside from the numerous deficiencies of the essentially mechanical estimating procedure, the use of 1966 as a base year seriously biases the estimates of dollar value changes. First, the existing volume of trade on which the estimates are based will itself change due to the implementation of the Kennedy Round tariff cuts. Thus, the formation of an FTA would eliminate post-Kennedy Round tariffs on an already expanded volume of intra-FTA trade. The effect of this omission is to bias downward the dollar amount estimates for both exports and imports, but not necessarily by the same degree.

Second, the 1967 devaluation of the pound sterling will also change the existing value of exports and imports so that trade totals and structure at the inception of an FTA would be systematically different from those in 1966. The pound deval-

Table 3

ESTIMATED CHANGE IN THE VALUE OF U.S. EXPORTS AND IMPORTS[1]

(millions of dollars)

	Change in Exports			Change in Imports		Net Balance-of-Trade Effect	
	Trade Creation	*Trade Diversion*	*Total*	*Assumption A*	*Assumption B*	*Assumption A*	*Assumption B*
Total	847.0	304.0	1.151.0	1,112.7	804.2	38.3	346.9
Crude Materials	2.2		2.2	3.2	9.1	—.9	—6.9
Semi-Manufactures	77.9	113.4	191.4	173.2	155.8	18.1	35.5
Manufactures	766.9	190.5	957.4	936.3	639.2	21.1	318.1

[1] Based on 1966 trade data and post-Kennedy Round (1972) tariffs described in the Appendix.

Source: Appendix Table A-9.

uation will tend to increase U.K. exports to members and reduce U.K. imports. The effect on the dollar value estimates in Table 3 is probably to overstate the increase in U.S. exports and understate the increase in U.S. imports; i.e., to overstate the improvement in the trade balance. Thus, the value estimates in Table 3 actually apply to a hypothetical situation in which post-Kennedy Round tariffs were eliminated in 1966 before the pound devaluation.

The shortcomings just described are partially remedied by expressing the changes as percentages of existing trade. Assuming that the tariff rates are valid, that the elasticities are correct, and that the assumed price behavior would be realized, the estimates may validly indicate the expected change in U.S. trade as a percentage of the trade existing at the time an FTA would be implemented. These percentages are summarized in Table 4.

Table 4

DIRECT EFFECT OF FTA TARIFF REMOVAL ON U.S. EXPORTS AND IMPORTS VALUE

	Per Cent Increase in U.S. Exports	Per Cent Increase in U.S. Imports: *Assumption A*	Per Cent Increase in U.S. Imports: *Assumption B*
All Commodities	3.8	4.4	3.1
Crude Materials	.1	0.07	0.2
Semi-Manufactures	4.0	3.3	3.0
Manufactures	6.4	10.3	6.8
Change in trade with Canada and the U.K. as a Percent of Existing Trade with Canada and U.K.			
All Commodities	13.9	14.8	10.6
Crude Materials	15.6	13.2	11.8
Semi-Manufactures	.1	0.2	0.5
Manufactures	18.7	26.1	17.8

Source: Appendix Table A-9.

Note: Assumption "A" is that no changes in export prices occur.
Assumption "B" is that Canadian and U.K. export prices change according to the schedule in the Appendix.

The upper half of the table expresses the estimated changes as percentages of U.S. trade with all countries. Total exports are predicted to rise by 3.8 per cent; total imports by 4.4 per cent under Assumption "A" and by 3.1 per cent under "B."[26] The percentage increases in both exports and imports of manufactured goods are considerably higher than in either of the other two categories, implying that U.S. trade would tend to become more concentrated in manufactured goods.

The lower half of Table 4 shows the predicted change in U.S. trade as a per cent of existing trade with Canada and the U.K. It is obvious that, under our assumptions, an FTA would expand the value of U.S. trade with the partners by significant amounts (14 per cent for exports, and 10–15 per cent for imports). Sizable increases in manufactures (18.7 per cent for exports, 18–26 per cent for imports) would likely occur, with sizable but lower increases for semi-manufactures, and little change in crude materials. Thus, bilateral trade between the U.S. and her proposed partners would become more concentrated in manufactured goods. Imports would become less concentrated in semi-manufactures under Assumption "A," but more under Assumption "B." Exports of semi-manufactures would rise more than total exports. Exports and imports of crude commodities would be little affected. The results reflect the structure of U.S. tariff rates which tends to give high effective protection to some domestic industries producing less sophisticated manufactures with low capital equipment and skilled labor requirements.[27]

Some tentative generalizations concerning exports and imports in individual SITC divisions may be drawn from Appendix Table A-9. First, the commodity divisions in which the estimated increases in imports are considerably greater than in exports tend to be those requiring little or relatively unsophisticated processing. Since the estimated change in imports accounts for both net increases in U.S. consumption and the decline in the share of the market for U.S. producers, the U.S. producers in these divisions will find their protected markets eroded by U.K. or Canadian competitors. Clear-cut cases using both "A" and "B" estimates are wood and lumber (SITC 24), essential oil and perfume materials (55), wood manufactures

(63), paper manufactures (64), nonferrous metals (68), and travel goods (83). These are the categories that one expects would be harmed by an FTA. It is notable, however, that with few exceptions (essential oils and perfumes and travel goods), U.S. trade in these divisions is very heavily concentrated with Canada, and the predicted increase in U.S. imports would come necessarily from Canada. As will be noted below, the estimated increase in imports in some of these divisions might be biased upward by the use of an unweighted average tariff, but this bias may be partially offset by a downward bias in the elasticities used, particularly in the more homogeneous commodity categories.

Among the commodity divisions in which sizable (absolute) expansions in exports, but not imports, are predicted are machinery (both electric and nonelectric, 71 and 72), transport equipment (73), and professional and scientific instruments (86). Again this is expected, since it is in these categories that the U.S. advantage in capital, research, and skill intensive products is manifested. It is interesting, however, that the predicted increase in U.S. exports due to trade diversion, while sizable, was less important than trade creation in the machinery and transport equipment categories (71–73).

The estimates for a number of commodity divisions indicate sizable increases in both exports *and* imports, under both assumptions. The more interesting appear to be chemicals and chemical manufactures (51–59 except 55), textiles (65), clothing (84), and footwear (85). While there can be little doubt that two-way trade in these broad commodity groups would expand, the estimates may be somewhat biased so as to favor the increase of U.S. exports as opposed to imports. The outlook for trade in some of these categories will be taken up below. The estimating procedure used here obviously cannot take into account the differences in demand elasticities and market conditions within and between commodity divisions which would be necessary to obtain a true picture of the likely changes in trade. Only a rough indication of the structure of the change in commodity trade is yielded by our method.

These estimates have not considered the increase in U.S. exports to the partner countries arising from the elimination of Commonwealth Preferences. This effect would likely not be sizable, since the degree of preference is low and the overlapping of U.K. and Canadian exports competitive with those of the U.S. in the other partner's market is not great. All the same, this omission has biased downward the estimates of U.S. export expansion. This bias may be important in those few categories in which Canadian exports competitive with U.S. exports now enter the U.K. duty free or at a low preference rate. The Canadian advantage in the U.K. is considerably greater than the U.K. advantage in Canada.[28] All the same, it seems likely that the total effect on U.S. exports of the elimination of preferences would not be sizable.

In summary, the estimates presented here indicate that the formation of an FTA would have relatively little direct effect on total U.S. trade, but a marginally important one. The structure of U.S. exports would tend to shift further to commodities intensive in technology, skilled and professional labor, and capital. Imports would further concentrate, to the extent possible with the U.K. and Canada as partners, in semi- and fully-manufactured commodities but of a generally less sophisticated variety than the exports. Roughly one-fourth of the estimated increase in exports would result from displacement of nonmember exports to member countries. The overall balance-of-payments effect of the FTA would be favorable, although the results must be qualified because of the changes in trade volume and structure resulting from the Kennedy Round tariff cuts and the pound devaluation.

THE DIRECT EFFECT ON THE U.S. LEVEL OF LIVING

The estimated changes in the volume of trade together with the tariff reduction may be used to calculate the change in "economic welfare" for the U.S. as a result of the direct effects of tariff reduction in an FTA. Ignoring the effects of the change in trade on the distribution of income and wealth, the direct effect of an FTA on the real national income has two parts.

First, prices of imported goods and domestic substitutes become lower, and the total *benefit* to the buyers (consumers' surplus) exceeds the sum of the losses to competing domestic industry (producers' surplus) and to the government (tariff revenue). This net gain to the consumer arises because resources are more efficiently allocated in production, i.e., the value of the increase in output in the export industry exceeds the value of the decline in output in the import-competing industry, and because consumer choice is widened, i.e., consumption is more efficiently allocated.

Second, there will be a change in the nation's terms of trade to the extent that export prices do not change in equal proportion to import prices. If import prices rise relative to export prices, the purchasing power of one unit of exports over imports declines, and real national income is harmed. The combination of the "allocation effect" and "terms-of-trade effect" yields the net change in economic welfare.

Using the estimates of the change in trade in Table A-9, the net effect on U.S. economic welfare was calculated.[29] Under assumption "A," wherein the supply price of both U.S. exports and U.S. imports remain unchanged (thereby making the terms-of-trade effect nil), U.S. real income in 1966 prices would be higher by about $50 million, or about .01 per cent of 1966 GNP and about 25 cents per capita per year.

Under Assumption "B," the net effect on economic welfare is to reduce it marginally, because the loss from the adverse movement in the terms of trade exceeds the gain from improved resource allocation. The rise in supply price of U.S. imports from the partner countries while U.S. export prices are assumed constant results in a negative terms-of-trade effect which more than offsets the gain from improved allocation of consumption and production. The net loss from both effects under Assumption "B" is about $250 million dollars (1966 prices). Of this, $30 million is the gain from improved allocation, while $280 million is the loss as a result of higher import prices. The latter, while a loss to the U.S., would be a gain to the FTA partners. Thus, the welfare of the three countries combined would improve.

These calculations further confirm that the direct impact of an FTA on the U.S. economy would be rather minute. The indirect effects must also be considered, however, and may, in the long run, be significant. Before turning to such factors, a more detailed but highly selective examination of the direct impact on certain industries will be made.

IV. IMPORT COMPETITION AND DOMESTIC ADJUSTMENT

While the estimates of Section III imply that the direct impact of an FTA on U.S. trade would be relatively small, some import-competing industries with protected domestic markets could suffer sizable adverse effects. This section, using the results of Section III, attempts to examine the relationship between the estimated import changes and the domestic industry. In addition, the industries that are likely to suffer increased competition from imported manufactured goods and imported crude materials are identified and the impact of the increased competition briefly evaluated. Finally, the possible arrangements for facilitating adjustment to increased imports are reviewed.

The SITC commodity divisions in which major increases in U.S. imports are predicted can easily be seen in Table A-9. Data for the more important commodity divisions are reproduced in Table 5. The table also shows the Standard Industrial Classification (SIC) industries which roughly conform to the particular SITC commodity divisions.[30] The final column shows the estimated change in imports expressed as a per cent of the pre-FTA (1966) output of the U.S. industry.

The increase in imports would result from two effects. First, the lowered domestic price (assuming foreign prices do not rise by the full amount of the tariff) due to removal of the tariff would increase the quantity consumed domestically. Second, the lower price of imported commodities would force marginal domestic producers to leave the industry, to reduce output, or to adjust to the foreign competition. To the extent that the latter occurs, sales by the domestic industry will not decline although profits may be adversely affected in either case. The percentages in the final column of Table 5 can thus be deemed as an upper-limit impact on the sales of the domestic

Table 5

ESTIMATED CHANGE IN IMPORTS IN RELATION TO DOMESTIC PRODUCTION—SELECTED IMPORT COMPETING INDUSTRIES

SITC Commodity Division *Number*	*Title*	Estimated Increase in Imports[1] (millions of dollars)	Corresponding SIC Industry Group	Value of Shipments, SIC Industries[2] (millions of dollars)	Estimated Change in Imports as a Per Cent of Shipments
51	Chemical elements & compounds & dyeing tanning, etc.		281 (except 281.4-5)		
53	Materials	22.2	285, 286	15,879,533	0.1
63	Wood & cork manufactures excluding furniture	7.5	243, 244, 249	5,438,418	0.1
64	Paper, paperboard & manufactures thereof	233.3	264, 265, 266, 276 277	13,314,076	1.7
65	Textile yarn, fabrics, etc.	15.8	22	19,599,852	0.0
66	Nonmetallic mineral [illegible]	55.5	[illegible]	14,629,434	0.3

68	Nonferrous metals	80.3	333, 334	5,975,226	1.3
71	Machinery, other than electric	143.8	35	46,633,641	0.3
73	Transport equipment	231.1	37	71,511,772	0.3
84	Clothing	23.2	23	19,971,042	0.1
85	Footwear	5.6	3021, 314	3,222	0.1

[1] From Table A-9, assumption "A'

[2] Department of Commerce, *Annual Survey of Manufactures, 1966*

Note: The coverage of the SITC and SIC data, which are derived on different bases, are not identical for any case. However, the degree of difference in coverage is not so great as to make the calculations meaningless.

industry since it assumes that all of the increase in imports would result from displacement of sales by domestic producers.[31] The analysis here, however, is no substitute for a thorough industry-by-industry analysis of the effects of an FTA for each member.

The estimated changes in imports are all relatively small compared to existing sales of the corresponding U.S. industries. The largest relative change, 1.7 per cent in paper and paperboard, while significant does not imply a major displacement of domestic output. The other case of significant import competition is in nonferrous metals. In every other industry division, the estimated change in imports is less than 0.5 per cent of existing domestic output, which indicates that the magnitude of adjustment to increased imports would not be a major problem for most industries. Even so, some subdivisions of the industries in Table 4, and firms within those subdivisions, would be severely harmed by the import competition and there would be little comfort for the owners and their employees in the knowledge that the relative adjustment for the entire economy was minimal.

Manufactured Goods

The increased competition from imports of manufactured goods will be felt in those U.S. industries which are not highly intensive in research and skilled labor; i.e., those industries which produce commodities in which the U.S. has a competitive disadvantage vis-à-vis Canada and the U.K. and which also are favored by relatively high tariffs. The major portion of U.S. trade expansion (both exports and imports) would occur in semi- and fully-manufactured commodities. Because of this, and since the factors governing increased imports of crude materials are different from those for manufactured goods, the two categories will be briefly reviewed individually. Since manufactures covers such a broad spectrum of commodities, two instances of significantly increased import competition under an FTA will be treated as illustrative cases, and the findings of others relating to possible U.S. import competition will be summarized.

To obtain an impression of the possible impact of increased imports on firms and employees, more narrowly defined industries and commodity groups are needed. Paper and paperboard (SITC 641) and woolen fabrics (SITC 653.2) have been chosen, primarily because other studies have shown that these two industries, the former in Canada and the latter in the U.K., would have especial success in penetrating the U.S. market under conditions of free trade.[32]

A summary picture of the impact of an FTA on these U.S. industries is presented in Table 6. Since the earlier elasticity

Table 6

ILLUSTRATIVE MAXIMUM "IMPACT" OF FTA ON TWO U.S. MANUFACTURING INDUSTRIES

	SITC 641 Paper & Paperboard	SITC 653–2 Woolen Fabrics
U.S.—Average Tariff (1972)	6%	32%
1966 Imports as % of U.S. output	7.3%	7.9%
Estimated decline in U.S. output due to FTA if increased imports displace U.S. production	2.4%	3.4%
Loss of employment due to FTA assuming employee-output ratio remains constant	10,000	1,500
Imports as % of domestic output after FTA	9.9%	11.7%

Source: Appendix Table A-9 and Department of Commerce, *Annual Survey of Manufactures*, 1966.

assumption (3.5) is surely too low for such commodities due to their relatively homogeneous and substitutable nature, it was decided that 7.0 would be more nearly correct, and would provide a "maximum" import estimate. The U.S. paper and paperboard industry could be substantially "injured" by the freeing of trade with Canada. U.S. imports from Canada amounted to 7.3 per cent of U.S. domestic production in 1966. Assuming that the price in the U.S. would fall by the full amount of the 6 per cent tariff as a result of an FTA, and that the elasticity of import demand was 7.0, imports from Canada would jump to the equivalent of 9.9 per cent of U.S. domestic production. Assuming that the entire increase in imports results in the displacement of domestic production, and that employment in the industry would change in the same ratio as output, the expected decline in domestic output would be 2.4 per cent of the 1966 level, and employment would decline by 10,000. Both these assumptions tend to overestimate the impact of a given change in imports on the domestic industry since there would not be a complete substitution of imports for domestic production; some part of the increase in imports would satisfy an increase in the quantity demanded caused by the fall in the import price. Similarly, the loss of employment would probably be less than in proportion to decline in production due to "fixed" employment categories which do not vary directly with output such as technical and administrative workers.

With respect to woolens, the complete removal of the U.S. tariff would raise imports from 7.9 per cent of domestic output to 11.7 per cent. This expansion, in turn, would cause a decline in domestic output of 3.4 per cent and a loss of employment of about 1,500.

These "upper limit" estimates of the displacement of domestic output and employment by cheaper imports show that even extreme assumptions as to the vulnerable U.S. industries yield results that imply relatively little harm to U.S. import-competing industries from an FTA. Expanding domestic markets would permit much of the predicted increase in imports to be absorbed by increases in total sales rather than by reductions in the sales of domestic firms. For these and other reasons, import competition in manufactures would pose no insurmountable problem for U.S. industry, even in those industries which are likely to be hardest hit.

Other studies concerning the international competitiveness of Canadian and the U.K. manufacturing, and the likely consequences of export performance under trade liberalization, have yielded results in broad agreement with those presented above. Balassa has ranked various commodities on the basis of "revealed comparative advantage."[33] On this basis, an FTA would likely permit the U.K. to expand exports to the U.S. in such manufactures as pigments and paints, woolen fabrics, tractors, trucks and buses, and power-generating equipment. Increased competition from Canadian exports should fall heavily in paper, organic chemicals, railway construction materials, and power generating machinery. Wells[34] also found U.K. exports of power generating equipment, woolen textiles, and chemicals as likely to benefit from an open U.S. market. A survey of a sample of British firms by Maxwell Stamp Associates found that the majority expected no major impact on sales from an FTA with the U.S. Only 17 per cent thought a substantial gain in sales could occur, and these were scattered through the machinery—(electric and nonelectric), metal manufactures, chemicals, and textiles industries.[35]

Careful attention has been given to the impact on Canadian industry, and therefore implicitly on U.S. imports from Canada, of a U.S.-Canada Free Trade Association in studies by English and by Wonnacott and Wonnacott. English[36] foresees the possibility of a major restructuring of Canadian industry as a result of a Free Trade Association, with the reduction of product lines produced in Canada permitting the adoption of more efficient techniques and longer production runs. As a result, one expects that both U.S. imports from Canada and exports to Canada would increase more than these mechanical estimates based on simple tariff elimination suggest in those product categories affected by this reorientation of Canadian industry. Industries examined by English which would likely be affected positively are chemicals, consumer durable goods, and machinery and equipment.[37]

The Wonnacotts[38] have attempted to estimate the low-cost location of various broad industries in a tariff-free North American market. On the basis of cost calculations alone,[39] certain regions in Canada would offer lower production costs than any regions in the U.S. for a broad range of industries. Although certain of the assumptions underlying their analysis are tenuous, the conclusion that Canadian locations had cost advantages for such industries as wood products, electrical equipment, leather goods, and transport equipment are all consistent with the findings of others that such industries would likely benefit from free trade with the U.S.

The analyses by English and the Wonnacotts implicitly take into account the advantage of economies of scale and modernization in Canadian industry which would likely result from a North American free-trade area. They thus deal with effects not contained in the earlier parts of this study. However, their general conclusions are consistent with the structure of the estimated change in imports of manufactures in Tables 3 and A-9. To the extent that the broader market permits significant economies of scale in particular industries in the U.K. or Canada, such as transport equipment, chemicals, or electrical machinery, the estimates of changes in U.S. imports in Table 3 may be too low, and the import competition to be faced by U.S. industry might, in fact, be higher.

Crude Materials

Separate discussion of possible U.S. import competition from imports of crude materials under an FTA appears justified on a number of grounds. Resource endowment and transport costs permit the discussion to be confined to Canadian-U.S. trade. This is especially true if Britain could win a concession to prolong her protection of domestic coal mining, thus continuing to block U.S. coal exports to the U.K. after an FTA.

The estimates of net trade change in Table 3 indicate a deterioration in the trade balance for crude materials of $.9 million under assumption "A" and $6.9 million under assumption "B." Under the former, the divisions which would experience major increases in imports are nonferrous metals (SITC 68), metalliferous ores and scrap (8), textile fibres (26), and fixed vegtable oils (42).

In each case, except textile fibres, trade with Canada dominates the total estimated change. It is obvious that the major impact on U.S. imports of crude materials lies in resource-based commodities—especially metals—of Canadian origin. Aside from petroleum,[40] which has been excluded from this study, the other nonmetallic crude material of interest is coal. Again, the freeing of trade in coal between the U.S. and Canada would likely increase U.S. exports rather than the reverse.

Trade in metallic crude materials is influenced by nontariff, as well as tariff barriers. Quotas, however, have been of no particular significance since the U.S. quota on lead and zinc was suspended in 1965. While government tax policy in both countries tends to favor domestic mineral production vis-à-vis nonmineral industries, it is likely that Canadian producers receive greater subsidies (direct and indirect) than do their U.S. counterparts.[41] Harmonization of these relevant nontariff policies would therefore reduce the estimated increase in U.S. imports.

The principal crude commodities affected by an FTA would be aluminum, and to lesser extents, lead and zinc, magnesium and molybdenum. The U.S. (post-Kennedy Round) tariff on crude aluminum will be less than 5 per cent, and although low, is still sufficient to protect a portion of U.S. aluminum output.[42] Also, elimination of the remaining tariffs on lead and zinc in an FTA would affect U.S. marginal producers. In addition, remaining U.S. duties on magnesium and molybdenum remain effective in screening out some Canadian imports. The remaining metal and nonmetal crude material imports would be relatively little affected by an FTA. Trade is already essentially free in iron ore, nickel, asbestos, potash, etc. and the U.S. tariff on copper has been suspended. Although the tariff on pig iron would tend to make steelmaking locate in the U.S., it is unlikely that U.S. steel imports would change drastically under free trade since the Canadian industry is still at a fuel-cost disadvantage.

The U.S. tariff structure, which gives preference to little-processed, crude materials, is largely responsible for the relatively small change to be expected in crude material imports. The predicted increase in imports would be concentrated in those few nonferrous metal and mineral imports (cited above) from Canada for which effective protection currently exists for marginal U.S. producers.

ADJUSTMENT ASSISTANCE AND IMPORT COMPETING INDUSTRIES

This section has concentrated on the possibility and degree of Canadian and U.K. exports capturing domestic markets from domestic producers as a result of an FTA. This problem for the U.S. would not be of major proportions, and would likely be considerably more severe in Canada and Great Britain. For the U.S., the probability of U.S. producers losing as much as 5 per cent of any broadly defined domestic market is very low. Unless one defines the market—and the commodity bundle comprising it—very narrowly, the adjustment problem is minimal.

Furthermore, the estimates and discussion have been concerned solely with relative changes. In an absolute sense, U.S. producers may suffer little absolute reduction in sales due to increased import competition. Should the U.S. economy grow at the rate of 4 per cent per year in real terms, the increase in consumption of most commodities *in one year* would equal the total expected relative displacement of domestic output by increased imports of that commodity. Thus, a rapidly growing economy would reduce the burden of adjustment to increased imports and facilitate the reallocation of resources and production.

Since the elimination of tariffs and the harmonization of the appropriate domestic policies in an FTA would not occur in one giant step, but would be spread out over at least a five-year period, the amount of adjustment required in any one year would be even smaller. Assuming that the increase in imports due to the FTA were spread evenly over five years, total merchandise imports would increase at most 1.0 per cent[43] faster than they would have without an FTA. For the economy as a whole, this is almost trivial; especially since exports would increase at a similarly accelerated rate.

The specific bearers of the adjustment, however, may undergo severe economic difficulty to permit the economic gain of an FTA to the entire U.S. Some workers with the wrong skills, associated with the wrong firm, or in the wrong region will become unemployed. The capital equipment of the marginal firm which owes its existence to tariff protection will become idle. These instances must occur, or no static gain from an FTA due to improved allocation of resources and consumption will accrue to the U.S. at all. Equity dictates that the entire society bear these costs of adjustment rather than the individuals and firms directly affected.

The principal means of transferring the costs to the society is through "adjustment assistance" financed from general tax revenues.[44] Increased unemployment compensation, subsidized retraining to provide useable skills, and the provision of moving expenses are among the benefits which should be provided for the displaced employees. The firm which finds its sales significantly reduced by import competition as a result of tariff reductions should also be aided with long-term low-interest loans subsidized by the government, government-assisted corporate planning with respect to product diversification, new production techniques, and other such benefits. The adjustment-assistance schemes, patterned after an existing and successful one, should be a part of any FTA agreement, and the provisions should be similar (though not necessarily identical) among the members.

A less tangible avenue for assisting harmed industries and employees would be advance study and advice by a government-sponsored agency. Its function would be to carefully consider, before implementation, the impact of an FTA on an industry and its employees and to communicate the findings to industry leaders, trade associations, and union and employee leaders so that the response to the probable effects could be incorporated into corporate and employee planning. This would permit more intelligent adjustment, with foresight, to both increased imports and larger export markets by those industries significantly affected. It might also increase the likelihood that potential indirect benefits from scale economies, product development, and technological change would be realized. A mystical "anticipatory" or "expectational" response among industries and firms may not only accentuate the benefits of an FTA but minimize the amount of government adjustment assistance needed.[45]

One other possibility deserves consideration as a means of alleviating the worst effects of adjustment. If an industry, defined in negotiations, is shown to face severe adjustment problems for which the means discussed above would be insufficient, the tariff reductions on the relevant commodities could be stretched out over a longer period, say ten years rather than five. Such a possibility would provide an avenue for avoiding snags in the negotiation of an FTA, and would be a reasonable substitute for completely excluding commodities from the free trade provision.

V. INDIRECT PRODUCTION EFFECTS

The analysis of the direct effects of an FTA in the foregoing sections has assumed that production techniques would remain the same. However, the economic forces set up by tariff elimination and the tendency toward further international specialization may induce changes in production techniques and in the real costs of production. These "indirect" effects, in turn, would affect the economic welfare and trade balance of the participating nations.

The potential indirect production effects resulting from a wider market in an FTA include economies of scale (both internal and external), and the effects of increased competition on production efficiency, technological change, the rate of investment, and the rate of spending on research and development.[46] Each of these possible responses to an enlarged market is likely to increase economic welfare of the individual member country and the group as a whole.[47] Capturing internal economies of scale because of larger production facilities, longer production runs, or the more economic use of research and development facilities would lower the cost of output, and thereby provide a once-over increase in welfare and in the volume of external trade. Similarly, external economies resulting from large-scale production complexes permitted by a larger market would tend to increase economic welfare through lower social costs of production. And increased competition from duty free imports might "shock" previously protected firms into modernizing, adopting least-costs production techniques, and developing new processes and products in order to preserve their existing domestic market. To the extent that this reduces costs, provides better-quality products, or increases the rate of investment or innovation, a gain in economic welfare results.

The relative importance of indirect effects in economic integration remains a matter of much debate. Some economists assign the major impact to them,[48] while others[49] indicate that their impact would be minimal. The failure to reach a consensus among economists of their importance is the result of a complete lack of, or totally inadequate, empirical measurement. Quantification of the indirect effects of an FTA on the U.S. would be extremely difficult even if these effects had already transpired and could thus be observed,[50] while the present task of indicating the prospective effects can go little beyond indicating the likely direction of change.

The "indirect" impact of an FTA on the U.S. would consist of a number of effects. First, economies of scale—internal and external—arising from the expansion of U.S. export industries to serve tariff-free markets in Canada and the U.K. would represent an increase in U.S. economic welfare. Second, increased foreign competition may force an improvement in the "efficiency" of U.S. import-competing industries, and thus increase welfare and limit the expansion of imports resulting from the removal of U.S. tariffs. Third, widening the market by tariff elimination, where tariffs remain a retarding factor, may instill an aura of stability in the size and growth of the relevant market so as to induce a greater *volume* and more productive investment (real and intangible) than otherwise would have occurred. The result would be to increase the potential rate of growth of the affected industries and the economy. Fourth, the U.S. may benefit in welfare terms from lower import prices due to indirect effects which occur in the partner countries. At the same time, the latter would tend to affect the U.S. trade balance adversely. These effects will be considered below.

POSSIBLE INDIRECT EFFECTS IN THE U.S.

The indirect effects of scale and competitive factors would be, in most cases, limited by the actual increase in the size of the market resulting from the removal of trade barriers. Only the goods-producing industries would be directly influenced by tariff removal in an FTA, and since we have excluded agriculture and petroleum from consideration, not even all of those.[51] The impact of these indirect factors which occur in the U.S. would affect U.S. economic welfare—and increase the rate of economic growth in the period in which they are manifested—as well as the volume of exports and imports. However, their impact on U.S. trade differs with the type of effect.

ECONOMIES OF SCALE

The size of most markets in the U.S. are already a multiple of the optimum plant size,[52] which implies that increasing the size of the export market would generally not affect the average cost of U.S. output greatly. While this appears to be the general case, there may very well be specific instances where an increase in the size of the freely accessible market would lower costs. Balassa[53] contends that some U.S. industries could still benefit from the vertical and horizontal specialization which larger markets could support. In addition, the rationalization of the location of production facilities without consideration of tariff barriers might well yield cost reductions for various multinational corporations with existing facilities in both the U.S. and Canada or the U.K. Also, it can be argued that industries making highly sophisticated products (computers, aircraft, lasers, etc.) would reap economies of scale by spreading research-and-development costs across greater output permitted by tariff-free foreign markets. Finally, there is some indication that a significant portion of past U.S. economic growth has resulted from an increase in the size of the economy.[54]

The scope for economies of scale accruing to the U.S. is constrained by the increased access to U.K. and Canadian markets. In 1966, the U.S. GNP was $739.6 billion, which at official par exchange rates was over eight times that in the U.K. and almost fourteen times that in Canada. Potentially "tradable goods" industries[55] produced 31 per cent of total output in the U.S., 37 per cent in the U.K., and 29 per cent in Canada. It is clear that the scope for reaping *major* economies of scale from an FTA reside in Canada and the U.K. rather than the U.S.

Economies of scale (both internal and external) in the U.S. due to an FTA would be triggered by an increase in the size of export industries as a result of increased exports to the U.K. and Canada. In order for a net gain to be obtained, the export industries must have increasing returns to scale while the import industries—which would be contracting (relatively) due to increased imports and releasing resources to export industries—must have constant, decreasing, or smaller increasing returns to scale. The gain to economic welfare results because the expansion in exports lowers (real) unit costs on *all* production in the industry affected (by assumption) without raising the unit costs on output in contracting industries. Thus, the U.S. gains due to reduced real costs for the output utilized domestically while the FTA partners, or the domestic industry (if profits rise) gains as a result of a lower real cost of exports.

The magnitude of the internal welfare gain due to economies of scale from U.S. membership in an FTA cannot be determined with any reasonable degree of precision. However, an exercise in numbers might provide an impression that must otherwise be left entirely to imagination.[56]

Assuming that economies of scale are evenly distributed among the export industries undergoing expansion, and that no losses accrue due to diseconomies of scale in contracting industries, Denison's[57] assumption of a 10 per cent accretion from increased size to the growth contribution of other sources may provide a basis for estimating the order of magnitude. On an aggregate level, the expansion of U.S. exports predicted in Table 3 was $1.15 billion. Assume that the actual increase in exports due to an FTA would be, in fact, twice that, or $2.3 billion. This doubling of the predicted values is partially justified by the potential indirect factors under consideration, including economies of scale, and the downward biases in our estimating procedure. This entire increase would, of course, occur in the "tradable goods" portion of output which constitutes about 30 per cent of total output in the U.S.

If the expansion in export industries were subject to economies of scale in the magnitude presumed by Denison, the welfare gain—for the U.S.—can be calculated very simply. The expansion of the export industries would be equivalent to an increase of about 1 per cent in the production of tradable goods. By Denison's method, this 1 per cent increase in the output of tradable goods in export industries would permit a saving in real resources in the expanding industries of about one-eleventh of the expansion, or about .001 per cent of total tradable goods output. In 1966 prices, this U.S. domestic gain from economies of scale would exceed $200 million.

It should be stressed that this exercise has value only in providing a very rough indication of the effects of scale economies operating in the U.S. There is no way of knowing what *past* gains from economies of scale were, and the assumption followed here is justifiable only in that it seems reasonable. Also, the assumed increase in U.S. exports might in fact be higher or lower by as much as 50 per cent. Thus, while the estimate of over $200 million gain in U.S. economies of scale appears reasonable, the true value could be zero or five times that amount. Unless, however, this "reasonable" guess is very far from the mark, the indirect benefits from scale economies to the U.S. will exceed the direct effects from improved resource allocation. This, of course, is to be expected, but by *how much* the indirect benefits exceed the direct effects must remain a matter of conjecture.

Economies of scale realized would benefit the U.S. consumer through reduced prices, lower real costs of production, and increased output. The balance-of-payments effect would be an increase in U.S. exports (assuming export prices decline and foreign demand is elastic) and thus a more favorable balance-of-payments effects than predicted in Section III would be likely. This adjustment should, however, be small and certainly less than the doubling of the earlier estimates assumed above.

RESPONSES TO INCREASED IMPORT COMPETITION

The probability of significant gains from induced changes in previously protected, import-competing industries may be greater than from scale economies in export lines. The potential disappearance of domestic sales because of foreign competition may stimulate a number of cost-reducing, output-increasing actions by American firms. The success of any of these actions would imply that prior to an FTA, U.S. firms were not producing with the optimum input mix or production methods, were being poorly managed, or had failed to anticipate and supply the kind of products that were being demanded. Thus the gains accruing to the U.S. in this category would arise because foreign competition would do what domestic competition in a protected market had not, i.e., to stimulate efficiency and, in the process, economic growth.

There is considerable evidence that losses in potential output because of poor management, use of antiquated techniques, and failure to modernize are very much greater than the loss in output because of misallocation of resources from tariffs, monopolies, and other distortion.[58] Empirical estimates indicate that the loss in potential national output from monopolies and tariffs are a small fraction of 1 per cent of total output, while other studies have shown that changes made as a result of increased competition *without changing the amount of inputs* has, in individual instances, raised output by as much as one or two times. If those responses which would *change* inputs—such as investment in more capital per worker, investment in more modern capital equipment, and increasing the expenditure on market research and product development are also considered, the *potential* gains from import competition appear sizable indeed.[59]

The difficulty, however, rests in determining how many of these potential gains would actually be realized in an FTA. Not all, or even a great part, of industrial inefficiency rests in import competing industries, although certain specific industries which enjoy tariff protection could be cited. Within such industries as chemicals (especially benzenoid products), steel, and aluminum, the large diversified U.S. firms appear to be in a favorable position to effectively meet increased import competition, at least in many individual product lines. If true, then the potential effects of increased competition will be larger than those from scale economies, but still limited by the rather narrow range of U.S. output competitive with potential exports of FTA partners. It should also be noted that a successful competitive response of American industry to elimination of tariffs would lower the direct cost of adjustment to increased imports. The meeting of import competition with domestic products of equal cost and equal quality would tend to make the net increase in U.S. imports due to an FTA lower than the estimates in Table 3, but as with scale economies, not greatly so.

SUMMARY OF INDIRECT EFFECTS IN THE U.S.

Economies of scale and defensive responses to increased import competition appear to be the major indirect effects to be expected in the U.S. from an FTA.[60] The scope for reaping such advantages from an FTA in the U.S. is small because of the already large size of the American economy. In general, indirect effects for a given country will be larger: (1) The smaller the size of the country relative to the other member countries; (2) the lower the existing level of efficiency; and (3) the greater the protection to be eliminated.[61] On this score, the U.S. has relatively less to gain than Canada and the U.K. on the basis of size and efficiency. Canada and the U.K., on the other hand, could expect relatively sizable indirect effects.

INDIRECT FACTORS IN CANADA AND THE U.K.

The indirect factors in Canada and the U.K. are anticipated to be of two different types. *Canadian industry* has been forced, by U.S. and Canadian tariffs, to produce only for Canadian markets while more than one firm has shared that limited Canadian market. As a result, less-than-optimum-size firms, each producing full product lines, now exist in many industries. It is argued that production could be rationalized so as to reduce the number of product lines, lengthen production runs, and reap economies of scale if free access to the U.S. (and U.K.) markets were permitted.[62] Thus the principal Canadian advantage would rest in economies of scale. If a part of these scale economies were reflected in lower prices, U.S. imports from Canada would rise by a greater amount than predicted in Section III. This would also produce a welfare gain to the U.S. as its terms of trade would improve as a result.

The proponents of *U.K. integration* into the EEC, and presumably also into an FTA, expect a major dynamic advantage from increased import competition, although possible economies of scale exist in certain industries. The exposure of U.K. industries to increased import competition would, it is expected, cause the adoption of labor-saving techniques, accelerated investment in modern capital equipment, and increased expenditure on product and process development. Should, in fact, U.K. business, with the help of government, make significant response along the lines indicated, the tendency would be for U.S. export expansion to the U.K. to be lower than predicted above. However, to the extent that the U.K. growth rate were enhanced, a second-order tendency for U.S. exports to increase as a result of higher U.K. income would occur.

The forces operating on U.S. trade as a result of dynamic effects in Canada or the U.K. are complex. Economies of scale in Canada (and the U.K.) would tend to increase U.S. imports, and competitive cost reductions would tend to reduce U.S. exports, especially to the U.K. These first-order effects, all of which tend to adversely affect the trade balance, would, however, be *partially* offset by increases in U.S. exports due to rising real income in Canada, but especially in the U.K. Whether any of these effects would be large depends on the magnitude of the indirect effects in the partner countries. Given the geographical structure of U.S. trade, economies of scale in Canada would likely have the larger impact on U.S. trade. The effects on trade with the U.K. would not be sizable since a much greater proportion of her imports come from nonmembers.

In summary, the indirect factors, although impossible to

predict precisely, require two general alterations in the estimates of trade balance and welfare effects of Section III. First, indirect effects in both the U.S. and in the partners would increase U.S. economic welfare and thus provide the main economic advantage of U.S. membership. Second, the effects of the indirect factors on the U.S. trade balance is composed of two opposing parts. Factors operating in the U.S. would tend to improve the trade balance by reducing imports and increasing exports. Forces in the partner countries, on balance, would tend to increase U.S. imports more than U.S. exports. For the U.S., one of these effects is likely to be relatively large because of the large size and relatively closed nature of the U.S. economy. Whether the combined influences would tend to improve or deteriorate, the trade balance cannot be unequivocably determined. It seems likely that, on balance, indirect factors would tend to deteriorate the trade balance, thus offsetting a part of the estimated improvement in Table 3.

VI. U.S. FOREIGN INVESTMENT AND AN FTA

The removal of tariffs on intra-FTA trade and the responses of affected firms to the wider markets and increased competition would likely affect capital movements between the U.S. and her partners. This seems particularly true in the case of Canada since many of the Canadian firms which would be expected to respond favorably to tariff removal are subsidiaries of American parent firms.

A Free Trade Association would not necessarily imply the removal of restrictions on capital movements among the members. Indeed, it might not be possible, given the U.K. balance-of-payments position for that country to undertake such extensive liberalization. However, such action would have considerable merit, to the extent possible, both in its own right and as a measure complementary to tariff elimination. It would facilitate the financing of investment required to realize the potential gains from the direct and indirect effects on trade which were discussed earlier. In addition, relatively free movement of funds between the three countries could assist in the solution of any balance-of-payments problems which changes in trade flows might engender. This section, therefore, assumes that the proposed FTA would provide for a substantial elimination of restrictions on intra-FTA capital movements, and the complete removal of existing U.S. restrictions. However, much of the analysis would stand even if the *status quo* were maintained, so long as existing restrictions were no more stringent than those in effect in 1967 or 1968.

For the U.S., removal of restrictions on capital flows to FTA members would involve excluding the U.K. from the interest equalization tax and excluding both the U.K. and Canada from the voluntary restraints on foreign loans by bank and nonbank financial institutions. In addition, the limits applied to foreign direct investment would be made to exclude completely Canada and the U.K.

If restrictions on foreign investment were removed by all members, the U.K. would be the most affected since capital outflow regulations there are more restrictive. Britain would be required to remove the restrictions on direct investment in the member countries and to free all (domestic and foreign) sterling accounts for portfolio investment in Canada and the U.S. The latter might prove impossible for the U.K., and thus only a limited movement to free capital flows could be achieved for the U.K. The long-term end sought should, however, be one or no restrictions at all. Canada, which has no direct discrimination on external investment, might be required to remove discriminatory tax treatment of income on foreign investments in Canada, but similar adjustments would likely be necessary in the U.S. and U.K.

Recent U.S. Capital Movements to Canada and the U.K.

An indication of the order of magnitude of recent flows of U.S. long-term private investment to Canada and the U.K., and their importance to lender and recipient, is contained in Table 7. The focus is on long-term capital since movements of short-term funds are relatively transitory, and are affected by temporary interest differentials and the confidence in existing exchange rates. It should be borne in mind while interpreting

Table 7

U.S. LONG-TERM PRIVATE INVESTMENT IN CANADA AND GREAT BRITAIN, 1964–1966
(*millions of U.S. dollars and per cent*)

		1964	*1965*	*1966*
Total U.S. Foreign Investment in				
	Canada	1,126	1,429	1,651
	U.K.	249	360	385
Direct Investment in				
	Canada	253	912	1,087
	U.K.	214	317	384
Portfolio Investment including Long-Term Bank Loans				
	Canada	873	517	564
	U.K.	35	43	1
U.S. Investment in Canada and U.K. as Per Cent of U.S. Investment in all Countries				
Total	Canada	28	32	44
	U.K.	5	8	10
Direct Investment				
	Canada	10	27	31
	U.K.	9	9	11
Portfolio				
	Canada	44	45	220
	U.K.	negligible		
U.S. Investment as a Per Cent of Domestic Gross Fixed Investment in Plant and Equipment[1]				
	Canada	13.5	14.9	14.0
	U.K.	1.9	2.6	2.6

Sources: U.S. Department of Commerce, *Survey of Current Business* (June, 1967), and Bank for International Settlements, *Annual Report*, 1967.

[1] U.S. gross private investment in each country as a per cent of domestic public and private expenditure on plant and equipment; i.e., excluding dwellings and inventory change. The plant and equipment figures were converted to U.S. dollars at par rates of exchange.

Table 7 that data for the years shown (1964–1966) have been influenced by U.S. policy toward foreign investment. The interest equalization tax has affected the results for all three years, while the "voluntary restraints program" was in force in 1965 and 1966. The impact of these policy measures has been to reduce the magnitude of capital outflows to all countries and to affect the flow to the U.K. more than to Canada. Despite these distortions, some valid inferences can be made. Canada is by far the largest recipient of U.S. private long-term investment, ranging from 28 per cent of the total in 1964 to 44 per cent in 1966. Investment in the U.K. is much less important, amounting to 10 or less of the total. Of the investment inflows to Canada, direct investment normally represents the major proportion, although portfolio investment has been sizable.[63]

Compared to U.S. investment in Canada, the U.K. has received very little U.S. capital in the years shown. Portfolio investment has been negligible, partially as a result of the highly developed London issue market and British restrictions on foreign borrowing. Direct investment, despite the "voluntary guidelines" on direct-investment corporations in 1965 and 1966 has increased, but still remains below $400 million per year.

The final rows in Table 7 relate U.S. investment in Canada and Great Britain to the volume of financing necessary for fixed capital formation in the two countries.[64] U.S. investment in Canada has been equal to 13 to 15 per cent of plant and equipment expenditure, a figure which illustrates the dependence of Canadian capital formation on external financing. In the U.K., U.S. investment has remained below 3 per cent of plant and equipment expenditure, implying relative independence from the U.S. as a source of investment funds.

The intimate connections between the Canadian and U.S. capital markets and the degree of U.S. ownership of Canadian industry (to be discussed further below) suggest that an FTA would likely change the volume and nature of capital flows to Canada. On the basis of the evidence shown here, and given the sophisticated London financial market, one would expect substantially less change in capital flows between the U.S. and the U.K.

Expected Change in U.S. Direct Investment

Changes in direct investment flows between the U.S. and her FTA partners as a result of tariff removal would primarily affect U.S. direct investment in Canada or the U.K., and not the latters' investment in the U.S. The flow of foreign direct investment to the U.S. by these countries, and the existing stock of their investments in the U.S., are small absolutely (although large relative to total foreign investment in the U.S.), and likely to be little affected by an FTA. If direct investment in the U.S., is affected at all, it would tend to decline. Partner country firms which would have found it necessary to jump the U.S. tariff in order to gain access to the U.S. market could serve it with exports without the tariff. This effect, which would adversely affect the U.S. balance of payments, would probably be negligible.

As was seen in Table 7, the preponderance of the flow of U.S. direct investment has been to Canada, and has equaled a significant percentage of domestic fixed-capital formation there. The flow to the U.K. has been of much less importance. The stock of U.S. direct investments in the two countries also indicates that the major impact of an FTA on new U.S. direct investment is likely to be concentrated in Canada. Table 8 shows the amounts (in Canadian dollars) and the percentages of particular industries controlled in the U.S. and other countries. The U.S. control in many Canadian manufacturing industries exceeds 50 per cent. Some of these industries are the same as those which the analyses in Sections III and V predicted would be considerably affected by an FTA. The pervasiveness of U.S. control of industry in Canada is much greater than in the U.K., although the U.S. presence in some U.K. industries is signficant, e.g., computers and automobiles. Traditional international trade theory, which implies that trade is a substitute for capital movements, and vice versa, would predict that the removal of tariffs under an FTA would induce firms to serve foreign markets with exports rather than establish foreign production facilities. On the basis of traditional theory, the increase of U.S. exports estimated in Section III would, to some extent, substitute for future direct investment.[65] The flow of U.S. direct investment in Canada and the U.K. would thus tend to fall, exerting a positive effect on the U.S. balance of payments (at least temporarily).

Indirect factors also may influence the flow of direct investment, and would in general tend to expand direct investment outflows.[66] Section III noted that Canadian exports to the U.S. of paper and paper products, certain chemical products, electrical equipment, and some nonferrous metals would likely expand under an FTA. From Table 8, it may be seen that 35 per cent of the Canadian pulp and paper capacity is controlled in the U.S., 66 per cent of the electrical apparatus capacity, 54 per cent of chemical manufactures, and 55 per cent of nonferrous metal refineries. If Canadian industry is to be transformed and rationalized by gaining access to the

Table 8

U.S. CONTROL OF SELECTED CANADIAN INDUSTRIES, 1961

Industry	Total Investment in the Industry (*millions of Canadian $*)	Total Capital Controlled in the U.S. (*millions of Canadian $*)	Per Cent of Total Controlled in *U.S.*	Per Cent of Total Controlled in *Other Foreign*
Pulp & paper	2,223	773	35	11
Transport equipment excluding automobiles & parts	225	70	27	44
Electrical apparatus	595	394	66	12
Chemicals	1,183	638	54	25
All manufacturing	12,668	5,671	45	14
Smelting and refining of nonferrous Canadian ore	968	534	55	—

Source: Dominion Bureau of Statistics, *The Canadian Balance of International Payments, 1961 and 1962.*

U.S. market, a considerable part of the transformation must be carried out by U.S. owned and controlled firms. Decisions to reduce the product lines and increase the length of production runs in Canadian facilities in order to serve U.S. and Canadian markets must be made by U.S. multinational firms. New funds (and technology) will be needed to accomplish the alteration and expansion of Canadian production, and with the parents' access to U.S. sources of funds, it is likely that U.S. direct investment would increase.[67] Also, if scale economies were to be captured by Canadian firms in serving their own and the U.S. market, U.S. firms might respond by establishing competitive facilities in Canada in order to maintain their global market share and to better serve Canadian tastes.

Thus, the elimination of tariffs may well increase the outflow of U.S. direct investment to Canada rather than reduce it. Conflicting tendencies will be set up, but the greater the extent to which Canadian industrial structure is transformed, the more likely that U.S. direct investment there will increase rather than fall.

The U.K. has higher tariffs on imports of manufactured goods and the tendency for U.S. direct investment there to decline because of easier access through exports would be stronger than with Canada. If dynamic factors are of less importance, U.S. direct investment in the U.K. would, on balance, likely decline. It is possible, however, that other considerations will override the tariff effect. If an FTA instilled a new competitive spirit in U.K. firms, and increased the rate of capital formation and economic growth, it might well be expected that the lure of a dynamic, growing British market would increase the small existing inflow of U.S. direct investment to the U.K. Much might depend on the British government's policy toward corporate takeovers by U.S. firms. In some instances, the British could benefit from the injection of U.S. management techniques and production technology, and encouragement of U.S. direct investment via mergers and joint ventures might increase direct investment. Thus, one factor will tend to reduce the already slow rate of direct investment in the U.K. while other factors involved with government policy and the success in raising the U.K. growth rate would tend to increase it. Whatever the direction of net change which would result, it would likely be small relative to the change in U.S. investment in Canada.

Changes in Portfolio Capital Movements

Changes in the volume of portfolio capital movements between the U.S. and her FTA partner countries could arise for two reasons: The removal of existing restrictions on foreign investment; and the change in the relationship between ex ante domestic savings and investment in Canada and Britain brought about by adjusting to an FTA.

The elimination of interference by all three governments over portfolio investments and bank loans would, on balance, likely increase these forms of U.S. capital outflow. The removal of the "spirit" of restraint over Canadian issues in the U.S. capital market would result in some increase. This effect would likely not be sizeable since the degree to which the New York market is used as a source of funds by Canada depends heavily on Canadian credit conditions.

The net flow of portfolio capital between Britain and the U.S. as a result of the removal of restrictions could conceivably be in either direction. The exclusion of the U.K. from the interest equalization tax and the provisions of the voluntary guidelines would tend to increase U.S. investment in U.K. debt instruments. An opposing force would arise as a result of the U.K.'s removal of exchange control (investment sterling) and other restrictions on the purchase of U.S. securities by British nationals, if, in fact, this could be accomplished. Presumably there is some pent-up demand for American stocks and bonds in the U.K. which has been unsatisfied because of government control. There is no way of knowing the size of either of these opposing forces, but it seems reasonable that neither would be large relative to existing U.S. capital outflows.

The second factor affecting portfolio capital movements as a result of an FTA is the impact on credit markets brought about by the industrial change resulting from tariff removal. As noted earlier, the impact of tariff elimination would not be sizable in the U.S., and given the relative size of U.S. financial markets, the influence of tariff removal on U.S. credit conditions would be imperceptible.

In Canada and the U.K., as noted above, both the direct and indirect effects of tariff removal would be relatively large. And as a result, the demand for funds in each country is likely to increase faster than the supply. The excess demand for funds in Canada and the U.K. at interest rates (appropriately adjusted) prevailing in the U.S. would be transferred to the

U.S. market. Thus, U.S. portfolio outflows would tend to increase.

THE LONG-RUN EFFECT OF INVESTMENT CHANGES ON THE U.S. BALANCE OF PAYMENTS

The expected changes in capital flows noted earlier include: (1) An increase in the outflow on account of portfolio investment both as a result of elimination of barriers to capital movements (especially to the U.K.) and as a result of tighter credit conditions in the partner countries (especially Canada); (2) An increase in direct investment in Canada; (3) An increase, decrease, or no change in direct investment in the U.K., depending on whether U.K. growth accelerated and U.S. investment was encouraged by government policy. Thus, the U.S. net capital outflow would probably rise, at least while the economic responses induced by the FTA continued in the partner countries.

A capital outflow, while harmful to the balance of payments when it occurs, is beneficial in the long run since return flows of interest, dividends, and principal will ultimately exceed the initial outflow. With direct investment, induced exports of capital equipment and raw materials and other similar considerations must also be included to estimate the net balance-of-payments effect of the investment.

There can be little doubt that any increase in U.S. foreign investment due to an FTA would, in the long run, have a favorable net effect on the U.S. balance of payments. What is of concern for balance-of-payments policy is *how favorable* an effect, and *how soon*. For portfolio investment, this depends on the interest rate and maturity of the debt. For direct investment, estimates of the repayment period, in the balance-of-payments sense, for all U.S. investment abroad cluster in the five-to-ten-year range.[68] Given the extended period over which tariff reductions would take place under an FTA, the change in capital outflow would likely be gradual, and a part of the return flow would occur before a major adverse balance-of-payments movement was felt.

If this were the case, the adverse balance-of-payments effect of an FTA would be temporary, and would provide a long-run stimulus to foreign-exchange receipts for the U.S. In the process, partner countries would receive the benefit of U.S. funds, and where direct investment is involved, U.S. technology and skills. The latter would facilitate successful adjustment to an FTA in the partner countries.

The net increase in U.S. capital outflow is likely to be small as was the improvement in the trade balance estimated in Section III and tentatively scaled down because of indirect factors in Section V. Table 3 estimated a minimum *increase* in the trade surplus of $38 million on the basis of 1966 data. *Total* U.S. long-term investment in Canada and the U.K. averaged about $1.7 billion per year in the 1964–1966 period. An increase of, say, 10 per cent in that flow, or $170 million, would imply a deterioration in the overall balance of payments, assuming that opposing indirect effects on the balance of payments offset each other. It should be emphasized that these estimations are purely illustrative, and indicate only that the likely *net* balance of payments effect will be small since it would be the net result of a *small* improvement in the trade balance and a *small* increase in capital outflows. In the long run, receipts generated by increased capital outflows make the total balance-of-payments impact of an FTA favorable.

VII. ADJUSTMENT BURDENS OF FTA MEMBERSHIP

Adjustment to the changed pattern and volume of trade and investment as a result of an FTA must be carried out on two levels. First, some firms and employees will find their profits, wages, and ability to find employment affected as import competition increases and exports expand. Second, the monetary authorities of the member countries (and nonmember countries) will find their international reserves affected because of changes in their balance of payments, which must be financed and eventually adjusted toward equilibrium. Ultimately, balance-of-payments adjustment involves adjustment at the firm and employee level, but for the brief consideration given here, it is convenient to treat them as separate problems.

Adjustment to Import Competition at the Micro Level

Adjustment burdens to increased imports in the U.S. as well as various means of easing adjustment and compensating the losers were examined in Section IV. It was noted there that a "high" estimate of the needed adjustment in severely affected U.S. import-competing industries would be to a loss of 2 to 3 per cent of sales and employment. At a less aggregative level, the burden would be greater. The indirect effects analyzed in Section V would not require increasing these "high" estimates by much.

Significantly greater adjustment burdens relative to national income and employment would seem likely in Canada and Great Britain and the importance of devices to lengthen and smooth the adjustment is correspondingly greater. The available devices, such as slowing the rapidity of tariff reductions on specific products, delaying the commencement date of tariff reductions on certain commodities for individual members, and the provision of government assistance for the retraining and moving of employees and the diversification of firms are all well known. In addition, independent analysis of the impact of an FTA on the individual industries in each country, while the FTA is still in the planning stage, would do much to minimize the adjustment burden.

Because the relative magnitudes of the required adjustment would be different for each member, and since the amount of the required adjustment by a member need not be proportional to the amount of its gain from the FTA, consideration should be given to a *multinational fund* from which the necessary adjustment-assistance benefits could be paid. Such a fund, together with a multinational administrative board, would insure uniform criteria for adjustment assistance in the respective countries and would permit the allocation of the costs of adjustment assistance among the member countries on a basis, such as the ability to pay, which would be more equitable than having the magnitude of adjustment dictate the incidence of assistance costs.[69] For the U.S., however, agreement of the allocation of adjustment costs among the countries would not be critical for the implementation of an FTA. The U.S. would have few adjustment costs to bear and would likely be a larger contributor to an adjustment fund than a recipient.

Adjustment to Balance-of-Payments Effects

The second level of required adjustment involves the national responses to the balance-of-payments effects of an FTA.[70] This aspect of international adjustment is particularly important with reference to acceptability of an FTA as a viable approach to freer trade because of the balance-of-payments problems of the U.S. and U.K. Any commercial policy alternative which would have a sizable adverse impact on either of these countries' balance of payments would clearly have a low probability of official acceptance in the near future.

A number of possible international monetary arrangements within an FTA are possible. One would be to leave the existing situation unchanged, as was essentially done with the EFTA, thereby leaving the solution of any FTA generated balance-of-payments problems to the individual countries. Another possibility, which appears preferable if the FTA is to include provisions for liberalizing intra-FTA capital movement, would involve specific provisions for mutual consultation on policy measures for balance-of-payments purposes and for increased bilateral credit lines between members to provide assistance in temporary balance-of-payments problems.

The amount of adjustment to balance-of-payments effects will be largely determined by the effects of an FTA on the individual members' balances of payments. One possible result of discriminatory tariff elimination is that the balance of payments of *every* member may improve due to the diversion of trade with nonmembers. An FTA among the countries considered would likely approximate that result. The estimates reported in this study suggest that the change in the U.S. trade balance would be small but positive, while the initial effects on capital account would be negative but temporary, and result in an additional improvement through time. Independent studies also indicate an improvement in the external balance for the U.K.,[71] and it is perhaps feasible that Canada would find her balance of payments improving as the combined result of trade-balance changes and increased capital inflows. Thus, there seems little likelihood that an FTA would accentuate the balance-of-payments problems of the group as a whole, or individually, but on the contrary would probably tend to improve the external accounts of each member.

This does not, of course, rule out temporary setbacks at the inception of tariff cuts for individual countries, or due to staggered timing of tariff reductions among the members. These types of problems of individual members, whether originating from FTA implementation or from other sources, should be shared among the members through bilateral credit lines. This would permit the avoidance of unnecessary deflationary policies, foreign payment restrictions, and currency devaluations, all of which would tend to stifle a part of the potential gains from freer trade through an FTA. A solid commitment to permanently fixed exchange rates among the member currencies would facilitate the flows of trade and capital which an FTA would tend to stimulate. This, of course, does not rule out exchange-rate changes of member currencies vis-à-vis nonmember currencies.

To the extent that the group's balance of payments improves, the solution to the balance-of-payments problems of the one or two individual members will be lessened since the other member(s) external balance will be in surplus. In addition, the improvement of the FTA balance with the rest of the world would ease some of the tension on the existing payments system since the two reserve-currency and major-deficit countries would be members.

The FTA should, of course, carry with it appropriate provision for the coordination of macroeconomic policies among the members. This is especially vital if free capital movements are an objective. In addition, a formal arrangement among the members to facilitate the financing of the payments imbalances of individual members would be highly desirable. This could

take the form of increased swap lines between central banks together with a provision for lending gold and foreign exchange to other members. Of course a more formal plan such as a payments union patterned after the European Payments Union would be feasible, but the difficulty involved in reaching agreement and in incorporating additional FTA members would make a more simple and informal arrangement preferable.

VIII. ADDITIONAL FTA MEMBERS AND THE IMPACT ON THE U.S.

While the analysis in this study has been confined to a Free Trade Association encompassing Canada, the U.K., and the U.S., it should not be inferred that such limited membership is advocated. On the contrary, the national interest of the U.S. likely lies in encouraging broad membership and should presuppose membership of Britain's EFTA partners at the inception.[72] An open-ended FTA would help avoid the creation of another "rival group" among Western countries and the political fragmentation which might go with it. Economically, a broader FTA would provide for the members, including the U.S., *more* of the direct and indirect benefits discussed above while limiting the adverse effects of trade diversion on total world welfare. While a broader Free Trade Association carries with it more economic advantages, so does it carry with it additional adjustment costs. The latter, however, would still be minimal for the U.S., and intelligent government policy would make them easily sustainable.

An FTA may be considered as a means or technique of moving toward the widest possible free trade consistent with the national interest. A high degree of success would imply that the membership ultimately include all of the Western industrial countries including the EEC.[73] It is likely, however, that political considerations and powerful economic vested interests will make the realization of that goal a slow, step-by-step process. A successful narrower FTA would increase the appeal and incentives for other potential members and also facilitate their inclusion, should it prove impossible to achieve broader membership initially.

An FTA should give explicit recognition of special trading arrangements for developing countries so as to accomplish a coordination of policies by the advanced members. This could involve the extension of some (temporary) trade preferences to UDC's under FTA auspices as a special provision of the agreement. Another possibility would be to include certain groups of UDC's under the general tariff-cutting provisions of the FTA with speical concessionary clauses covering the speed and timing of their tariff cuts.

The advanced countries, aside from the EEC, from which additional members could likely come, include the EFTA countries besides the U.K., Australia, New Zealand, and Japan. The degree of concentration of these countries' trade, and that of Latin America, with the U.S., Canada, and the U.K. are shown in Table 9. Figures for trade with the EEC are also shown for comparison.

Existing trade of the EFTA members is much more highly concentrated with the EEC than with the three potential FTA members. The trade of the Scandinavian members of EFTA is less concentrated than for total EFTA trade due to their higher percentage of trade with the U.K. Austria and Switzerland, however, have a very high concentration of trade with the EEC. From a purely economic view, the latter would benefit most from EEC membership.

The uncertainty of widening EEC membership leaves little alternative for the non-U.K. EFTA members but to pursue liberalizing trade arrangements elsewhere. U.K. membership in an FTA would exert a strong force on other EFTA countries to become members. The elimination of EFTA preferences vis-à-vis the U.S. and Canada in the U.K. market would be potentially harmful to their exports, and the opening of the U.S. market to Canadian and U.K. exports without doing the same to other EFTA members would tend to compound the harm. Thus, barring a change in EEC membership policies, it is likely that other EFTA countries would desire to enter an FTA with the U.K., and they should be encouraged to do so by the U.S.

Table 9

PER CENT OF EXPORTS AND IMPORTS OF ADDITIONAL POTENTIAL MEMBERS WITH U.S., CANADA, AND U.K., 1966

Potential Members	% of total exports (X) or imports (M)	*U.S.*	*Canada*	*U.K.*	*IFTA Members*	*ECC*
EFTA	X	8.4	1.4	12.5	22.3	32.3
(excl. U.K.)	M	8.0	1.2	11.7	20.9	43.2
Sweden, Norway,	X	7.6	1.3	16.9	25.8	27.7
and Denmark	M	8.4	1.5	14.5	24.5	33.6
Australia and	X	10.7	2.0	22.0	34.7	11.7
New Zealand	M	23.3	3.0	29.5	55.9	10.8
Japan	X	30.7	2.6	2.3	35.7	6.1
	M	27.9	4.8	2.2	34.9	4.7
Latin America	X	43.6	2.9	4.4	51.0	2.5
	M	36.2	3.0	7.0	46.3	1.6
EEC	X	7.8	1.0	4.8	13.6	
	M	11.2	1.2	5.2	17.6	

(Columns U.S. through ECC are grouped under "Trade With".)

Source: Calculated from IMF, *Direction of Trade,* and OECD, *Overall Trade by Countries* (Series A).

On the other side of the world, widened membership would be also desirable but perhaps more difficult to attain. Existing exports of Australia and New Zealand to potential FTA members constitute over one-third of their total, while imports from the FTA members are 55 per cent of the total. Furthermore, the loss of the advantage of Commonwealth preference vis-à-vis the U.S. as a result of an FTA would be an additional incentive for their membership.

Japan, because of its heavy bilateral trade with the U.S., is also a potential candidate for membership. Certainly considerable mutual gain would accrue from such membership, but the existing degree of Japanese tariff and nontariff protection might make early membership difficult. Encouragement by the U.S. to dismantel some of the protectionist devices plus the lure of freer access to the U.K. market are factors encouraging eventual Japanese membership. An even stronger factor is the potential loss of exports to the U.S. due to a substitution of tariff-free imports from the U.K. and Canada. This effect could be sizable[74] and might constitute sufficient reason for Japan to reexamine its protection policy so as to be able to accept FTA membership.

Additional members of the FTA would enhance the favorable impact on U.S. economic welfare by extending tariff reductions to a greater volume of imported goods, and would thus permit a broader scope for import competition to induce favorable dynamic responses by U.S. industry. Also, both U.S. exports and imports would increase by more than would be the case if Canada and the U.K. were the only partners. A determination of whether the net effect on the trade balance would be favorable or unfavorable would require more detailed study than can be given here, and would depend on precisely which additional countries were included. Whereas a positive effect on the U.S. trade balance would be likely if Australia and New Zealand were included (partially due to the loss of preferential treatment for U.K. manufactured goods exports), inclusion of Japan might well affect the U.S. trade balance adversely. Japanese membership, however, would have by far the greatest aggregate effect on U.S. trade of any of the possible additional members, and also the greatest potential benefit. This is true because the existing volume of U.S. trade with that country is considerable, and likely to be significantly affected by the removal of the existing protective tariffs in the two countries. The inclusion of EFTA countries would require relatively little adjustment to the estimates made in this study.

In all cases, so long as the EEC is excluded, additional members would require relatively little alteration on an aggregate basis of the earlier estimates for a three-country FTA. Specific U.S. industries would be significantly affected by increased import competition, e.g., cotton textiles and electronic components by Japanese membership; glassware, flatware, and furniture by Scandinavian membership. Also, specific U.S. export industries would be significantly benefited, depending on the assumed membership configuration. The adverse effects of competition on some protected U.S. industries would require adjustment assistance, but these instances of severe hardship would not be numerous, especially if an extended period were allowed for adjustment. The economic and political benefit of an expanded FTA would pay the cost of adjustment many times over, but, as the subject is one of infinite expandability and is beyond the scope of this pilot project, no more can be done than indicate the general trend of further inquiry.

IX. SUMMARY

One major conclusion of this study is that a British-Canadian-U.S. FTA would *not* have a major general impact on the U.S. economy. It would provide marginal economic benefits—an increased volume of trade would increase the efficiency of the U.S. economy and the level of U.S. economic welfare; some isolated economies of scale could be captured and the shock effect of increased import competition in some industries might well stimulate labor and capital-saving techniques, increased research-and-development expenditures, or simply improved management.

In the political sphere, an open-ended FTA, while recognizing the current proclivity for regional trading schemes, would serve to mediate the worst effects of tight and inward-looking regional integration arrangements. By tending to move closer to free trade, an FTA would serve to tighten political relations with our traditional allies and provide the U.K., which has traditionally had a special place in U.S. relations, a viable alternative to sitting on the doorstep of the EEC for an extended period.

Because the U.S. economy is relatively closed, and the degree and structure of tariff protection not overly restrictive of trade with Canada and the U.K., the direct effects of an FTA on the U.S. would probably be relatively small. The crude estimating procedure employed indicated that exports would increase by 3.8 per cent while imports would increase by 4.4 per cent if foreign supply prices remained constant and 3.1 per cent if such prices rose. The direct effect on U.S. economic welfare under the first case would be a small increase; in the latter case, a small decline. The balance of payments would tend to improve from these direct factors.

The adjustment of industry and labor to such small changes would be small in the aggregate, but the localized impact in certain industries and areas could be sizable. The estimate of the maximum displacement of sales and employment by increased imports in broadly defined import-competing industries was 2 to 3 per cent. The most likely candidates for significantly increased imports appear to be the paper and paperboard industry, woolen textiles, some chemical products, transport equipment other than automobiles, electrical machinery, and aluminum.

Although impossible to quantify precisely, indirect effects could be of significant benefit to the U.S. Some benefit from economies of scale in the U.S. would be expected, and the response of U.S. firms to increased competition could conceivably be economically beneficial. The amount of U.S. industry touched by foreign competition is not great, but where an FTA would face U.S. firms with no alternative to extinction except to lower costs or change product quality, the *potential* benefit is considerable. These possible indirect effects occurring in the U.S. would tend to increase U.S. economic welfare and improve the trade balance.

Indirect effects operating in Canada and the U.K., which a broad group of economists foresee as the means to introduce significant changes in their respective economies, could indirectly affect the U.S. Economies of scale in Canada would tend to increase U.S. imports. Modernization and better management in the U.K. would tend to reduce U.S. exports. These factors would suppress the improvement in the U.S. trade balance, but because of lower import prices, provide an additional improvement in U.S. welfare.

In total, the indirect factors are likely to reduce the trade balance, offsetting a part of the improvement predicted from the estimates of the direct effect. However, the welfare gains from the indirect and dynamic factors would probably be more important than the static gains.

The influence of the FTA on U.S. capital outflows would be measurable, and perhaps larger than the impact on trade flows. Outflows of private U.S. capital for portfolio investment in the member countries would likely increase, especially if the U.S. restrictions on foreign investments are removed. Tighter credit conditions in Canada and the U.K. as a result of industrial change brought on by tariff elimination would induce greater outflows of U.S. capital. U.S. direct investment in the member countries would also likely increase, since many of the firms which would undertake change in Canada are subsidaries of American parents. This effect would likely be greater than the reduction of direct investment due to direct access of U.S. exports in tariff-free partner markets. The certainty of these predictions is low since the complex factors governing direct investment make prediction hazardous.

In sum, the balance-of-payments effect of an FTA would be small, but probably negative initially. It would increase slightly through time as a result of returns on increased investment outflows. This prediction must be deemed tentative since it is a result of the implicit netting out of much larger gross effects.

The implications of the FTA for the balance of payments of the member countries and the possible means of facilitating the requisite adjustment to deficits and surpluses were examined. It is probable that the payments balance of the members as a group would improve. This would facilitate the financing of the deficits of any individual member, if this proved necessary. An arrangement for extension of credit between the members should be negotiated and implemented, although it need not be complicated.

Wide membership of the FTA should be encouraged. For the U.S., little additional effect would be likely unless the additional members included Japan. Some special arrangements with developing countries would be desirable in any event. The possible economic and political gains, together with the small economic cost, would make the active promotion of an open-ended free-trade area a policy worthy of the careful consideration of the U.S.

APPENDIX: DIRECT EFFECTS OF FTA ON U.S. EXPORTS AND IMPORTS

ESTIMATING EQUATIONS

The estimates of trade changes resulting from the elimination of tariffs on intra-FTA trade shown in Tables 3 and 4 in the text ignore any induced changes in imports or exports from income growth, economies of scale, and improved methods resulting from an increase in the size of the market and its effects on trade. For any commodity class, the change in U.S. imports (exports) depends on the elasticity of import demand in the U.S. (export demand in other members), the height of the U.S. (other members) tariff, and the existing level of U.S. imports from (exports to) the partners.

For an import commodity, the change in price to U.S. buyers as a proportion of the existing price is equal to

$$[t/(1+t)]\cdot(1-p)$$

Table A-1

COMMODITY STRUCTURE OF U.S. TRADE, 1966

Commodities	Per Cent of Total Imports	Per Cent of Total Exports
Agricultural	17.4	23.0
Nonagricultural	82.2	76.9
Food & livestock	15.4	15.2
Beverages & tobacco	2.5	2.0
Crude materials (except fuels)	12.7	10.2
Mineral fuels & related goods	8.8	3.2
Animal & vegetable oils & fats	0.5	1.1
Chemicals	3.7	8.9
Machinery (except transp. equipment)	10.5	25.6
Transportation equipment	8.3	11.6
Other manufactured goods	33.8	17.6

Source: U.S. Government Printing Office, *Overseas Business Reports.*

Table A-2

GEOGRAPHICAL STRUCTURE OF U.S. IMPORTS FOR CONSUMPTION BY BROAD COMMODITY GROUPS, 1966

Commodity Groups	By Country as a Percentage of Total U.S. Imports in the Commodity Group						
	Canada (%)	*U.K.* (%)	*Canada & U.K.* (%)	*E.E.C.* (%)	*Rest of Western Europe* (%)	*Japan* (%)	*Latin America* (%)
All commodities	24.0	6.9	30.9	16.1	6.9	11.6	15.5
Agricultural commodities	5.3	0.6	5.9	6.8	8.0	0.8	39.3
Nonagricultural commodities	28.1	8.2	36.3	18.1	6.6	13.9	10.4
Food & livestock	8.8	0.7	9.6	3.9	6.7	3.0	44.1
Beverage & tobacco	19.9	37.5	57.4	16.1	22.1	0.1	1.5
Crude materials inedible (except fuels)	41.4	1.5	43.0	3.8	5.5	1.5	15.6
Mineral fuels & related goods	19.9	0.2	20.1	0.8	0.0	0.0	44.3
Animal & vegetable oils & fats	0.6	0.6	1.3	10.2	7.5	3.4	15.7
Chemicals	26.5	7.6	34.1	28.2	8.6	7.5	8.8
Machinery (except transp. equip.)	24.8	13.2	38.1	25.4	8.9	23.0	0.4
Transportation equipment	37.3	13.4	50.8	36.0	3.4	9.3	0.0
Other manufactured goods	20.6	7.8	28.4	20.8	11.5	21.3	5.9

Source: See Table A-1.

Table A-3

GEOGRAPHICAL STRUCTURE OF U.S. EXPORTS BY BROAD COMMODITY GROUPS, 1966

	Country as Per Cent of Total U.S. Exports in the Country Group						
Commodity Groups	*Canada* (%)	*U.K.* (%)	*Canada & U.K.* (%)	*E.E.C.* (%)	*Rest of Western Europe* (%)	*Japan* (%)	*Latin America* (%)
All commodities	21.9	5.7	27.6	18.1	8.4	7.7	13.9
Agricultural commodities	9.1	6.8	15.9	2.2	10.7	13.6	7.0
Nonagricultural commodities	26.9	5.3	32.3	16.9	7.3	6.2	16.7
Food & livestock	9.8	6.2	16.1	21.3	9.4	10.5	8.5
Beverages & tobacco	1.4	22.1	23.5	22.7	18.7	6.7	5.2
Crude materials	13.8	4.1	18.0	27.0	9.0	25.2	5.7
Mineral fuels	23.8	2.8	26.6	25.8	6.9	2.8	3.4
Animal & vegetable oils & fats	5.3	3.0	8.4	15.4	10.9	10.9	13.4
Chemicals	15.3	6.3	21.7	22.3	5.9	6.7	20.2
Machinery (exc. transp. equip.)	28.2	6.0	34.2	15.6	8.0	4.1	16.3
Transportation equipment	38.7	1.3	40.0	9.9	7.2	3.8	19.6
Other manufactured goods	27.6	7.1	34.8	16.9	7.5	3.8	16.2

Source: See Table A-1.

Table A-4

FREE AND DUTIABLE U.S. IMPORTS, VARIOUS YEARS

Average	Total Imports	Dutiable Imports	Dutiable as % of Total
	(millions)		
1946–50	6,602	2,741	41.5
1956	12,674	6,281	49.6
1960	15,014	8,872	59.1
1964	18,600	11,576	62.2
1966	25,360	15,962	62.9

Source: Department of Commerce, *Overseas Business Reports* (February, 1966, and October, 1967).

Table A-5

TOTAL AND DUTIABLE IMPORTS BY COMMODITY CLASS, 1966

	Total Imports	Dutiable Imports	Dutiable as % of Total
	(millions)		
Chemicals	941	538	46.5
Machinery (except transport equipment	2,662	2,020	75.8
Transport equipment	2,132	1,374	64.4
Other manufactured goods	8,664	6,228	71.8
Food & livestock	3,937	2,052	52.1
Beverages & tobacco	601	599	99.6
Crude materials inedible (except fuels)	3,195	928	29.0
Mineral fuels and related items	2,241	1,858	82.9
Animal & vegetable oils & fats	136	79	58.0

Source: See Table A-4.

Table A-6
GEOGRAPHICAL STRUCTURE OF U.S. TARIFF PROTECTION, 1966

Imports from	Total	Dutiable	Dutiable as % of Total
	(millions)		
World	25,360	15,962	63
Canada	6,106	2,112	35
U.K.	1,761	1,357	77
Canada & U.K.	7,867	3,469	44
EEC	4,048	3,640	89
EFTA	2,919	2,319	79
Japan	2,947	2,832	96
Latin America	3,942	1,867	47

Source: See Table A-4.

where t is the U.S. ad valorem tariff and p is the proportion of the tariff by which foreign export prices rise. Under assumption "A," that partners export prices remain constant, p is zero, and the landed price of U.S. imports declines by the full amount of the tariff.

Assuming that p is zero, the proportional change in U.S. import volume *and* value in a commodity division is

$$dM/M = [t/(1+t)]e \qquad (1)$$

where e is the U.S. elasticity of demand for imports in that division. The absolute change in imports (dM) from the base year level of imports from the members (M) is then

$$dM = M[t/(1+t)] \cdot e \qquad (1)'$$

This equation was employed for estimating the change in imports under assumption "A."

Assumption "B" was that foreign supply prices rise by some proportion of the tariff (positive p) as a result of increased quantity exported; i.e., the elasticity of export supply in Canada and U.K. is less than infinite. In this case, the proportional change in the *volume* of imports in a commodity division is

$$(dM/m)_q = [t/(1+t)] \cdot (1-p)e \qquad (2)$$

The proportional change in the *value* of imports is[75]

$$dM/M = \frac{t}{(1+t)}(1-p)e + pt + pt\frac{t}{1+t}(1-p)e \qquad (2)'$$

This equation was used for the assumption "B" estimates of import changes.

Similar equations, using separate Canadian and British tariff rates, imports from the U.S., and elasticity estimates, were used to estimate the increase in U.S. exports due to trade creation. In each case, U.S. supply price was assumed constant ($p = 0$). The increase in U.S. exports to both Canada and the U.S. as a result of trade diversion was estimated in the following equation

$$dX = C[t/(1+t]s \qquad (3)$$

where dX is the change in value of U.S. exports due to trade diversion, C is the value of imports by Canada (or the U.K.) from nonmembers which are in competition with U.S. exports, t is the MFN tariff to be eliminated on U.S. exports and retained on nonmember imports, and s is the assumed elasticity of substitution of U.S. exports for nonmember exports to the country. Value estimates were made using Equation 3 for those commodity divisions where *a priori* reasoning suggests substantial nonmember competition with U.S. exports. Separate calculations were made for export changes to the U.K. and to Canada, and only the sum is shown in Table A-9.

Estimates for SITC two-digit commodity divisions were derived for almost all nonagricultural commodities. As noted in the text, it is assumed that trade in agricultural and petroleum products would be handled under separate provision in an FTA agreement, and thus not be subject to general tariff elimination provisions. The appropriate commodity divisions were omitted from the calculations.

In addition, tobacco was excluded for reasons similar to those for agricultural commodities. Beverages, mainly alcoholic beverages, were excluded on the rationale that government policy as to consumption taxes and other nontariff controls were so important as to make an estimate highly unreliable. It seems clear, however, that should discriminatory treatment of imported beverages be eliminated, U.S. imports would rise more than U.S. exports.

It was also decided to exclude trade in all energy-producing commodities (electric power, gas, and coal in addition to petroleum) due to the special conditions surrounding trade in each. Trade in electric power and gas occurs only between Canada and the U.S. where existing tariffs are zero, and trade policies relating to each are made by the appropriate government agencies by direct negotiation. U.S. coal is certainly competitive in both Canada and the U.K., and a complete freeing of discriminatory treatment would permit substantial increases in U.S. coal exports. However, the Canadian tariff is zero on most types of coal but Canadian coal is heavily favored by the Government's practice of absorbing much of the cost of transport from mine to markets. Thus, the elimination of the few tariffs on special coal products would affect U.S. exports very little, while elimination of the Canadian government transport "subventions" would have a significant impact. Estimation of the effects of the latter by methods used here is not possible. In addition, the U.K. prohibition of coal imports certainly restricts U.S. exports, but an estimate of the magnitude of protection would involve much closer analysis than can be given here. Finally, all special category items (SITC Group 9) are excluded from the calculations.

The values for the parameters in Equations 1′, 2′, and 3 have, in most instances, both conceptual and empirical problems attached. These problems and the data sources will be discussed in turn.

TARIFFS

The fact that each trade-data commodity classification includes many individual items while tariff rates often apply to single items necessitates the use of an average tariff for each commodity class in the trade data. Any average results in some distortion, and the objective is to minimize that distortion. The tariff average for a trade category could be derived by weighting the individual tariffs which it covers by each item's weight in the country's imports, in world imports, or some particular regional group's imports. Weighted averages have the general drawback of giving little weight to restrictive, high-tariff rates and too much weight to unrestrictive low rates, and thus yield an average rate lower than the actual level of protection afforded. This downward bias may be reduced by weighting the tariffs on a broader basis than the imports of the country in question.[76]

Unweighted tariff averages have been used in this study. These have the advantage of availability and ease of computation. Further, it is likely that the extent of bias arising from inappropriate tariff averages are relatively small. However, it remains that these unweighted averages have a possible upward bias, since "excess" protection may exist in some U.S. categories; i.e., the existing tariffs could be reduced with little or no increase in imports. To the extent that this is the case, the increase in trade has been overestimated. But unweighted averages do avoid the downward biases of the small or zero weights accruing to prohibitive tariffs.

The tariffs used in the computations are shown in Table A-7. The rates for the U.S. and U.K. SITC Divisions 51 and above were taken from *The Free Trade Area Option: Opportunity for Britain.* The remaining averages were derived by reclassifying items in the U.S., U.K., and Canada tariff concordances to the SITC (mainly on the basis of commodity description), and taking unweighted averages. Where possible, the "reasonableness" of these averages was checked against the rates in *Atlantic Tariffs and Trade* (London: Political and Economic Planning) which were based on 1961 tariff rates.

The following special adjustments were made:

1. Chemical elements and compounds and dyes (SITC 51 and 53) and footwear (SITC 85) harbor the main items subject to the "American Selling Price" valuation method, and these comprise a considerable portion of imports in these divi-

Table A-7

AVERAGE (UNWEIGHTED) TARIFF RATES USED IN CALCULATION OF DIRECT EFFECT ON U.S. TRADE

	SITC Division	U.S. Tariff	Canadian Tariff	U.K. Tariff
21	Undressed hides & skins	4.0	0	6.0
22	Oil seeds & oil nuts	3.9	0	0
23	Crude rubber	0.5	3.0	4.0
24	Wood, lumber, cork	1.2	0	3.5
25	Pulp & waste paper	0	0	3.0
26	Textile fibres	7.0	5.0	9.0
27	Crude fertilizers & minerals	3.0	2.5	2.5
28	Metalliferous ores & scrap	1.0	1.0	0
29	Crude organic materials n.e.s.	2.7	7.0	6.0
41	Animal oils & fats	4.5	11.0	6.5
42	Fixed vegetable oils	9.0	0	0
43	Processed animal & vegetable oils & fats	8.0	2.0	4.5
51	Chemical elements & compounds	9.4	7.0	8.8
52	Tar & crude chemicals—oil & coal	3.9	3.5	6.0
53	Dyeing & tanning materials	11.8	6.5	6.9
54	Medical and pharmaceutical products	10.3	7.5	7.8
55	Essential oils and perfumes	7.8	8.0	10.6
56	Fertilizers—manufactured	4.6	1.5	4.6
57	Explosives	4.7	—	8.3
58	Plastics	10.5	5.0	6.4
59	Chemicals n.e.s.	8.8	9.5	6.4
61	Leather & dressed furs	7.8	11.0	9.7
62	Rubber manufactures n.e.s.	6.9	10.0	8.5
63	Wood & cork manufactures	8.2	8.0	7.5
64	Paper & paperboard manufactures	8.9	9.5	12.6
65	Textiles & fabrics	18.6	16.0	16.3
66	Nonmetallic mineral manufactures	10.5	9.0	9.1
67	Iron & steel	8.7	8.5	9.0
68	Nonferrous metals	12.2	9.0	7.4
69	Metal manufactures n.e.s.	12.7	10.5	11.5
71	Machinery—nonelectric	5.8	6.0	8.8
72	Electric machinery	8.1	13.0	10.4
73	Transport equipment	7.2	9.0	10.5
81	Plumbing, heating fixtures	14.9	11.0	11.5
82	Furniture	10.1	15.0	12.5
83	Travel goods, etc.	13.0	14.0	17.5
84	Clothing	22.6	16.0	19.9
85	Footwear	11.8	19.0	19.6
86	Professional & scientific instruments	15.4	13.0	13.6
89	Miscellaneous manufactures	10.9	9.0	8.9

sions. It was assumed, on the basis of recent sentiment in the U.S., that ASP would not be removed. The ASP procedure raises the actual rate of tariff by considerable amounts. Grubel and Johnson[77] have recently estimated actual ad valorem rates on certain chemicals. Using their estimates, I found the approximate proportion of benzenoid chemicals in the total imports in SITC 51 and 53, and adjusted the tariff rate in the table upward (by 20 per cent for SITC 51 and 40 percent for SITC 55) to reflect the ASP valuation on the average tariffs. For footwear, an arbitrary 10 per cent upward adjustment in the tariff was made.

2. The U.S.-Canadian automotive agreement, which eliminated tariffs on passenger vehicles and certain parts, was reflected in these calculations by eliminating trade in autos and parts between these two countries from SITC 73. The average tariff in the table was applied to the remainder.

3. Since the U.S. tariff on imports is applied to FOB values in the exporting country, the per cent decline in price in the U.S. as a result of tariff removal would be less than the U.S. ad valorem tariff. Adjustment has been attempted for this. It is assumed that freight, shipping, and insurance amounts to 10 per cent on all imports—a not completely valid, but still reasonable assumption—and the ad valorem rates were reduced accordingly. Since the Canadian tariff is also applied on an FOB value, the same procedure has been used to adjust that country's tariffs on U.S. exports.

A lack of data on an appropriate commodity classification basis made it impossible to include explicitly estimates of the expansions of U.S. exports because of the elimination of discrimination by Canada and the U.K. through the Commonwealth Preference system. As noted in the text, some types of

---

Sources:

1. For U.K. and U.S., Division 51 and above: Maxwell Stamp Associates, *The Free Trade Area Option* (London: The Atlantic Trade Study, 1967), p. 41.
2. For U.S. Divisions 21–43: Derived asd adjusted by averaging rates and reductions reported in Office of Special Representative for Trade Negotiations, *Report on U.S. Negotiations*, Vol. II, *List of Tariff Concessions Granted by the United States.*
3. For U.K. Divisions 21–43, and all Canadian tariff rates: Estimated by the author. The procedure was to adjust downward, for Dillion and Kennedy Round reductions, the average tariffs in *Atlantic Tariffs and Trade* (Political and Economic Planning, 1962). In general, reductions of one-third were made, but greater or lesser adjustments were made for certain divisions on the basis of press reports and other sources.

U.S. exports may benefit noticeably, but in most categories, the low rate of preference and the noncompetitiveness of U.S. exports with those of the partner countries, makes this omission of negligible proportions.

Finally, our use of nominal tariff rates rather than the "effective rates of protection" as a basis for estimating the direct effect on U.S. trade is also the result of limited time and the unavailability of tariff, trade, and input-output data all on the same bases. Effective rates of protection, by explicitly considering the effect of tariffs on imported inputs in the production process, provides a more valid theoretical basis for identifying the degree of protection in an industry and the possible result of the elimination of all tariffs. Our estimates using nominal tariffs fails to consider directly the effect on the domestic industry of the reduction in the cost of inputs, while the reduction in the cost of competitive imports is considered.

Elasticities of Demand for Imports

Estimating the elasticities of demand for a country's imports may be done either directly or indirectly. Direct estimation generally involves deriving, by regression techniques, coefficients relating observed movements in the time series of import volume with import prices. This technique may be done on various levels of aggregation.[78]

The indirect method makes use of the fact that, given the elasticity of domestic demand for a commodity, the elasticity of demand for imports of that commodity varies directly with the ratio of domestic consumption to imports, the elasticity of domestic supply, and the ratio of domestic production to imports.[79]

In either method, a valid statistical estimate is needed either of the import-demand elasticity directly, or of the price elasticity of demand in the domestic market. All existing statistical estimates of either of these are at least partially unreliable. Further, there is no set of elasticity estimates of either type on a commodity classification comparable to the detail used in our estimates of trade changes.

Because of these and other problems, the estimates used

in the text are based on elasticities derived in previous studies which utilized both methods. The elasticities used are shown in Table A-8. For U.S. imports, the Ball and Marwah estimates for the types of commodities (crude materials, semi-manufactures, and manufactures) were used without alteration.

For the elasticities of demand for imports into the U.K. and Canada, this study uses the values derived by Balassa (*Trade Liberalization, op. cit.*, p. 190). He used the indirect method to adjust the Ball and Marwah estimates for the U.S. to fit other countries. Since both Canada and the U.K. have ratios of consumption to imports and production to imports which are generally lower than the U.S., their import demand elasticities are proportionately lower.

For each commodity division, some degree of bias in our trade estimates is introduced by applying the same elasticity of import demand to all commodity divisions; some divisions should have higher and some lower elasticities of import demand. While some qualitative allowances have been made for these biases in the text, the factors governing these systematic errors are straightforward. Commodities with higher than average domestic price elasticities of demand are likely to have higher import-demand elasticities than the average used in the estimates. Likewise, commodity divisions for which imports are a very low proportion of domestic consumption will probably have higher than the average import-demand elasticity.

For the elasticity of substitution of U.S. exports for nonmember exports to Canada and the U.K. (as in equation 3), Harberger's estimate (see Table A-8) of 2.5 was scaled down to 2.0 for competition with nonmember imports in the U.K. and to 1.0 in Canada. These arbitrary adjustments to Harberger's value seemed needed in order to make the estimates more realistic. Many of U.S. exports of manufactured goods to Canada enjoy a market sheltered by transport-cost differentials, and those non-U.S. goods that enter Canada must either have a considerable competitive edge or be highly differentiated from the nearest U.S. competition. Judging the latter to be widely the case, the substitution elasticity of 1.0 between imports from the U.S. and those from nonmember countries appears a fair guesstimate. For basically the same reasons, but

Table A-8

DEMAND ELASTICITIES USED IN CALCULATIONS OF CHANGE IN U.S. TRADE

	Crude Materials	Semi-Manufactures	Manufactures
Elasticity of demand for U.S. imports:[80]	.26	1.38	3.50
Elasticity of demand for U.S. exports to:[81]			
United Kingdom	.25	1.06	2.68
Canada	.20	.82	2.06
Elasticity of substitution of U.S. exports for competitors exports in:[82]			
United Kingdom		2.00	2.00
Canada		1.00	1.00

with the different transport-cost conditions, the value of 2.0 for U.K. imports seems to be a conservative assumption. Furthermore, as will be seen below, we exclude a number of commodity divisions from the trade diversion estimates on similar grounds, thus the estimated export expansion from trade diversion is as low as could be objectively expected.

Nonmember Exports Subject to Displacement by U.S. Exports

While the elasticity of substitution relates the discriminatory tariff advantage acquired by U.S. exports to the displacement of nonmember exports, it is certain that not all nonmember exports are competitive with those of the U.S., and thus would be unaffected by the FTA. A host of considerations govern the susceptibility of nonmember imports to trade diversion including the market structure in the nonmember industry, relative transport costs to the member market, and the like.

In order to be as realistic as possible, separate assumptions have been made for each country and each broad commodity category, i.e., crude materials, semi-manufactures, and manufactures. Again, each assumption is designed to be conservative, i.e., to give a low view of the expansion of U.S. exports from trade diversion. This is warranted on a number of grounds, the main one being that the mechanical estimating procedure cannot account for competitive response from the exporters being displaced.

No trade diversion in crude materials is expected because of the unique supply conditions which prevail in the markets for such commodities. Thus, only SITC divisions in the semi-manufactured and manufactured categories are estimated. The following outlines the procedure.

1. All SITC divisions with an average U.K. or Canadian tariff of 5 per cent or lower are presumed to be unaffected by trade diversion.

2. For Canada, if the U.S. already supplies 75 per cent of total Canadian imports in a commodity division, it is assumed that no diversion can take place. Aside from the fact that only 25 per cent of total imports are left to divert, it is realistic to assume that product differentiation and loyalty will make the last 25 per cent (at a two-digit level) hard to conquer by U.S. exports.

3. a) For manufactured goods imports to the U.K., U.S. exports are assumed to be competitive with EEC exports only. Japan is excluded due to transport-cost differentials, and other EFTA countries already enjoy no-tariff treatment.

b) For imports of semi-manufactured goods to the U.K., only the EEC is considered. It is assumed that discrimination in favor of U.S. exports at the expense of exports from the under-developed countries will be avoided with some arrangement with the latter. Again EFTA exports are free of restrictions already.

4. For Canada, trade diversion by U.S. exports is assumed possible for both manufactured and semi-manufactured imports from all OECD countries excluding the U.K.

Since the U.S. is the major supplier of Canadian imports in all categories among the OECD countries and in most instances supplies in excess of 75 per cent of Canadian imports, little displacement of nonmember exports to Canada is expected. Much of this displacement is of Japanese origin. However, as noted earlier, the main portion of trade diversion is likely to be EEC exports of manufactured goods and chemical products in the U.K. market.

CHANGES IN THE PRICE OF MEMBER EXPORTS TO U.S.

The estimates of U.S. export expansion were made on the assumption that U.S. prices remained the same. The low ratio of U.S. exports to domestic production, the small estimated change in exports relative to U.S. output, and the relatively dynamic market structure in the U.S. all indicate that this is a tenable approximation, and more tenable than any assumption of increased export prices as a result of the tariff elimination. The structure of the changes in the exports among divisions shown in Table 3 indicate that the largest absolute changes in U.S. exports are in mammoth U.S. industries which could easily adjust output or product lines to the changed export conditions without necessitating any sizable price adjustments.

As noted in the text, the assumption ("A") that the prices of exports from Britain and Canada to the U.S. will remain constant is tenable only under very limited circumstances. These circumstances include a critical adjustment of aggregate demand in the two countries by economic policy plus an industrial structure in the adjustment of domestic demand which matches closely the industries in which export demand would expand. These hairline adjustments would be very difficult in these countries because the projected changes in exports are significant proportions of the existing output and exports in some of these industries in Canada and the U.K. If one also considers the increase in export demand due to trade diversion in the U.S. market, the result that at least some export prices in Canada and the U.K. will rise is almost inevitable.

Recognizing this possibility, assumption "B" involves estimates of the increase in U.S. import value assuming that export prices in Canada and the U.K. rise (as a proportion of the tariff, namely, "p" in equations 1′ and 2′) in accordance to the following schedule:

% of Total U.S. Imports in 1965 Supplied Jointly by Canada and U.K.	Assumed Increase in Export Prices as % of t
50% or more	25%
25–49%	50%
10–24%	75%
less than 10%	100%

This schedule is, to a considerable extent, arbitrary. But any assumption concerning changes in export prices as a result of foreign tariff reduction must be arbitrary since empirical evidence concerning the subject is hopelessly deficient or lacking. The forces which govern such price increases include industrial structure in the exporting country, the possible existence of economies of scale in production, R & D, or external economies, and so forth. Extensive data on an industry basis simply do not exist.

The schedule used here can be justified only on a priori grounds, and then only in the sense that it appears as good as any. The economic rationale is simple. If the U.K. and Canada combined are supplying a small portion of the U.S. import market before tariff elimination, it is likely that the export industries are small, noncompetitive, and unable to use the favorable tariff discrimination to expand exports without price rises; and the smaller the existing share, the relatively greater the expected price rise. Alternatively, supplying a large share of U.S. imports suggests a large domestic industry in one or both of the partner countries, and is thus assumed to be able to switch to the U.S. market with relatively smaller price changes. Partial disaggregation along these lines seems more justifiable than extending the same fractional assumption across all industries.

The Trade Data

Consistent multilateral trade figures were obtained from OECD, *Commodity Trade: Exports* and *Imports,* Jan.-Dec. 1966. The choice of year is critical only with reference to the existence of unusual distortions. For our purposes, 1966 seems to be "normal" and is also the latest year for which complete data is available.

As discussed in the text, tariff reductions in an FTA would certainly not be accomplished immediately. This introduces a major problem in the absolute (dollar) estimates of trade changes since two major events will alter the volume and structure of trade before an FTA could be initiated. These are the tariff reductions under the Kennedy Round and the devaluation of the pound sterling. The impact of each is complex and difficult to predict. Kennedy Round reductions will affect most tariffs, but those for some SITC categories much more so than others. Ideally, what is needed is an estimate of the trade volume by SITC division after all Kennedy Round results are implemented.

A similar problem—and solution—arises with respect to the devaluation. Here, the biases from omission are perhaps more serious for our estimates since the impact on U.S. exports and imports will be in opposite rather than the same directions.

Results

The estimates of changes in the value of U.S. exports and imports by SITC Division is shown in Table A-9. Import changes are given both for the assumption that supply price does not change ("A") and for the assumption that supply prices rise according to the schedule in Appendix subsection 5 ("B"). Export increases resulting from trade creation and trade diversion are shown separately.

Although the total increase in exports resulting from trade creation is over twice that from trade diversion, quite a number of divisions show the opposite result. Export increases from trade diversion assume the inability or unwillingness of nonmember supplies to reduce prices and meet the competitive advantage afforded U.S. exporters by the Free Trade Association. In those cases where nonmember producers do attempt to offset the FTA advantage, the U.S. export increase would be less than that estimated.

It will be noted that a large portion of the increased exports and imports occur in a few major categories—and often the same divisions (e.g., transport equipment and nonelectric machinery). This in part reflects existing patterns of trade, and implies that an even greater intra-divisional specialization would result from an FTA. In these cases, many large firms would both face increased import competition and increased exports—but in different product lines.

THE ESTIMATION OF CHANGE IN ECONOMIC WELFARE:

The net balance-of-payments changes derived from the estimation procedure above is not directly connected to the change in output and absorption from given resources which is the measure of change in economic welfare. No doubt the balance-of-payments change has an indirect impact on welfare to the extent that the projected improvement in the current account balance would permit more single-minded policies for output maximization. But this is a problematical gain which assumes unused resources and the expansion in export demand to bring them into production.

The change in economic welfare arises because resources and consumption are reallocated, and because the terms of trade change. The reallocation gains can be crudely estimated by assuming that the demand for import-type goods is linear and the supply function of import competing goods is upward sloping and linear. Then, the gain arises through a decline in the price of imported goods, increased purchases of imports to displace imperfect domestic substitutes, and the reapplication of the released resources in the import competing industry to other industries where the value of their contribution to output is higher. The equation for estimating this reallocation gain assuming linear demand and supply functions, is:[83]

$$.5[t/(1+t)]\, dQ - .5[t/(1+t)]\, dC = .5[t/(1+t)]\, dM$$

where dQ is the decline in output of import competing goods and dC is the increase in consumption of the import goods. The sum of dC and dQ is the estimated change in imports shown in Table 3.

The change in the terms of trade also directly affects the

Table A-9

DIRECT EFFECT OF FREE TRADE AREA ON U.S. IMPORTS AND EXPORTS, BASED ON 1966 TRADE FLOWS AND AVERAGE POST-KENNEDY ROUND TARIFF RATES
(millons of dollars)

(1) SITC Division	(2) Title	(3) Change in Exports (F.O.B.)	(4)	(5)	(6) Change in Imports (F.O.B.)	(7)	(8) (F.O.B.) Net Effect	(9)
		Trade Creation	*Trade Diversion*	*Total*	*Assumption A*	*Assumption B*	*Assumption A*	*Assumption B*
21	Hides, skins, & furskins	8.2	—	.2	.3	1.0	—.2	—.9
22	Oil seeds & oil nuts	—	—	—	.7	1.3	—.7	—1.3
23	Crude rubber	.1	—	.1	—	.1	—	—
24	Wood, lumber, & cork	—	—	—	.2	.6	—.1	—.5
25	Pulp & waste paper	.2	—	.2	—	—	.2	.2
26	Textile fibres	1.0	—	1.0	1.3	4.3	—.3	—3.3
27	Crude fertilizers & minerals	.4	—	.4	.2	.4	.2	—.1
28	Metalliferous ores & metal scrap	.1	—	.1	.3	.8	—.1	—.7
29	Crude animal & vegetable materials, n.e.s.	.2	—	.2	.1	.2	.1	—.2
41	Animal oils & fats	.6	1.8	2.5	.3	.3	2.1	2.1

42	Fixed vegetable oils & fats	—	—	—	1.4	1.2	—1.4	—1.2
43	Animal & vegetable oils & fats, processed, & waxes of animal or vegetable origin	.6	—	.6	.5	.4	.1	.1
51	Chemical elements & compounds	12.7	14.1	26.8	18.5	17.1	8.3	9.7
52	Mineral tar & crude chemicals from coal, petroleum & natural gas	.1	.1	.3	.2	.2	—	.1
53	Dyeing, tanning & coloring materials	2.0	2.6	4.6	3.8	2.0	.8	2.6
54	Medicinal & pharmaceutical products	1.9	2.1	4.0	.6	.5	3.4	3.5
55	Essential oils & perfume materials	5.9	3.5	9.4	72.6	22.2	—63.2	—12.8
56	Fertilizers, manufactured	.2	2.5	2.7	5.9	5.6	—3.2	—2.9
57	Explosives & pyrotechnic products	—	.1	.1	.8	.7	—.7	—.7
58	Plastic materials, regenerated cellulose & artificial resins	6.5	7.2	13.7	11.9	10.9	1.8	2.8
59	Chemical materials & products, n.e.s.	5.3	4.0	9.4	1.3	1.1	8.1	8.3
61	Leather, leather manufacturers n.e.s. & dressed furskins	1.4	1.5	2.9	2.2	2.0	.7	.9
62	Rubber manufactures, n.e.s.	9.6	2.0	11.6	2.9	1.4	8.7	10.2

Table A-9 (continued)

DIRECT EFFECT OF FREE TRADE AREA ON U.S. IMPORTS AND EXPORTS, BASED ON 1966 TRADE FLOWS AND AVERAGE POST-KENNEDY ROUND TARIFF RATES
(millions of dollars)

	(2) Title	(3) Change in Exports (F.O.B.)	(4)	(5)	(6) Change in Imports	(7)	(8) (F.O.B.) Net Effect	(9)
		Trade Creation	*Trade Diversion*	*Total*	*Assumption A*	*Assumption B*	*Assumption A*	*Assumption B*
63	Wood & cork manufactures	2.5	2.6	5.1	7.5	6.8	—2.4	—1.7
64	Paper, paperboard & manufactures thereof	25.4	42.2	67.5	233.3	196.5	—165.8	—128.9
65	Textile yarn, fabrics, made-up articles & related products	19.6	43.9	63.5	15.8	13.4	47.7	50.1
66	Nonmetallic mineral manufactures, n.e.s.	20.6	14.3	35.0	55.5	37.7	—20.5	—2.8
67	Iron & steel	13.4	18.5	31.9	22.1	18.8	9.7	13.0
68	Nonferrous metals	11.0	12.4	23.4	80.3	74.7	—56.9	—51.3
69	Manufactures of metal, n.e.s.	45.7	8.9	54.6	33.6	17.1	21.0	37.5
71	Machinery, other than electric	225.5	6.7	232.2	143.8	120.0	88.4	112.2
72	Electric machinery, apparatus & appliances	137.1	20.7	157.9	47.5	23.4	110.4	134.4

73	Transport equipment	170.1	32.9	203.0	170.1	142.6	32.9	60.4
81	Sanitary, plumbing, heating & lighting fixtures & fittings	5.0	.7	5.7	.5	.2	5.2	5.5
82	Furniture	5.1	.7	5.8	7.9	5.4	—2.1	.4
83	Travel goods, handbags & similar articles	.7	1.2	1.9	76.2	24.3	—74.3	—22.4
84	Clothing	5.0	14.8	19.7	23.2	8.0	—3.5	11.7
85	Footwear	.8	13.0	13.7	5.6	1.8	8.1	11.9
86	Professional, scientific & controlling instruments; photographic & optical goods, watches & clocks	57.8	11.7	69.5	13.7	4.5	55.8	65.0
89	Miscellaneous manufactured articles, n.e.s.	52.6	17.4	70.0	50.0	34.1	20.0	35.9
Totals		847.0	304.0	1,151.0	1,112.7	804.2	38.3	346.9

"economic welfare" of the FTA members. An increase in prices of imports from members while export prices are constant obviously denotes a loss, while rising prices for exports to members denotes a gain. The net terms-of-trade effect (Z), using our earlier symbols, becomes

$$[(t/(1+t)]_x \cdot P_x(dX+X) - [t/(1+t)]_m \cdot P_m(dM+M) = Z$$

The subscripts indicate tariffs and price changes on domestic exports to member countries (x) and imports from member countries (m). The total terms of trade change is thus Z and depends on the volume of trade and the proportion by which price changes offset tariff reductions. In our calculations, P_x was zero; thus the terms of trade effect under assumption "B" was negative. Should a different set of assumptions involving a rise in U.S. export prices be made, the net terms-of-trade effect could easily turn positive since U.S. exports to the partners considerably exceed imports from them.

The total change in welfare is the sum of the terms-of-trade and reallocation effects. As noted in the text, assumption "A" yields a small gain in welfare in static terms while assumption "B" yields a small loss.

As was emphasized in the text, however, these welfare measurements apply to the *direct effects* only. Welfare benefits of economies of scale, increased competition, and more rapid economic growth are ignored in these calculations.

NOTES

The author was immeasurably assisted in the calculations in this paper by Helen Waehrer and William Schneider. In addition, particularly helful suggestions were made on earlier drafts by Professors Gordon Bjork, Norman Mintz, Ingo Walter, and Harry G. Johnson, and by Messrs. Sperry Lea and David Steinberg, and by the members of the N.Y.U. Seminar on a Free Trade Association.

1. The other alternatives, broadly defined, include (1) to pursue another major round of GATT-most-favored-nation negotiations; (2) to attempt to negotiate free trade in certain major products or

sectors among many countries; or (3) to do nothing except consolidate the gains resulting from the Kennedy Round. See the other papers in this volume. Also, Ralph Straus, "A Proposal for New Initiatives in U.S. Foreign Trade Policy," *Orbis* (Spring, 1967), pp. 20–23, and T. Geiger and S. Lea, "The Free Trade Area Concept as Applied to the U.S." in *Issues and Objectives of U.S. Foreign Trade Policy,* compendium of statements to the Joint Economic Committee (September, 1967).

2. A Free Trade Association involves the elimination of trade barriers on essentially all trade among members but permits each member to establish its own treatment of imports from nonmembers.

3. It is not intended to suggest that UDC's should be excluded from a Free Trade Association among advanced countries which included the U.S. Indeed, their membership—either with special status or with a preferential adjustment period—should be welcomed. It would be preferable if all advanced members maintained the same treatment of the UDC associates than a disparate individually determined policy.

4. The results of that research, directed by Bela Balassa, is reported in B. Belassa, *Trade Liberalization among Industrial Countries: Objectives and Alternatives* (New York: Council on Foreign Relations, June, 1967). See also Mordechei Kreinin, "Effects of an Atlantic Free Trade Area on the American Economy," *Southern Economic Journal* (July, 1966), pp. 96–111.

5. See, among others, Sperry Lea, *A Canadian-United States Free Trade Area: A Survey of Possible Characteristics* (Washington and Montreal: Canadian American Committee, 1964), and *A Possible Plan for a Canada-U.S. Free Trade Area* (Canadian-American Committee, 1965). For a survey of these and other studies see R. A. Matthews, "A North American Free Trade Area," *M.S.U. Business Topics* (Winter, 1967).

6. R. Wonnacott and P. Wonnacott, *Free Trade Between the United States and Canada* (Cambridge: Harvard University Press, 1967).

7. *A Possible Plan for a Canadian-U.S. Free Trade Area, op. cit.*

8. See S. Green and K. Gabriel, *The Rules of Origin* (Geneva, EFTA, 1967). It should be made clear, however, that rules of origin necessitate the maintenance of a customs frontier between the FTA members, and this in itself may be a significant psychological barrier to free trade which would not exist in a customs union.

9. "Other manufactured goods" consist of manufactured goods classified chiefly by material (SITC Section 6) and miscellaneous manufactured articles (SITC Section 8).

10. The theory of tariff structure and the advantages of effective tariff rates are discussed in W. M. Corden, "The Structure of a Tariff System and the Effective Protective Rate," *Journal of Political Economy* (June, 1966), pp. 221–37.

11. B. Balassa, "Tariff Protection in Industrial Countries: An Evaluation," *Journal of Political Economy* (December, 1965), pp. 573–94, and Giorgio Basevi, "The U.S. Tariff Structure," *Review of Economics and Statistics* (May, 1966), pp. 147–61.

12. On this point, see M. Kreinin, " 'Price' vs. 'Tariff' Elasticities in International Trade—A Suggested Reconciliation," *Ameri-*

can Economic Review (September, 1967) pp. 892–93.

13. The U.S. quotes on lead and zinc were suspended in 1965. The U.S., however, does effectively impose export quotas on the export of certain commodities (cotton textiles, etc.) to the U.S. by Japan and others.

14. These are often referred to as "dynamic effects." See B. Balassa, *The Theory of Economic Integration* (Irwin, 1961), Part II.

15. Jacob Viner, *The Customs Union Issue* (New York: Carnegie Endowment for International Peace, 1950), pp. 50 ff.

16. This ignores the complications introduced by trade diversion and its effect on the distribution of gains and losses.

17. H. E. English, *Industrial Structure in Canada's Internation Competitive Position* (Montreal: Canadian Trade Committee, 1964).

18. A detailed discussion of the estimating technique and its shortcomings is provided in the Appendix to this paper. The procedure followed is essentially the same as in Balassa, *Trade Liberalization . . . , op. cit.*, Chapter IV, and pp. 189–205, and Kreinin, *op. cit.*, pp. 96–105.

19. See Appendix for a justification of these exclusions.

20. The actual tariff rates employed for each commodity division and the sources are given in the Appendix.

21. The original estimates for U.S. imports are from R. J. Ball and K. Marwah, "The U.S. Demand for Imports, 1948–1958," *Review of Economics and Statistics* (November, 1962), pp. 395–401, and A. Harberger, "Some Evidence on the International Price Mechanism," *Journal of Political Economy* (December, 1957), pp. 506-21. These have been used for the U.S. and applied in adjusted form to the U.K. by Balassa, *Trade Liberalization, op. cit.*, pp. 187–89. See Appendix to this paper.

22. Separation of the forty SITC divisions into three groups was based on the degree of processing of the important components in each division, although this is partly arbitrary. The divisions included in each group were indicated in Table 1. The elasticities of import demand (with minus sign omitted) for the three countries for each category are:

	Crude Materials	Semi-Manufactures	Manufactures
U.S.	.26	1.38	3.50
Canada	.20	.82	2.06
U.K.	.25	1.06	2.68

23. It was assumed that substitution for imports from nonmembers occurred only in semimanufactures and manufactures, and then only if certain tariff and market-share criteria were met. These are explained in the Appendix, but the procedure was designed to give a conservative estimate of the expansion of U.S. exports from this source. The elasticity of substitution between U.S. and nonmember exports is assumed to be 2.00 for U.K. imports and 1.00 for Canadian imports. These are also conservative as Harberger (*op. cit.*) estimated the substitution elasticity between U.S. and European exports in third markets to be 2.5.

24. The proportion of the tariff by which the U.K. and Canadian supply price is postulated to rise was assumed to vary inversely with the per cent of the U.S. import market already supplied by the

partner country, i.e., a small market share indicated noncompetitiveness, and supply price would thus rise by a high percentage of the tariff. For more detail, see the Appendix.

25. *The Effect on Prices of Tariff Dismantling in EFTA* (Geneva, 1966), pp. 13–22.

26. The impact on U.S. trade of a Free Trade Association encompassing *all* non-communist industrial countries under pre-Kennedy Round tariffs estimated by Balassa and Kreinin was 10.1 per cent for exports and 11.2 per cent for imports. (See Balassa, *Trade Liberalization, op. cit.*, Table 4.3, or Kreinin, *op. cit.*)

27. Basevi, *op. cit.*, Tables 1 and 2.

28. See "The Free Trade Option," *op. cit.*, p. 40, for a comparison of U.K. MFN and preference rates. For all manufactures, the average (unweighted) MFN rate is 10.2 per cent, while the Commonwealth preference rate is 1.2 per cent. The degree of preference afforded the U.K. by Commonwealth members is considerably lower. See First National City Bank, New York, *The Changing Commonwealth*, for some very rough estimates of the degree of existing preference. Also, Balassa, *Trade Liberalization, op. cit.*, p. 192. The failure to take explicit account of the preference system in the estimates is simply the result of the absence of preference tariff data on an SITC basis. Construction of such data was not warranted, given the relatively low rates remaining.

29. See the Appendix for a more explicit statement of method.

30. The matching of the commodity coverage on the two bases is by no means perfect, but the rough correspondence achieved is sufficient for the purpose here.

31. This assumes that the increased imports do *not* lower or raise costs in the partner countries' export industries (Assumption "A").

32. Balassa (*Trade Liberalization, op. cit.*, Appendix Table 4.6 and 4.7) ranks woolens as a top export performer for the U.K., and paper and paperboard as the same for Canada. On U.K. competitiveness in woolens, see also Wells, *op. cit.*, p. 69, and *The Free Trade Area Option, op. cit.*, pp. 70–71.

33. Comparative advantage is "revealed," for Balassa, by the position of a commodity in a rank ordering of the change between two periods in the export share of the commodity in total exports relative to the share of the country's total exports to world exports. See *Trade Liberalization, op. cit.*, Appendix to Chapter 4, especially Tables 4.6 and 4.7.

34. Wells, *op. cit.*, pp. 69–96.

35. *The Free Trade Area Option, op. cit.*, Chapter V.

36. H. Edward English, *Industrial Structure in Canada's International Competitive Position* (Montreal: Canadian Trade Committee, 1964).

37. The Canadian-U.S. automotive agreement and the already essentially free trade in farm machinery limits the scope for rationalization in machinery and equipment.

38. *Free Trade Between the United States and Canada: The Potential Economic Effects*, especially Chapter 10.

39. The U.S. and Canada were divided up into a number of regions. On the basis of 1958 regional wage and other cost data, and using U.S. production coefficients, the average cost per unit of output on a broad industry basis was cal-

culated for each region. The inter-country comparisons assumed an exchange rate of parity between the U.S. and Canadian dollars. See *Ibid.,* Part I.

40. The problems of U.S.-Canadian trade policy with respect to petroleum and petroleum products has been considered in Roy A. Matthews, "Energy," *Canadian-American Planning,* "The Seventh Annual Conference on Canadian-American Relations, 1965" (Toronto: University of Toronto Press, 1966), pp. 65 ff. He suggests that the most fruitful approach would involve, first, federal cooperation between the two countries since the multiplicity of lower governmental regulations and the structure of the industry and its multinational firms makes a more direct approach to free trade in oil largely unfeasible.

41. Among other things, the depletion allowance in Canada is higher, and the treatment of depreciation for tax purposes of mining and quarrying equipment is more liberal. (See "Summary Review of Federal Taxation and Legislation Affecting the Canadian Mineral Industry," Mineral Information Bulletin 82 [Ottawa, 1966].)

42. In addition, an indirect subsidy to U.S. primary aluminum through subsidized electric power from the Bonnewille generating complex benefits the U.S. industry.

43. Taking assumption "A" estimates from Table 4, and dividing it evenly over five years yields 0.9 per cent per year. Therefore 1.0 per cent is a conservative figure which could reflect additional increases due to indirect effects of the FTA discussed in the following section.

44. This is the procedure under the Trade Expansion Act of 1962 and used in the European Common Market.

45. There is considerable evidence of such responses in the EEC, and their reflection in very few claims on the "common market adjustment fund." See I. Walter, *The European Common Market: Patterns of Trade and Production* (New York: Praeger, 1967), Chapter 7.

46. For more detailed discussions see J. Viner, *The Customs Union Issue* (New York: Carnegie Endowment for International Peace, 1950), T. Scitovsky, *Economic Theory and Western European Integration* (Stanford: Stanford University Press, 1958), and B. Balassa, *The Theory of Economic Integration* (Illinois: Irwin, 1961).

47. A possible negative factor would be a potential increase in the degree of economic monopoly, extending across national frontiers, and the resulting distortions in resource allocation.

48. Besides Viner, Scitovsky, and Balassa (*Ibid.*), L. Krause has concluded that dynamic factors of the type considered here have been of major importance in the EEC. See *The Meaning of European Economic Integration for the U.S.* (Washington: Brookings, forthcoming), Chapter II. Also Wonnacott and Wonnacott (*op. cit.*, Part I), foresee various dynamic factors, e.g., adoption of U.S. production techniques, external economies, and research stimulation as important effects for Canada in the event of a U.S.-Canada Free Trade Association.

49. For example, Harry G. Johnson has argued the U.K. would reap little gain from dynamic factors in joining the EEC. See his "The European Common Market—Risk or Opportunity," *Weltwirtschaftliches Archive* (Cambridge:

Harvard University Press, 1957), pp. 267–78. And J. Vanek is of the opinion that the dynamic (long-run) factors are of little importance relative to the static effects. See his *General Equilibrium of International Discrimination* (Cambridge: Harvard University Press, 1965), pp. 9–10.

50. An attempt at quantifying the net effects for the EEC can be found in Krause, *op. cit.*, Chapter II.

51. For an extended discussion of the potential for international trade to permit an economy to exploit economies of scale, see the papers in E. A. G. Robinson (ed.), *The Economic Consequences of the Size of Nations* (New York: St. Martins Press, 1963), Part 6.

52. Empirical studies have been almost unanimous in this conclusion. In particular, see Joe Bain, *Barriers to New Competition* (Cambridge: Harvard University Press, 1956). For summaries of this and a number of other studies, see Balassa, *Trade Liberalization, op. cit.*, Chapter 7.

53. *Ibid.*

54. For example, E. F. Denison, *Sources of Economic Growth in the U.S.* (C.E.D., 1962), Chapter 16, makes the assumption, after weighing the arguments and evidence, that increases in the size of the economy increased the contribution of all other sources of growth by 10 per cent. See also his *Why Growth Rates Differ* (Washington D.C.: Brookings, 1967).

55. The relevant industries are taken to be manufacturing and mining excluding petroleum.

56. The possibility of a calculation of this sort was suggested to me by Professor Harry G. Johnson.

57. *Op. cit.*, p. 175.

58. See Harvey Leibenstein, "Allocative Efficiency vs. 'X'-Efficiency," *American Economic Review* (June, 1966), pp. 392–415.

59. A peripheral advantage in the U.S. would be easing the administration of the antitrust laws.

60. Other peripheral effects, such as reduced uncertainty of commercial policy treatment of trade and changes in the structure (concentration) of domestic industry seem trivial for the U.S. because of its small foreign sector. For consideration of these factors, see Balassa, *The Theory of Economic Integration, op. cit.*, Chapter 8.

61. Krause, *op. cit.*, Chapter 3.

62. See particularly English, *op. cit.* Similar implications exist in Wonnacott and Wonnacott, *op. cit.*, Parts I and II.

63. Borrowing by Canadian provincial governments in New York is commonplace, and the lower level of U.S. portfolio investment in Canada in 1965 and 1966 reflects an unofficial agreement by the Canadian government to limit these and other Canadian issues in the New York market.

64. These measures should be taken only as rough indications of importance. The data on foreign investment (from U.S. sources) is certainly not comparable to the domestic investment data (from Canadian and U.K. sources). The time of reporting is quite different. Furthermore, foreign capital can finance housing, inventories, government consumption or private consumption, in addition to plant and equipment.

65. In a survey conducted as part of the Atlantic Trade Project, some U.S. firms indicated that their direct investment abroad would decline in the event of a Free

Trade Association encompassing all Western industrial countries, due to the ability to serve a tariff-free market from the U.S. This, of course, confirms the predictions of traditional trade theory. An almost equal number of firms indicated that their investments would expand for reasons similar to those indicated below. See M. E. Kreinin, "Freedom of Trade and Capital Movements—Some Empirical Evidence," *Economic Journal* (December, 1965), pp. 748–58.

66. The apparent inability of static equilibrium theory to explain observed foreign direct investment has caused considerable reevaluation of its causes and its net effects on the balance of payments and national welfare. Among the recent contributions which are consistent with the analysis and conclusions here are J. Polk *et al.*, *U.S. Production Abroad and the Balance of Payments* (New York: NICB, 1966), and B. Balassa, "American Direct Investments in the Common Market," *Banca Nationale del Lavoro* (June, 1966), pp. 121–46. On the welfare effects of foreign investment see John Dunning, "Does Foreign Investment Pay" and "Further Thoughts on Foreign Investment," *Moorgate and Wallstreet* (Autumn, 1964, and Autumn, 1966, respectively). Also of interest is the theory developed in Raymond Vernon, "International Investment and International Trade in the Product Cycle," *Quarterly Journal of Economics* (May, 1966), pp. 190–208.

67. One result of this which many Canadians would not welcome is the perpetuation and perhaps extension of the existing degree of U.S. ownership of Canadian industry.

68. For example, see W. Salant, *et al.*, *The U.S. Balance of Payments in 1968* (Washington D.C.: Brookings, 1963), pp. 142–47.

69. The Development Bank suggested by the Canadian-American Committee could perform this function. See *A Possible Plan for a Canada-U.S. Free Trade Area*, *op. cit.*, pp. 45–46.

70. A more detailed discussion can be found in the paper by Harry G. Johnson in this volume.

71. *The Free Trade Area Option*, *op. cit.*, pp. 41–49.

72. This, in fact, was assumed in the Atlantic Trade Study. See *The Free Trade Area Option*, *op. cit.*

73. This configuration of members was analyzed in Balassa, *Trade Liberlization*, *op. cit.*; Wells, *op. cit.*; and Kreinin, *op. cit.*

74. See *The Free Trade Area Option*, *op. cit.*, p. 44.

75. This can be seen as follows. Let π be the foreign price of imports (initially equal to 1) and M be the volume and initial value of imports.

$$d(\pi M) = \pi dM + M d\pi + d\pi dM$$

Equation 2 yields dM while

$$d\pi = pt$$

Thus,

$$d(\pi M) = \left[\frac{t}{1+t}(1-p)eM\right] + [Mpt] + \left[pt\frac{t}{1+t}(1-p)eM\right]$$

which is equivalent to 2′.

76. This was the procedure used by Balassa, *Trade Liberalization*, *op. cit.*, Appendix to Chapter 4.

77. See H. Grubel and H. Johnson, "Nominal Tariff Rates

and U.S. Valuation Practices: Two Case Studies," *Review of Economics and Statistics* (May, 1967), pp. 138–40.

78. This method is employed in Ball and Marwah, *op. cit.*

79. The derivation of the formula summarizing these relations is in Guy Orcutt, "Measurement of Price Elasticities in International Trade," *Review of Economics and Statistics* (May, 1958). The formula for the elasticity of import demand of a commodity (e) is:

$$e = E_d \cdot (C/M) + E_s \cdot (Q/M)$$

where E_d is the domestic price elasticity of demand for the commodity, E_s is the elasticity of domestic supply, and C/M and Q/M are the ratios of domestic consumption and production to imports. This formula has been used, assuming ostensibly "reasonable" values for E_d and E_s, by John Floyd ("Overevaluation of the Dollar: A Note on the International Price Mechanism," *American Economic Review* [March, 1965], pp. 95–107) to estimate the elasticities of demand for U.S. exports and imports.

80. U.S. demand elasticities are taken from R. J. Ball and K. Marwah, "The U.S. Demand for Imports, 1948–1958," *Review of Economics and Statistics* (November, 1962).

81. Estimates of demand for U.S. exports to the U.K. and Canada are assumed to be the same as the average elasticity of demand for imports of the respective countries. The latter were obtained from Bela Balassa, *op. cit., Trade Liberalization among Industrial Countries*, p. 190.

82. The elasticities of substitution are based on Harberger's estimates of 2.5 for substitution between U.S. and European exports in third markets. See A. Harberger, "Some Evidence on the International Price Mechanism," *Journal of Political Economy* (December, 1957), pp. 506–26. This value is adjusted downward for both countries to be conservative and because Harberger's estimate appears high in the present environment. Transport costs and highly developed communication between the U.S. and Canadian markets appears to justify the much lower value for exports to that country.

83. More extensive discussions of the theory underlying this formula can be found in H. Johnson, "The Cost of Protection and the Scientific Tariff," *Journal of Political Economy* (August, 1960), or Balassa, *Trade Liberalization, op. cit.*, pp. 195–97.

The Economic Consequences for Britain of a Free Trade Association

by Harry T. Cowie
Maxwell Stamp

I. THE MULTILATERAL ALTERNATIVE

The recent veto by President de Gaulle of Britain's second bid for membership in the European Economic Community has reopened the great debate concerning the various alternative strategies that lie open to the U.K. There are several variations that can be discussed, but broadly speaking there are four major policy alternatives that present themselves.

In the first place, Britain can press for further multilateral reductions of tariffs in the GATT and by these means try to achieve international free trade. This policy would in effect represent a return to the traditional policy pursued by successive Secretaries of the Board of Trade in the years since the end of the Second World War. As such, it must be regarded as not necessarily being the best policy option open to Britain; for these years, for example, from 1950 to 1966, have witnessed a steady reduction in the U.K.'s share of manufactured exports of the industrial nations from 25.5 per cent to 13.0 per cent.

Britain has a very real interest in freer world trade. But the lesson that must be drawn from postwar trade history is that Britain herself cannot bring sufficient pressure to bear to generate free trade between industrial nations through a multilateral reduction of tariffs in the GATT. This situation became evident in the five rounds of worldwide tariff negotiations that were conducted prior to the Kennedy Round when the results were rather unsatisfactory, at least from a British viewpoint insofar as the U.K. had one of the highest tariffs in the Western world but seemed unable to negotiate away this seemingly important ace.

It was the formation of the Common Market that broke the logjam in worldwide tariff negotiations, by prompting a new initiative from the American administration in the shape of the 1962 Trade Expansion Act, which prepared the way for the Kennedy Round. Furthermore, the actual negotiations at the Kennedy Round amounted to a confrontation between the delegations from the U.S. and the EEC, with the British, for the first time, relegated to a role of a poor second fiddle. This situation is indicative of the changed situation at the world trade conference table. Although Britain continues to remain a nation with a high ratio of international trade to national income, the possibilities that the U.K. market can offer cannot match up to the opportunities provided by freer trade in the U.S. and the EEC.

The multilateral approach must therefore be assessed in terms of the likelihood that the EEC and the U.S. will successfully be able to conduct another Kennedy Round at the GATT. It is too early to be dogmatic about whether another Kennedy Round can be mounted. Officials in the various major countries have the situation under review at the present time. Nevertheless, recognition must be made of a change in the climate of opinion since the last round of negotiations. These discussions were conducted as the climax to an era of trade liberalization that started with the OEEC in western Europe, which in turn created the basis for steps toward an economic union in the form of the Rome Treaty, a process which finally reached world level at the Kennedy Round and its ensuing substantial reduction of world trade barriers.

Various experts have suggested that the Kennedy Round has taken the MFN (Most Favored Nation) approach to tariff negotiations about as far as it can go. Mr. Eric Wyndham

White, at that time the Director-General of the GATT, was quoted by *The Times* of London as saying on May 16, 1967, "The Kennedy Round is probably the last of the major pure tariff exercises. The next stage may come, in establishing free trade among major international industries."

Mr. Wyndham White had already suggested that the role of the GATT must change after the Kennedy Round. In an address at Bad Godesberg in October, 1966, he spelt out that future tariff negotiations would be of a different kind:

> I see progress in the field of tariff reductions as being best sought through the promotion by the major industrialized countries of a free trade arrangement covering, (a) the consolidation of all existing duty free items, (b) the "nuisance" duties I have referred to, (c) certain sectors of industrial activity which are ripe for a move towards free trade, and (d) additional sectors or products on which duties could be eliminated from time to time through negotiation or agreement, or by unilateral action.

He said then that in his opinion arrangements of this kind should be negotiated in the GATT and the benefits extended through the MFN clause to other GATT countries. Nevertheless, in previous GATT negotiations the rate of progress has been determined by those major trading nations least willing or able to offer meaningful concessions. As a recent paper prepared at the request of the subcommittee on foreign economic policy of the Joint Economic Committee of the United States Congress has pointed out:

> The unconditional application of the MFN principle has committed the multilateral approach to proceed like a wartime convoy, at the speed of its least active participant. Otherwise such a country would have been given through the operation of the MFN principle a "free ride."[1]

For a long time in the lengthy Kennedy Round negotiations, it seemed very likely that the opposition of the French government (and as a reflection of this attitude the EEC Commission) to very substantial tariff cuts, would jeopardize the whole outcome of the negotiations. In the event the French government and the EEC Commission agreed to go further along the road to trade liberalization than most people expected. The explanation that is usually given for this change is that the exclusion of Britain from the EEC would no longer be quite so painful a process. Whether this is the case or not, there seems little justification for expecting, at least at this juncture, that another round of unilateral negotiations at the GATT would achieve anything like the same success as the Kennedy Round.

The whole climate of world economic policy has deteriorated since the summer of 1967. The two world reserve currency countries, Britain and the United States, have been forced to impose restrictions which cannot fail to affect world trade. These restrictions, which are sometimes interpreted as beggar-my-neighbor policies by the French government could easily be used as an excuse for a failure on the part of the European countries to entertain another Kennedy Round.

In any case, the success of the Kennedy Round means that another multilateral negotiation would be confronted with hardcore problems such as textiles and the vexed questions of nontariff barriers. The failure of the American administration to secure the necessary legislation to revoke the notorious American Selling Price[2] restrictive device does not augur well for another GATT-style negotiation. Obviously, these factors could change over the next few years. There may well be scope for a limited initiative at the GATT in the direction of harmonization of tariffs. A certain amount may also be accomplished by sector negotiations where industries in the leading countries are ripe for free trade. The problem with this concept, however, would seem to be that there are very few sectors where reciprocity would be meaningful. For example, in many technologically advanced sectors the EEC is anxious to secure a base for expansion which is sometimes described in terms that amount to the "infant-industry" argument for protection. As long as this attitude continues, the European Commission, let alone the French government, will be able to find reasons for not being able to negotiate another round of multilateral tariff cuts.

Furthermore, there is the question of nontariff barriers. It is highly probable that nontariff barriers will be resorted to more and more by governments as tariffs are removed under the Kennedy Round agreement. The EEC countries, for example, have recently started to implement the decision to adopt a value-added tax.[3] The substantial export rebate that this tax incorporates has been accepted by the GATT. However, countries, such as the U.S. and the U.K., which do not have value-added taxes will find their exports increasingly at a disadvantage in third markets as a result of, say, the German government's recent move to adopt a VAT. In the case of West Germany, one estimate is that a VAT could be equivalent to a 7 per cent export rebate. This advantage could be substantial and from a British viewpoint would cancel out the approximate net effect of the recent sterling devaluation.

The GATT, however, has never had a very strong mandate in the field of nontariff barriers, and it seems unlikely that another round of negotiations will be able to deal with them adequately, especially as there are problems in ensuring reciprocity as the effect of the removal of nontariff barriers is particularly difficult to quantify. A Free Trade Association, on the other hand, would be well placed to adopt measures to control the discriminatory effects of the regulations and practices that are described as nontariff barriers. EFTA, for example, which intentionally limited the degree of economic integration among its members, found it necessary to establish some "rules of competition" in order to prevent tariffs from being replaced by nontariff barriers. Whereas the effects of removing tariffs can be assessed on certain assumptions, nontariff barriers are not so easily quantified. As a result, the liberalization of nontariff barriers would present a problem unless the countries concerned agreed to complete removal. This objective could be encompassed in a Free Trade Association but is unlikely to be achieved by a multilateral negotiation.

Nevertheless, the first alternative considered in this paper, namely the multilateral approach, could have some attraction in certain political quarters in Britain if it were dressed up in a guise of "Britain going it alone." This policy would, of course, stand on its head the multilateral objectives that the GATT embodies. Supporters of this kind of policy who believe that Britain should accept a role in the world more akin to Sweden would probably not oppose further multilateral reductions of tariffs. On the other hand, they would probably not give trade liberalization a very high priority and would consider that a higher priority must be given to cutting overseas commitments. Unfortunately a great deal of thinking along these lines tends to be mercantilist in outlook. If the "little Englanders" followed through the logic of their own argument about Britain accepting a role more akin to Sweden, and advocated unilateral reductions in tariffs and a massive redeployment of labor out of inefficient industries into areas where the U.K. has a comparative advantage, it would not be necessary to quarrel with their logic, although their assumptions would still be open to question. Too often, however, the argument that Britain should divest itself of its overseas commitments and investments is put forward as an excuse for little or no action on the home front of the kind required to eradicate the restrictive practices on both sides of industries which lead to considerable overmanning and inadequate investment in the U.K. domestic economy.

The Commonwealth Alternative

The second alternative open to Britain after the veto of Mr. Wilson's bid to join the Common Market is a revival of Commonwealth trade. This option has very few enthusiastic supporters in Britain today, not because the sentiment is not there, but because there is little support in either Britain or the Commonwealth for trade polices akin to the Ottawa Agreements of 1932. The Commonwealth preference system, like many other trade initiatives, was a reaction to an economic crisis. Britain had adopted specific tariff barriers during World War I in order to establish infant industries. These were extended after the war to protect national markets from outside competition and the threat of unemployment. The British tariff was generalized in the Ottawa Agreement and substantial preferences were created in order to protect Commonwealth trade. In return for free access to the U.K. market, the Commonwealth countries gave British manufactured goods a preferential position in their own markets. The system of Commonwealth Preference did provide a partial answer to the problems of the 1930's by maintaining the level of Commonwealth trade at a time when Britain's imports from other sources fell by about one-half in value.

Successful at a time when world trade was declining, the system has not maintained the British share of Commonwealth trade or the Commonwealth share of the British market when world trade is expanding. This is partly because the level of preference, which was expressed in many cases in specific terms, has been falling on account of rising prices. For example, it has been estimated that the average margin of preference on all imports into the U.K. was 10 to 12 per cent in 1937. By 1948 this margin had fallen to 6 to 7 per cent, and by 1957 to about 5.5 per cent. A more recent study by the Board of Trade, however, has estimated that the average margin in all exports is 6.5 to 7 per cent. The preference is greatest in the old Commonwealth countries, especially New Zealand, Australia, and Canada. On the other hand, as these countries expand it is inevitable that they should look to non-U.K. sources for their manufactured imports. Many people would agree with merchant banker Mr. Kenneth Keith who wrote recently:

> We should not forget that even today the overseas sterling area and other primary producers take about two-fifths of British exports and account for the same proportion of our imports. But it is difficult to believe that the Commonwealth countries would be willing, in the present circumstances, to commit themselves to giving Britain larger preferences for our exports and vice-versa. Such a move would be contrary to GATT. In any case I believe that the Ottawa agreements encouraged too many British firms to sell unsophisticated goods in what was mainly an unsophisticated market. This meant that when we started to re-equip our own industries in the 1950's we had to buy a great deal of our requirements from Europe or

> America. I am sure it is right therefore that British industry has set its sights on the continental markets of Europe and North America which have proved to be the most dynamic and challenging markets in recent years.[4]

In fact it is now generally recognized that the system of Commonwealth preferences has been an obstacle to freer trade for Britain in the postwar world. One of the problems posed by British membership of the Common Market, for example, is that the adoption by Britain of the EEC Common External Tariff would convert the present preferences enjoyed by certain Commonwealth exports in Britain into an anti-Commonwealth preference for EEC goods. This problem does not present itself so severely in a Free Trade Association (such as EFTA) that would allow the U.K. to maintain preferential margins, although, of course, they would have to be extended to other members, thereby reducing the effective Commonwealth preference.

Whereas there is little support in Britain today for any design to revive Commonwealth trade on the basis of further discriminatory arrangements, there is nevertheless a desire to avoid placing restrictions on Commonwealth goods entering British markets, as far as possible, and also a desire to maintain a reasonable share of British goods in Commonwealth markets. The share of British exports taken by Commonwealth countries has fallen from 45.9 per cent in 1956 to 30.7 per cent in 1966 (including South Africa). The older Commonwealth countries, such as Australia, which are now entering a take-off phase of industrial development, could offer a rapidly growing market of British capital exports in the next decade. British commercial policy may therefore wish to give a relatively higher priority on trade arrangements that can avoid the anti-Commonwealth preference involved in British membership in the EEC.

THE THIRD ALTERNATIVE: ASSOCIATE STATUS OF THE EEC

The third alternative is to refuse to take no for an answer from the French government regarding Britain's application to join the EEC. There are several different postures that Britain can adopt. Firstly, there is the present official position of the British government, namely to continue to knock on the door and refuse to accept the French president's press conference as an official veto. It would seem that this tactic can only continue for an interim period. If the other members of the Common Market indicate that they are unwilling to rupture the EEC for the sake of British membership (and this seems to be the case), then the British tactic only makes sense as a form of disengagement from its previous stance. In other words, the U.K. Government, by this means, can underline that it was unequivocally seeking membership of the EEC and that the blame for the failure of this application must lie with the French government.

By itself, camping out on the Common Market doorstep cannot remain a continuing policy for a British government for long. Some people suggest that this position need only be maintained until President de Gaulle leaves office. However no time limit can be set to this event. Consequently it is necessary to consider alternatives that might be acceptable to the French government. This raises the question of associated status of the EEC which from time to time various French spokesmen and some British voices have suggested as an interim type of membership that Britain could apply for pending full membership.

Associated membership of the EEC is an undesirable role for Britain if there is no guarantee that full membership will follow. In the first place the application for membership both by Conservative and Labour Governments has been made on political grounds and only in the second place for economic reasons. According to one well-informed source[5] the original decision in Whitehall to apply for membership emanated from a top-level committee chaired by the Permanent Secretary to the Treasury that came to the conclusion that Britain should seek to join the Six, first, for fear of political instability among the Six which could lead to the disintegration of the EEC; secondly, because the EEC could become the main partner of the U.S., with a consequent loss of relative standing for the U.K. not only with the U.S. but with the overseas Commonwealth; thirdly, because it was felt that if Britain joined the EEC it would be possible to establish a real Atlantic partnership; and fourthly, because it was believed that membership would stimulate Britain's economic growth.

Political considerations largely determined the decision taken in Whitehall and by the government. But associated membership of the EEC would not make Britain party to the decision-making of the Six in the Council of Ministers. Indeed, associate membership of the Rome Treaty has hitherto served as a means of allowing countries like Greece and Turkey, which were not fully developed industrially or geographically, contiguous to the Six to participate in the customs union. For these reasons the proposal that Britain should apply for associate membership has been given a cool reception by the British government, which has made it clear that full membership was the only kind for which the U.K. wished to apply. In any case, in the next few years the final steps will be taken toward an economic union as set out in the Rome Treaty which provides a mere framework on which the European Commission must provide the flesh and bones. A great deal of the future character of the Six will therefore be decided in this process, and if Britain remained only an associate member, it must be presumed that she would play little or no part, although the U.K. would have to accept the consequences when she ultimately became a full member.

No one can ignore the fact that a process of consolidation is now going on in the Community which will make it very difficult for a major power like Britain to join without disturbing many delicately balanced arrangements. Furthermore, the forward planning of large companies inside the Six as well as the Commission itself is being made on the assumption that the EEC will consist of six countries. This kind of decision-making is weighing the scales against eventual British membership of the EEC as the years elapse and the final milestone of the transitional period, 1970, comes into sight.

For all these reasons, and many more, close consideration is now being given in the U.K. to a fourth alternative, the Free Trade Association option. This arrangement could bring to Britain the advantages of free access to the widest continental market in the world, the United States, while at the same time setting in motion a trade liberalizing dynamic which could eventually create a more outward looking European Economic Community which Britain could join.

THE FOURTH OPTION: A FREE TRADE ASSOCIATION

The fourth option under consideration is a Free Trade Association which would be open ended but whose initial members would consist of the United States, Canada, and EFTA. From the U.K. point of view there would be considerable advantages in a Free Trade Association with the widest possible membership. If the EEC could be persuaded to join from the outset, this would be to Britain's advantage. However it must be accepted that this seems unlikely at this stage, although this "happy event" could take place later. As trade is growing faster between members of either Continental Europe or the North American Continent, Britain would gain from the lowering of trade barriers with both these regions.

One disadvantage of such a wide tariff free area is that it would not be possible to accord significant preferences on manufactured goods or raw materials to developing countries or to the Commonwealth. But there would inevitably be a long transitional period—perhaps as long as fifteen years—to enable corporations to adjust to the new market with minimal disruption. In this period it would be possible for member countries to give the developing countries free access for their products from the beginning without demanding reciprocal concession. Such an arrangement could have a considerable benefit for developing countries as their goods would have a period, as long as the transitional period, in which they would enjoy a preferential position over the products of developed countries. This preferential margin would diminish throughout the transitional period, but by that time a foothold in the wealthy markets of the industrialized countries should have been established which the lower wage costs of the developing countries should help to maintain.

On the assumption that Britain is or can become reasonably competitive so that industry shall not be overwhelmed by competition either from Continental Europe or the U.S., a Free Trade Association as wide as possible but certainly including the U.S., Canada, and EFTA has much to offer. But is it feasible? In the next section an attempt is made to quantify some of the factors involved.

II. THE FREE TRADE ASSOCIATION OPTION

From time to time proposals have been put forward in Britain for freeing trade with North America. In September, 1957, Mr. Peter Thorneycroft, who was Chancellor of the Exchequer at that time, proposed in Ottawa what he described as "an adventurous proposal," namely the establishment of a Free Trade Association between Canada and the U.K. This proposal was a response to calls for a closer trade association with the U.K. that Mr. John Diefenbaker, the Canadian Prime Minister, had made earlier that year. There has always been considerable doubt cast as to whether the proposal was seriously intended by the British government, which at the same time was proposing a Europe-wide Free Trade Association that would include both the Six and the other OEEC members.

Since the Thorneycroft proposal was not pursued by officials on either side, it did encourage private groups in Canada to consider the problem of freer trade. A Canadian-American Committee was established by the Private Planning Association of Canada and the National Planning Association of the U.S. in order to investigate problems arising out of the growing interdependence between Canada and the U.S. In 1963, the various possible characteristics of a scheme for bilateral arrangements between the U.S. and Canada were examined in a paper, "A Canada-U.S. Free Trade Arrangement." This study assessed the possible scope and nature of a free trade arrangement by systematically examining a wide range of practical choices. A second paper, "A Possible Plan for a Canada-U.S. Free Trade Area," published in 1965, narrowed down the alternatives to a plan for a Canada-U.S. Free Trade Association. Although the plan aroused only mild curiosity in the U.S., the rigorous examination of the problems made it an interesting prototype for any future Canadian-American scheme. In Canada interest has been far more intense. The plan stimulated considerable comment there, providing a realistic basis for the Canadian Liberal Party's 1966 resolution which called for a Free Trade Association.

The breakdown of the first British attempt to join the European Economic Community in 1963 and the ensuing deterioration in international economic affairs caused the Canadian-American Committee to decide to consider the extension of the area plan into a wider trade strategy. In May, 1966, a statement entitled "A New Trade Strategy for Canada and the United States" was published that outlined the broad principles on which a wider Free Trade Association could be based. On membership the committee specified that the FTA should be based "on the principle of opening membership . . . to all eligible industrialized countries, and of extending some special 'one-way' trade privileges to all developing countries." The paper continues: "In view of the uncertainties and special problems of some of the prospective members of a broad free trade association, it would seem most appropriate for Canada and the United States to establish a nucleus for the larger grouping by encouraging at the outset the participation of the United Kingdom and its EFTA partners."

The work of the Canadian-American Committee is referred to here at some length because the statement left the ball in Britain's court. For as the American research director of the Committee, Mr. Sperry Lea, has pointed out: "Despite interest in some American circles, and a Canadian interest, a positive American response could only come after a positive expression of British interest."

The Atlantic Trade Study

Although a major postwar goal of British commercial policy has been the maintenance of British influence in the Atlantic alliance, little consideration has been given, until recently in the U.K., to the implications of a Free Trade Association which would include the U.S. Too often when proposed it has been dismissed without study as either impractical, a nonstarter for want of American support, or likely to be economically disastrous leading to Britain's absorption by the U.S. On the other hand, the work of the Canadian-American Committee demonstrated that in the context of the objectives of American and Canadian trade policy, a Free Trade Association consisting of the U.S., Canada, the U.K., and other EFTA countries could make a good deal of sense.

Accordingly, the Atlantic Trade Study, an independent and nonparty group, was formed in the U.K. in December, 1966, to sponsor studies on the implications for Britain of taking part in an open-ended free trade arrangement as proposed by the Canadian-American Committee.[6]

The Committee has sponsored a series of studies, the first being published in November, 1967, under the title "The Free Trade Area Option—Opportunity for Britain."[7] This study reviews the implications of a wide Free Trade Association for Britain in light of recent developments and quantifies the likely economic effects using the same statistical data as the study prepared by Professor Hawkins. Although it is assumed that the arrangement would be open-ended, the study considers that it is perhaps unlikely that the EEC would be interested in joining in the early stages, as the common external tariff is still widely regarded as a necessary protective wall behind which there is a greater chance of integrating the Six into an economic union. The Free Trade Association is assumed in the first place to consist, therefore, of the U.S., Canada, the U.K., and the other EFTA countries. Other countries—Japan, Australia, and New Zealand—might well join a Free Trade Association, but these countries in that case would probably want the program to include further steps toward a more general freeing of agricultural trade. As the analysis of a Free Trade Association is restricted in this study to industrial commodities and basic materials, the effects of membership of Australia and New Zealand are not examined.

Relative Heights of Tariffs

The classical case for free trade is based first on the gains achieved by selling commodities on better terms than would be possible in the absence of tariff reductions and, secondly, on the benefits that accrue from the opportunity to consume lower-cost imports in place of more expensive domestic goods. There are other effects from free trade, the dynamic effects, which take account of changes in production methods and economies of scale resulting from the increased size of the market. But the classical case is real enough and provides a useful starting point for our analysis.

The first task was to establish the relative heights of the tariffs of the possible member countries of a Free Trade Association in order that the gains from freer trade could be measured. This was a major undertaking as American and Canadian tariffs are not on the same Brussels Tariff Nomenclature (BTN) as the European countries and many other leading trading countries, such as Japan. The existence of various keys and concordances prepared during the Kennedy Round negotiations made it possible, however, for the first time to compare accurately, item-by-item, the tariffs of the U.K., the U.S., the EEC, and Japan. Calculations were made and unweighted arithmetic averages estimated for all BTN groups corresponding to the Standard International Trade Classification (SITC) divisions. In this way an assessment was made of the relative heights of the tariffs of the main industrial countries as they will be when the Kennedy Round reductions have been completed in 1972.

The table of industrial tariffs after the Kennedy Round indicates that the leading industrial countries by 1972 will have average tariffs in a range between 7 per cent and 12 per cent. The U.S. tariff at 11.2 per cent will be the highest, closely followed by the U.K. at 10.2 per cent, Japan at 9.8 per cent, and the EEC with 7.6 per cent. The actual U.K. level of protection is lower than these averages would imply because of the very low level of preferential duties averaging only 1.2 per cent on manufactures coming from the Commonwealth preferential area.

Trade Creating Effect

The direct effect of a Free Trade Association depends on the gains involved in the opportunity to sell manufactures on better terms than would be possible in the absence of tariff

INDUSTRIAL TARIFFS AFTER THE KENNEDY ROUND (1972)
Comparison of average tariffs by SITC divisions

(Per cent ad valorem)

SITC		US	UK (MFN)	UK (Pref.)	EEC	Japan
51	Chemical elements & compounds*	9.4	8.8	0.2	6.8	9.1
52	Crude chemicals	3.9	6.0	0	2.2	3.3
53	Dyestuffs & coloring materials	11.8	6.9	0	6.9	7.2
54	Medicinal & pharmaceuticals	10.3	7.8	0.4	6.7	9.0
55	Essential oils & perfumes	7.8	10.6	0	6.1	10.5
56	Manufactured fertilizers	4.6	4.6	0	3.0	2.5
57	Explosives	4.7	8.3	0	7.3	11.3
58	Plastics	10.5	6.4	0	7.5	9.5
59	Other chemicals	8.8	6.4	0.4	6.0	9.6
5	All chemicals	9.2	8.1	0.2	6.4	9.0
61	Leather manufactures	7.8	9.7	0.3	5.8	14.4
62	Rubber manufactures	6.9	8.5	1.8	5.7	7.7
63	Wood & Cork manufactures	8.2	7.5	0	7.3	9.0
64	Paper & board manufactures	8.9	12.6	0	11.0	8.6
65	Textile yarn & fabrics	18.6	16.3	7.3	10.5	10.9
66	Nonmetallic mineral manufactures	10.5	9.1	0.03	6.5	7.6
67	Iron and steel	8.7	9.0	0	7.2	8.9
68	Nonferrous metals	12.2	7.4	0	6.3	11.4
69	Other manufacures of metal	12.7	11.5	0.05	7.9	10.0
6	Manufactures classified by materials	12.3	12.0	1.2	8.0	10.0
71	Machinery nonelectric	5.8	8.8	0.4	5.7	9.4
72	Electrical machinery	8.1	10.4	0.7	7.9	9.5
73	Transport equipment	7.2	10.5	2.5	8.5	9.7

SITC		US	UK (MFN)	UK (Pref.)	EEC	Japan
7	Machinery & transport equipment	6.7	8.8	0.8	6.8	9.5
81	Sanitary, plumbing, heating	14.9	11.5	0	9.0	8.8
82	Furniture	10.1	12.5	2.1	8.1	11.9
83	Travel goods	13.0	17.5	0	11.3	15.0
84	Clothing	22.6	19.9	9.2	11.8	16.5
85	Footwear	11.8	19.6	2.7	10.7	10.8
86	Professional & scientific instruments	15.4	13.6	2.1	8.6	11.8
89	Miscellaneous manufactures	10.9	8.9	1.3	7.4	8.5
8	Miscellaneous manufactured articles	14.7	10.5	2.6	8.5	10.5
5–8	AVERAGE TARIFF ON MANUFACTURES	11.2	10.2	1.2	7.6	9.8

* Assumes abolition of ASP (American Selling Price)

reductions, and secondly, on the benefits that accrue from the opportunity to consume lower-cost imports in place of the more expensive domestic goods. In order to measure this trade-creating effect of dismantling tariffs, we assume that a 1 per cent fall in imports prices resulting from a reduction in tariffs would lead to an increase in imports of finished manufactures of 3.5 per cent in the U.S.; 3.1 per cent in Japan; 2.68 per cent in the U.K.; and 2.06 per cent in Canada. In the case of semi-manufactures it is assumed that a 1 per cent fall in the tariff would lead to a 1.38 per cent increase in the U.S., 1.42 per cent in Japan, 1.06 per cent in the U.K., and 0.82 per cent in Canada. These assumptions are made on the basis of studies by various economists and are believed to be as good estimates as possible.[8]

The first important conclusion that emerges from this analysis is that Britain's balance of trade in manufactures could improve quite substantially in a Free Trade Association, provided British export prices can be held down. We calculate that on the basis of 1966 trade flows, the U.K. would be able to export $311 million or more manufactured goods to the U.S., but in return would only increase imports of manufactures by $229 million. On this basis the trade balance would improve, for the U.K., by as much as $82 million. If, on the other hand, the greater export effort meant a price rise in Britain amounting to a quarter of the amount by which tariffs are reduced, with no corresponding American rise, the U.K. would only be able to export $230 million extra manufactures to the U.S., slightly more than the total increase in American exports to the U.K.

Britain would also benefit relatively from the direct effect of free trade with Canada. We are unable to make the same detailed comparison of the Canadian tariff as the other industrial tariffs, because no key is available to relate one to the other. However using the PEP study "Atlantic Tariffs and Trade" and adjusting the tariff averages in that report for Canada in order to allow for the Kennedy Round it is possible to arrive at averages for the main SITC groups for both the Canadian MFN tariff and preferential tariff.

In incidence the U.K. preferential tariff on Canadian manufactures is considerably lower than the Canadian preferential tariff on British manufactures. Britain should therefore be able to increase exports of manufactures by more (the estimates made in our study is plus $49 million) provided export prices remain stable. An increase of this order would represent an increase of about one-tenth of the 1966 trade flow. Canadian manufactured exports, which at present enjoy almost free entry, would only increase fractionally as a result of a Free Trade Association. Our study estimates that Canadian exports to the U.K. would increase by $2.9 million if export prices remain stable and by about $2.4 million if a rise in Canadian export prices absorb one quarter of the tariff reduction effect. Even if U.K. export prices go up by the same amount, Britain should gain less, but still substantially more than the Canadians, namely about $36.8 million.

Before going on to consider the wider implications of a Free Trade Association (FTA), it would be useful to summarize the trade creating effects, at least as far as the U.K. is concerned.

TRADE CREATION EFFECTS OF FTA ($ MILLION)

	USA		Canada		Total	
	A	B	A	B	A	B
U.K. Exports	311	230	49	37	360	267
U.K. Imports	229	229	3	2	232	231
	+82	+1	+46	+35	+128	+36

A = Export prices constant
B = Export prices rise in Canada and U.K. by 25% of tariff reduction

On the assumption that export prices do not rise, the U.K. trade balance would improve by $128 million. If export prices in Canada and the U.K. rise by 25 per cent of the tariff reduction with no rise in U.S. export prices, the net balance would be reduced from $103 million to $36 million.

Trade Diversion Effect

A Free Trade Association would not only create trade between members, it would also divert trade away from third countries to member countries. British exporters, for example, would benefit from tariff-free entry to the United States market, whereas EEC exports would continue to pay the U.S. tariff (unless the Common Market decided to join FTA). This trade-diverting effect could be important on account of the size of trade between the EEC and North America. In 1966 the EEC exported $3,660 million of manufactures[9] to the U.S. and $687 million to Canada.

We estimate that about 10 per cent of EEC exports to North America might be deflected as a result of the tariff differential. This calculation is based on a low elasticity of substitution of 1 and it should be noted that American economists have estimated that on elasticity of substitution between U.S. and European exports in third markets as high as 2.5. Nevertheless, even on fairly conservative assumptions we estimated that the U.K. on the basis of 1966 trade flows could deflect $531 million of EEC and Japanese exports from the U.S. market and $65 million from the Canadian market. The trade-diversion effect of a Free Trade Association consisting of the U.S., Canada, and EFTA could therefore be more important than the trade-creating effect, at least as far as the U.K. is concerned.

The U.K. could win trade away from the EEC and Japan in the North American market totaling $596 million compared with an increase in British exports through trade creation of $360 million.

Economists have sometimes suggested that common markets and free trade associations can be evaluated according to whether trade creation is greater than trade diversion. In the former case they are regarded as "good," whereas in the latter case they are regarded as "bad." This would seem an oversimplified analysis in the case of a Free Trade Association that is open-ended.

In the latter case any country or group of countries would be free to join the Free Trade Association and by so doing remove the discriminatory effect and increase the trade-creating effect of the whole arrangement. In this way a Free Trade Association should be recognized as an important initiative that could lead to maximum trade movement through the establishment of industrial free trade in the world.

The combined trade-creating and trade-diverting effects of an FTA (on the assumption that Japan was not a member) would amount to $956 million; that is 8 per cent of all British-manufactured exports representing about a 49 per cent increase in British manufactured exports to North America compared with the 1966 trade flow.

Britain would also lose a small share of her existing markets in EFTA to the U.S. and Canada as a result of an NAFTA (including the EFTA countries). It has not been possible to quantify this aspect of trade liberalization, but we consider that the effects would not be considerable because the Scandinavian and Swiss tariffs are already low even before the Kennedy Round. The U.S. would also capture a portion of the U.K. preferential market in Canada and likewise the Canadians could divert some existing British exports in the event of an FTA (although this latter effect seems likely to be small). If the U.S. captured 10 per cent of British exports to Canada, there would be a loss of around $50 million. On the other hand, it must be pointed out that although these factors could diminish the net trade effect of an FTA for Britain, we have assumed a low elasticity of substitution when calculating the trade diversion effect in order to allow for the factors which we have not been able to quantify in this study.

Comparison of U.K. Membership of FTA and EEC

What would be the trade-creating and diverting effects of the U.K. joining the EEC? We calculate on the same assumptions but on the basis of 1965 trade flows that the trade-creation effect would be slightly larger if Britain joined the EEC than if she joined FTA, despite the fact that the average tariff is lower, because the U.K. has a larger export trade at present with the Common Market than with North America. U.K. exports to the EEC would increase by $316 million if she joined that group against an increase to North America of $292 million if she joined FTA. On the other hand, British imports from EEC countries would rise by $286 million with the removal of the U.K. tariff on Common Market manufactures. This figure would be almost $100 million greater than the comparable increase in British imports from North America as a result of an FTA. Furthermore, the trade diversion effect to the U.K.'s advantage would not be nearly as large as in an FTA.

We estimate that the U.K., assuming the same elasticity of substitution, would take $16 million trade in manufactures away from the U.S. and $26.3 million away from Japan as a result of joining the EEC. The trade-diversion effect of Britain joining the Common Market would, therefore, be considerably smaller than trade diversion in FTA. It seems likely, moreover, that the U.K. would lose more to the EEC in Britain's "preferential" EFTA markets than the U.S. would take from Britain's preferential markets in Canada. Even ignoring the latter factor, it would appear that the direct effects of joining the EEC would not be as advantageous as joining an FTA.

EEC AND FTA COMPARED
(Increase in trade resulting from U.K. membership
based on 1965 trade flows)

$ million	FTA	EEC
U.K.		
Export Increase (trade creation)	292	316
Export Increase (trade diversion)	552	191
Import Increase	189	286
Net change	655	221

This comparison between an FTA and the EEC is, of course, restricted to the gains from free trade in manufactured goods. Membership of the EEC would involve Britain in wide areas of common policies including a common agricultural policy and greater mobility of capital movement. It is worthwhile pointing out that both these factors could be costly to the British balance of payments, at least in the short run. Probably for these reasons, British ministers have pointed out on several occasions that the overriding motives behind the British application to join the EEC are political. Nevertheless one suspects that most people would not have expected that trade effects of liberalization with North America would be more beneficial (at least on these assumptions) than freer trade with the Common Market.

Anglo-Japanese Trade

We also examined the direct effect of removing tariffs on the Anglo-Japanese trade balance in manufactures. In 1965 the total U.K. manufactured exports to Japan at $113.4 million were slightly higher than the $112.3 million imported from there. The lowering of tariff barriers between Japan and the U.K. would lead to an almost equal increase of trade both ways. British exports to Japan would increase by $25.2 million and Japanese exports to the U.K. by $24.8 million, assuming constant export prices. But if export price rises absorbed one-quarter of the tariff reduction, the trade increase for both countries would be smaller: about $18.9 million in British manufactured exports to Japan and $18.6 million in Japanese exports to the U.K.

British machinery exports should do best, especially non-electric machinery, which could rise by $11.5 million on the basis of constant export prices. British chemical exports could rise by 15 per cent. Transport equipment and professional instruments should do quite well, although in these sectors the imports of Japanese goods also should be greater.

As might be expected, the Japanese could look forward to a net gain in exports of clothing and footwear. But we calculate that on the basis of existing trade flows the gain would be fairly modest, although Japan limits existing export of cotton textiles to the U.K. Japanese clothing exports would rise by $4.65 million and footwear by $1.58 million. On the other hand, British exports of textile yarn and fabrics would rise by $2.09 million against an increase of Japanese exports to Britain of $1.66 million. The U.K. should also benefit from the removal of the quota and other nontariff barriers which extensively protect the Japanese market. This might decisively tilt the balance in Britain's favor.

NONTARIFF BARRIERS

The success of the Kennedy Round means that nontariff barriers will become larger obstacles to international trade than hitherto. Nontariff barriers have not been so important while trade has had to flow against considerable tariff protection, but as this level comes down, nontariff barriers are likely to show more above the surface. It seems highly probable that nontariff barriers will be resorted to more and more by governments as tariffs are removed under the Kennedy Round Agreement.

A Free Trade Association would probably have to establish "rules of competition" in order to ensure that nontariff barriers were removed as far as possible. The Canadian-American Committee's plan for a Canada-U.S. Free Trade Association envisaged that appropriate steps would have to be taken to control the discriminatory effects of nontariff regulations affecting freely traded products. This document stipulated that the partners would be expected to identify a number of obviously discriminatory government aids and settle on means of dealing with them before the founding date.

On the whole North American nontariff barriers seem more restrictive on trade than those used in the U.K. or other EFTA countries. On the other hand, the "Buy American" rules are published rules and hence visible and often cited. Americans rightly point out that government agencies (and public corporations) in western European countries (including the U.K.) rarely buy abroad when there are domestic suppliers. Many West European countries also severely limit imports of U.S. coal. The U.K., for example, has prohibited imports of coal from non-Commonwealth countries since 1958. However the U.S. provides an outstanding example of preferential buying through the well-known "Buy American Act" and special customs classification and valuation systems which have a very noticeable restrictive effect on trade. The notorious American selling price (ASP) procedure, which has the effect of doubling the level of the tariff on the categories where it applies, was a *cause celebre* in the Kennedy Round. It was generally agreed that this device would be abandoned but the necessary legislation has not yet been introduced and the attitude of Congress may well be hostile at this time. If this is so, then Britain should gain substantially from the removal of nontariff barriers in an FTA arrangement. While the coal industry would suffer as a result of American imports, the economy as a whole would gain.

Dynamic Effects

So far this paper has concentrated on the static gains from free trade in an FTA. There are other effects from free trade: the dynamic effects which take account of changes in production methods and economies of scale resulting from the increased size of the market. These effects are probably more important in the long run but they are also more difficult to quantify. Economists since Adam Smith have placed great importance on dynamic importance of the size of the market. Smith pointed out in "The Wealth of Nations" that

> The greatest improvement in the productive power of labour and the greater part of the skill, dexterity and judgement with which it is anywhere directed or applied, seem to have been the effects of the division of labour . . . this division must always be limited . . . by the extent of the market.

Even so, it is only in recent years that economists have been able to make tentative evaluations of the dynamic effects of trade liberalization. Until recently many British economists argued that the U.K. economy was large enough to permit the full exploitation of economies of scale. The work done by Professor Bela Balassa and other economists has drawn attention to the dynamic benefits that relatively well-developed economies can reap from trade liberalization. Balassa has pointed out that on these grounds Britain should benefit from freer trade. He writes:

> In general, it would appear that the gain from economies of scale is inversely related to the size of national markets. In relative terms, the exploitation of economies of scale following the liberalisation of trade would therefore provide the largest gains to small countries. Still, indications are that countries of the size of the UK can derive considerable benefits from economies of scale following the liberalisation of international trade.

In theory, exports can provide an indefinite enlargement of the market, and exports did provide the British cotton industry with large-scale economies through specialization and long runs in the mid-nineteenth century. Today manufacturers do not usually consider exports as an adequate substitute for a large home market. Exports tend to be highly precarious and do not provide the requirements of a market—stability and uniformity of product—on which mass production can safely be based.

The enthusiastic acception that British industry has given to successive governments' applications to join the European Economic Community stems partly from their realization that once Britain was inside the Common Market, the other member countries could not suddenly shut out British exports for political or balance-of-payments reasons, thus enabling manufacturers to plan accordingly.

American Mass Market

This point is actually far more valid as an argument for joining an FTA, since Europe, even after tariffs have been removed, will not be a very homogeneous market, natural differences—widely differing local tastes and other market imperfections—being likely to remain for many years. It could be a long time before Europe can be said to be a "home market" for Britain, in the event of membership being achieved, even if the Community does evolve into a true economic union. An FTA, on the other hand, would give British exporters access to the vast U.S. market free of tariff and other trade barriers. And the American market exhibits a remarkable level of demand for homogeneous products and would therefore provide British industry with the right kind of economic climate for taking full advantage of economies of scale. The increase in total U.S. imports between 1964 and 1965 was just over £1,000 million, almost double the total of British exports to the U.S. in 1965. Such is the size of the American market that although total imports amounted to £7,000 million in 1965, this represented only 3 per cent of GNP in the U.S.

There are several ways in which increasing the size of the market, and thus the size of the economic unit, could lead to increased efficiency in British industry. First, certain industries and companies can realize economies of scale by building larger plants. These are particularly crucial in technologically based industries such as petrochemicals, where labor costs have been shown to rise by only 20 to 30 per cent and capital costs by only 60 to 70 per cent as output doubles.

Secondly, a larger market permits a higher degree of specialization within an industry. The motor car industry is frequently cited in this connection. For instance, the specialized production of components in separate plants in the U.S. has allowed greater economies of scale to be reaped in electrical and ignition systems, radiators and heaters, steering wheels and transmission equipment.

Thirdly, a larger market permits the lengthening of production runs for individual commodities. This horizontal specialization has been cited as accounting for a considerable part of the differences in productivity between America, on the one hand, and Europe and Canada on the other. Higher productivity in the U.S. compared to Canadian textile plants has been explained by the fact that American firms can concentrate on a single fabric, while Canadian establishments often produce five to one hundred types of fabric. The Canadian-American Committee's plan for a Free Trade Association in North America drew attention, therefore, to the productivity gains that industry in Canada would achieve through greater specialization as one of the main reasons for Canadian participation in a Free Trade Association.

Salutary Jolt

Another dynamic effect of trade liberalization is the intensified competition that results from the lowering of tariff and other trade barriers. An argument that is often used regarding the benefits of British membership of the Common Market is that this would give British industry a "salutary jolt." The argument, however, would apply even more strongly to participation in an FTA arrangement. For American industry, in general, is more competitively minded than its European counterpart. Various explanations have been suggested. Professor Tibor Scitovsky, of the University of California, has pointed out:

> Much of European industry was established on a small scale at a time when the advantages of large-scale production were not yet known; and this has created vested interests and a tradition that are among the main obstacles that stand in the way of a transition to the now more economical large-scale production in a few plants.

Whatever the reasons, European industry in many sectors constantly tends to be more cartel-minded than competitive in outlook. There are, consequently, many areas where the Common Market's formation has not resulted in price reduction commensurate with lowered tariffs. American industry, by contrast, believes in a more effective form of competition. Antitrust legislation, the influence of the frontier, and pioneering traditions have played their part. If Britain wants the advantages of a competitive environment, she is more likely to achieve them under an FTA scheme than by joining a Common Market which remains in many fields cartel-minded and protectionist in outlook.[10]

Economic Growth

What effect would membership in an FTA have on Britain's rate of growth? Often it is suggested that Britain should adhere to the Rome Treaty because the EEC "is the most dynamic market in the world." The implication is that the rate of growth of GNP in the Six has been high in recent years and therefore Britain can expect to benefit from a free trade relationship with countries enjoying higher rates of growth than the U.K.

It has never been satisfactorily demonstrated that the EEC itself was responsible for accelerating the growth of GNP in member countries, or that if it did the effect was lasting. West German growth, for instance, declined from an average of 9.3 per cent in the period 1950–1955 to 4.8 per cent in 1960–1965; last year GNP there actually declined. The growth of some countries outside EEC (such as Japan) has also been exceptional. At the most the EEC can only be claimed as one of the factors responsible for growth performance.

Growth depends, first, on the rate of expansion of economic capacity and, secondly, on the change in the degree to which capacity is utilized. The first is more fundamental, depending, as it does, on the rate of growth of working population and of output per employed person. According to the OECD, the U.S. will experience a very rapid increase in working population rising from 111.2 million in 1965 to 136.30 million in 1980.[11] This increase is almost double what is expected in Italy (the west European country with the fastest-growing working population) and almost four times the increase expected in West Germany.

The Canadian working population is also forecast to increase even more rapidly than that of the U.S. In the years 1965 to 1970, the Canadian working population will rise, it is projected, by an average 9.2 per cent a year against 6.6 per cent in the U.S. and 2.3 per cent in West Germany.

1965–80 ESTIMATED INCREASE IN WORKING POPULATION

	Average per cent increase	
	1965–70	1965–80
Canada	9.2	na
U.S.	6.6	22.8
Italy	4.4	13.2
Sweden	3.5	10.6
U.K.	3.4	10.2
France	3.4	11.6
Germany	2.3	4.8

The rapid expansion of working population in North America will tend to be reflected in a faster rate of economic growth. Using official statistics of working population, we made estimates of employment in 1977 and prepared projections of GNP for 1972 and 1977 for FTA and the EEC.

In the absence of any adequate basis for estimating changes in productivity beyond 1970, we assumed that the forecasts of output per person made by the OECD would be achieved. We then adjusted the OECD figures for the forecast trend in hours worked and the anticipated effect of economic and social policies (but no allowance was made for the effect of an FTA).

The results are shown in the following table.

ACTUAL GNP AND PROJECTIONS
(Based on 1965 figures in U.S. $'000 million)

	Actual		Projected		Average Annual % Change
	1960	1965	1972	1977	1965–77
W. Germany	83.4	112.2	140.5	160.7	3.6
France	69.3	94.0	126.9	150.4	5.0
Italy	40.8	56.8	74.3	86.7	4.4
Belgium	13.8	16.9	21.6	25.0	4.0
Netherlands	14.4	19.0	24.9	29.3	4.5
Luxembourg	0.4	0.6	0.8	0.8	3.2
EEC (Total)	222.2	299.5	389.0	452.9	4.3
U.K.	82.2	98.9	120.4	135.7	3.1
Denmark	7.6	10.0	13.1	15.3	4.4
Austria	7.4	9.3	11.8	13.5	3.8
Norway	5.1	6.9	9.3	10.0	4.8
Sweden	14.7	19.3	25.1	29.3	4.3
Portugal	2.6	3.9	5.8	7.0	6.6
Switzerland	10.6	13.9	117.5	20.1	3.7
EFTA (Total)	130.2	162.2	203.0	231.8	3.6
EFTA (Continental)	48.0	63.3	82.6	96.1	4.3
U.S.	541.0	681.0	904.8	1065.1	4.7
Canada	39.6	48.3	65.9	78.4	5.2
NAFTA FTA	710.8	891.5	1173.7	1375.3	4.5

Source: The Free Trade Area Option

According to the projections in the table above, the U.S. and Canada will outperform the EEC countries (except France) in the period 1965–1977 (even on the restrictive assumption that nonemployment in North America will average more than twice the level in western Europe). An FTA, with the U.K. included, would be expected to have a 4.5 per cent rate of growth, about a quarter of 1 per cent greater than the EEC. If the U.K. was included in the EEC, then the Common Market's overall rate would be lower at 3.9 per cent. More interesting, perhaps, is the massive size of the FTA market. The total GNP of the FTA countries, on this basis, would be $1,375,000 million by 1977, with the U.S. move having a GNP of $1,065,000 million compared with a GNP for the EEC of $453,000 million.

AMERICAN INVESTMENT IN THE U.K.

Increased U.S. direct investment in British industry is another factor that could raise Britain's rate of economic growth under an FTA scheme. There is a historical pattern whereby American firms are induced to invest abroad as they become familiar with foreign markets through exports. Insofar as American exports are able to expand their share of the U.K. market, which could be expected in industries enjoying a comparative advantage, perhaps where know-how and capital are important, it seems likely that there would follow a tendency towards increased investment in Britain. The U.K. as a base for American industry in western Europe would presumably become more attractive if Britain were in an FTA. The U.K. could be a convenient place for servicing and exporting across the Channel, to countries within both an FTA and the Common Market (where the tariffs will be substantially reduced by the Kennedy Round). As the British market would be the largest western European one inside the FTA, and as American firms would no longer be hindered from exporting back to the U.S. by the tariff, the U.K. would be likely to continue to be a key area for American overseas investment.

Some people fear the large domestic U.S. market would afford American industry an unequal position from the outset in any freer trade scheme. The advantage from the existing extensive economies of scale would be so overwhelming that freer trade and the removal of restrictions on labor and capital mobility would result in an outward flow from the U.K. to the U.S. History records some examples of regions or countries that have suffered relatively from free trade groupings or economic unions. The classic one is provided by the Kingdom of Naples in the unification of Italy when the free trade policy introduced in 1861 probably ruined southern Italy and led to a capital flight to Milan and the north. Both Scotland and Northern Ireland have experienced lower rates of development than England, brought about by an emigration of labor and capital.

But this argument is based on a mistaken analogy. The southern Italy and Northern Ireland situations were largely due to deficiencies in social and economic infrastructure not found in Britain. As Professor Balassa has pointed out:

> The United Kingdom possesses a highly developed industrial structure; hence the relevant question is whether business firms would have sufficient incentive to carry out the transformation necessary to meet the challenge of foreign competition.

British Industry and an FTA

In order to discover how British industry would react to an FTA, Maxwell Stamp Associates as part of the study sent a questionnaire to a sample of commercial and industrial companies employing professional economists. Of the companies circulated, 54 per cent agreed to take part in the survey. Although a small sample cannot form the definitive assessment of the attitudes of British industry to the proposal, we regard the views expressed as significant, especially as thirty out of the forty-one participants in the survey are among the three hundred leading U.K. companies (including fifteen in the top one hundred).

This majority did not consider that adaptation to an FTA arrangement would create major problems for them. In answer to the question, "To what extent would your company be faced with a problem of adapting itself to an FTA scheme?" 65 per cent replied, "To a minor degree," 20 per cent replied, "Not at all," and 15 per cent replied, "To a major degree."

Only one industry foresaw a major problem of adaptation. That was the computer industry. But three out of the four companies in the industry considered that, changes notwithstanding, when all factors are taken into account, there would be a clear and progressive balance of advantage to their firm from U.K. membership in an FTA. The fourth replied that more detailed information and study were required. Only two other companies in the survey considered an FTA would involve a major adaptation problem. One was a chemical concern which candidly admitted that "the EEC would be a blow, particularly if monopoly and cartel legislation is enforced" and that "membership of FTA would spell the end of the road for the company as it is at present." The other was an American-owned company in the food industry. Their position, they pointed out, "may be atypical" because they have subsidiary companies in other potential FTA countries, as well as a parent company in the U.S.

In general, therefore, the companies questioned did not subscribe to the view that British industry would be "flattened" as a result of an FTA. On the contrary, the abolition of tariff and other trade barriers, they seemed to believe, would be unlikely to erode substantially British markets either at home or abroad. We asked, "U.K. membership of FTA would eliminate tariff protection against imports from, first the U.S. and, secondly, (possibly) Japan. To what extent would you expect your company's home market trade to be adversely affected?" With U.S. imports, "Not at all" was the reply of 22 per cent; with Japanese imports, that was the answer of 27 per cent; just over half expected that their U.K. trade would suffer a little from the tariff-free entry of American goods, but only 17 per cent expected theirs would suffer very much. As for Japanese goods entering freely, only 12 per cent would expect to suffer severely, 44 per cent taking the view that their home business would suffer only a little. The remainder either did not know or did not have sufficient information to form an opinion.

Economies of Scale

The companies which took part in the survey placed more importance on the dynamic aspects of a Free Trade Association. They were asked: "Does your company see advantages concerning economies of scale stemming from FTA?" More than three times as many considered that there would be advantages from such economies as the number who believed that the tariff reduction would lead to considerable expansion of sales. Three-quarters of the engineering companies, both mechanical and electrical, considered that they would gain from economies of scale. The chemical companies did not foresee the same advantage in an FTA, although a recent report by the National Economic Development Council on manpower in the chemical industry came to the conclusion that "The scale of operations is a major factor in the achievement of increased output per man in America." This apparent contradiction could stem from the fact that some major chemical companies have already set their sights on achieving economies of scale in a European market and have not yet considered in any depth the FTA proposal. The other major industry that envisaged advantages of scale was the vehicle industry.

The Overall Advantage

Finally companies were asked how they assessed the balance of advantage to their company in an FTA arrangement. "Firstly, how would you expect your company's costs on balance to be affected by British membership of FTA?" One company, largely engaged in merchanting, thought its costs would rise. About one-fifth visualized their costs being decreased; these companies were spread fairly evenly between the various industries. The majority of companies believed that costs would largely remain unchanged. On the question of profitability—how the companies expected their profits would be affected by British membership in an FTA—the breakdown was more interesting. Of the participants in the survey, 33 per cent believed that profits would rise as a result of an FTA, 40 per cent considered theirs would remain the same, and only 10 per cent believed that their profitability would fall.

The final question was posed as follows: "In the light of all the above, do you think there would be a clear and progressive balance of advantage to your company from membership of FTA?" Fifty per cent answered in the affirmative. There were 7 per cent who did not consider there was a clear advantage, and 10 per cent were unwilling to commit themselves at this stage. As pointed out at the beginning, the survey conducted as part of this study was too small to be conclusive. But it did include some of the largest British industrial enterprises. Very few believed that taking on the Americans in a Free Trade Association would lead to British industry being overrun; quite the opposite, half the companies in the survey believed that there would be a clear advantage to their company under an

FTA scheme and about one-third saw this working out in terms of improved profitability.

CONCLUSIONS OF U.K. STUDY OF FTA

So far as can be seen, and provided export prices can be kept competitive, an Atlantic-based free trade area would have beneficial effects both on the volume of British trade and on the country's balance of payments.[12] If there is no deterioration in the U.K.'s relative position, Britain should be able to compete with other participants, even in the face of superior American technology, in a large enough proportion of trade to enable her, in all probability, to improve her position. Having the big, rich, and homogeneous American market to "shoot at" would provide the stimulus and opportunity to enable British manufacturers to exploit to the full the economies of scale made possible in a large assured market. American competition in the U.K. market would, even more than European competition, administer the "salutary jolt" which would encourage or force British industry to improve productivity. But, as must follow if our trade balance with the U.S. improves, as we would expect, this "jolt" would be no more than Britain could healthily absorb.

A major problem likely to be the subject of increasing attention concerns assistance to less-developed countries. Of itself, an FTA would do nothing directly to help African, Asian, and Latin American nations to expand their exports; although they would benefit from the secondary effects of a higher level of world trade and faster economic growth. An FTA could also provide the developed countries with an opportunity to remove their tariffs to the developing countries on raw materials and semi-manufactures. Insofar as these items were not included in the freeing of trade between the developed countries, there would be an important and lasting preferential position created for the developing countries. However, it would be possible within the FTA framework to accord them preferential advantages also in manufactures over the next few years. If the FTA agreement provides, as it probably would, for a long period, say fifteen years, during which tariffs between members

IMPACT OF FTA ON U.K. EXPORTS AND IMPORTS

		U.S. Billions of $				
		Increase in Imports from:			Increase in Exports (Trade Creation) to:	
		U.S.	Canada		U.S.	
		I & II	I	II	I	II
51	Chemical elements & compounds	6,378	55	41	2,950	2,329
52	Crude chemicals	273			175	128
53	Dyestuffs & coloring materials	456			3,109	2,332
54	Medicinal & pharmaceutical products	580	1	1	932	689
55	Essential oils & perfumes	2,910			766	563
56	Fertilizers	11			4	3
57	Explosives & pyrotechnic products	22			67	49
58	Plastic materials	3,952			1,474	1,090
59	Chemical materials & products n.e.s.	2,527	7	5	629	464
61	Leather manufactures	178	5	4	1,492	1,119
62	Rubber manufactures	1,449	57	43	930	698
63	Wood & cork manufactures	1,255			70	53
64	Paper & board manufactures	13,388			1,110	832
65	Textile yarn & fabrics	4,562	790	603	11,731	8,798
66	Nonmetallic mineral manufactures	1,583	5	4	22,683	16,784
67	Iron & steel	1,758			9,191	6,775
68	Nonferrous metals	10,040			28,218	20,956
69	Other manufactures of metal	8,316	79	59	12,177	9,053
71	Machinery nonelectric	79,335	404	303	42,612	31,205
72	Electric machinery	40,801			14,047	10,340
73	Transport equipment	14,137	302	228	81,077	59,562
81	Sanitary, plumbing, heating & lighting equipment	338			117	87
82	Furniture	328	11	8	1,756	1,298
83	Travel goods, handbags, etc.	103			464	345
84	Clothing	200	680	521	16,703	12,657
85	Footwear	76	24	18	3,629	2,693
86	Professional & scientific instruments	23,604	291	219	12,415	9,280
89	Miscellaneous manufactures	11,111	220	166	40,561	30,039
	Total	229,671	2,931	2,223	311,089	230,221

Footnote: I = No rise in export prices; II = Rising export prices absorbing 25% of tariff cuts; + = net exports; — = net imports.

Increase in Exports (Trade Creation) to: Canada		Increase in Exports (Trade Diversion) to:			Net Change	
I	II	U.S.	Canada		I	II
600	450	17,271	760	18,031	+15,148	+14,391
		179	20	199	+101	+54
194	145	2,689	340	3,029	+5,876	+5,050
277	208	2,414	200	2,614	+3,242	+2,930
128	96	2,028	200	2,228	+212	−23
		484	10	494	+487	+486
		94	31	125	+170	+152
168	126	3,135	885	4,020	+1,710	+1,284
252	189	1,626	260	1,886	+233	+7
473	355	2,471	300	2,771	+4,553	+4,063
596	447	3,325	610	3,935	+3,955	+3,588
25	19	6,235	710	6,945	+5,785	+5,762
539	405	1,518	200	1,718	−10,021	−10,433
3,806	2,855	57,253	8,770	66,023	+76,208	+72,511
1,421	1,066	28,518	3,110	31,628	+54,144	+47,891
1,160	870	67,512	10,440	77,952	+86,545	+83,839
796	597	22,803	375	23,178	+42,152	+34,691
3,976	2,982	26,821	3,200	30,021	+37,779	+33,681
13,615	10,212	32,460	4,650	37,110	+13,598	−1,111
5,267	3,950	43,754	5,500	49,254	+27,767	+22,743
7,711	5,784	58,965	8,950	67,915	+142,264	+118,896
135	101	2,715	250	2,965	+2,879	+2,815
200	150	1,818	190	2,008	+3,625	+3,120
91	68	3,509	400	3,909	+4,361	+4,219
1,958	1,469	53,008	4,840	57,848	+75,629	+71,253
619	465	12,986	1,710	14,696	+18,844	+17,760
1,437	1,078	29,603	3,950	33,553	+23,510	+20,088
3,843	2,882	46,595	5,950	52,545	+85,618	+74,189
49,287	36,969	531,789	66,811	598,600	726,374	633,896

were to be gradually reduced, it would be possible to remove tariffs against the manufactured products of developing countries in a much shorter time, say five years. Developing countries would then enjoy a preferential rate for several years, during which time they could develop industrial production. An FTA would, therefore, be a useful instrument for helping all developing countries, free from the complications of entrenched preferences for a few (the former French colonies) in the EEC.

Finally, a Free Trade Association can be an effective instrument, as EFTA has shown. By comparison, however, they lack glamor. "Building Europe" has a fine ring to stir the imagination. "Building a Free Trade Association" would mean little to the man in the street. A vision, though, of an economic community of the free world, with hope of sweeping away the trade barriers that do so much to prevent the world reaching its full economic potential, could all the same stir imagination in Britain and the U.S. And so to the final question, "Would the Americans accept the Free Trade Association concept of a new grand design?"

As the world political scene changes, so shifts in policy can be expected, particularly from the U.S. With Congressional hearings often a guide to how American opinion is shaping, it is very interesting to note the relevant, early conclusion of the subcommittee of the Joint Economic Committee, referred to earlier, which has been reviewing U.S. trade policy:

> While the USA should pursue the multilateral approach reducing trade barriers, we recognize that conditions may arise in the future that would favor US participation in a regional trading block. . . . The possibility that Britain will not be accepted as a new member of the EEC raises questions that are not going to be answered satisfactorily by economic measures alone. Should she not be accepted, it is possible that Britain would consider joining an Atlantic free trade area in which the USA would be the leading member.

NOTES

1. Theodore Geiger and Sperry Lea, "The Free Trade Area Concept as Applied to the United States"; submitted July 28, 1967.

2. The American Selling Price (ASP) was applied to benzenoid chemicals after World War I to afford added protection to the coal tar sector of the U.S. chemical industry. Customs duties are fixed on the basis of the wholesale price of the comparable American-made product. On average, ASP has the effect of doubling the level of the tariff. As a result 43 of the 108 categories covered by ASP carry effective duties exceeding 50 per cent.

It was agreed in the Kennedy Round that an automatic and unconditional 50 per cent cut in chemical duties would be made by the U.S. (except for duties already below 8 per cent), but until ASP is abolished, the tariffs of other countries will only come down by 20 per cent. So far the U.S. administration has been unwilling to introduce the necessary legislation for fear that the bill would become a vehicle for protectionist lobbies in the Congress.

3. A value-added tax is a general tax on consumption levied on all stages of the economic process, but in such a way that it falls only on the value added at each stage of the process. Thus a company manufacturing automobile body shells, for example, pays the tax only on the difference in value between the sheet steel it buys in and the body shells it sells to the final car manufacturer. The latter in turn pays the tax on the difference in value between the shell and the assembled car. In the EEC the tax is payable on imported goods but is refunded on exports.

4. Kenneth Keith, "British Industry Week," *Journal of the Confederation of British Industries* (January 5, 1968).

5. Miriam Camps, *Britain and the European Community 1955–63* (London: Oxford University Press, 1964).

6. The Chairman of the Committee is Sir Michael Wright, formerly permanent head of the British Delegation to the ten-Power and eighteen-Power Disarmament Conferences. Other members include Sir George Bolton, a prominent banker, and several eminent economists, including Sir Roy Harrod, Professor Harry Johnson, and Professor James Meade.

7. "The Free Trade Area Option—Opportunity for Britain," by Maxwell Stamp Associates for the Atlantic Trade Study (London: Moor House, 1967).

8. Bela Balassa "Trade Liberalization among Industrial countries: Objective and Alternatives," Council on Foreign Relations (New York: McGraw-Hill, 1967), and R. J. Ball and K. Maswah, "The U.S. Demand for Imports, 1948–58," *Review of Economics and Statistics* (November, 1962).

Professor Robert G. Hawkins assumes the same elasticities of import demand in his study of the Economic Implications for the United States of a Free Trade Association.

9. Manufactures are defined in this study as SITC Divisions 5–8 in order to have a comparable basis with the U.S. study prepared by Professor Hawkins. In *The Free Trade Area Option* (London: Maxwell Stamp Associates, 1967), a slightly different definition of manufactures was used (see page 84 of that study).

10. Mr. Michael Shanks (*The Times* (London) December 4, 1967) has argued that the U.K. would only be competitive with the U.S. in industries with a high labor-capital ratio. In other words, the comparative advantage of Britain over the U.S. lies in only one thing: the cheaper cost of labor. He says, "The United States by contrast would greatly increase penetration of the British market in high-technology, capital intensive industries—computers, electronic capital goods, scientific instruments and the more sophisticated types of machinery."

Shanks' thesis is not supported by recent trends in British exports to the U.S. or by empirical studies. The most rapidly growing British exports to the U.S. in the last ten years have been aero-engines and machine tools. The U.K. exports which would benefit most from trade liberalization are capital intensive industries such as transportation (+ $116 million) and iron and steel (+ $96 million). These findings are supported by the views of business economists as expressed in the answers to the questionnaire summarized on pp. 48–50 of this study.

11. "Demographic Trends, 1965–80" (Paris: Organisation for Economic Co-operation and Development, 1966). These figures may need to be revised downwards because of more recent trends in North America and western Europe.

12. The devaluation of sterling in November, 1967, has made U.K. export prices competitive in world markets. As long as this advantage is maintained, Britain should benefit even more from an FTA than the calculations in this study indicate (which necessarily had to be based on predevaluation trade statistics).

Canada's Economic Interests in Trade Liberalization*

by H. Edward English

Canada's interest in participating in a North Atlantic Free Trade Association or in any other comparably substantial move toward fuller integration of Canada in the world economy will be determined primarily on economic grounds. In recent years, there has been a rising crescendo of concern over the competitive position of the Canadian economy. In part, this was a response to the inevitable restoration of the competitive strength of foreign economies that were more disrupted by war. In part it was the consequence of policies that generated an overvaluation of the Canadian dollar in the late 1950's and up to 1961. But insofar as comparisons with the United States are concerned, the comparison has been particularly meaningful in recent years of prosperity. It has become apparent that, far from reducing the gap in per capita productivity in response to the opportunities provided by expanded domestic and external markets, Canadian industry has experienced a relatively poorer record of productivity gains.

In its Annual Reviews, the Economic Council of Canada

* The author is indebted to Mrs. Dian Cohen, economist on the staff of the Private Planning Association of Canada (Montreal), for her extensive assistance in the preparation of a first draft of this chapter.

has analyzed the factors which may have contributed to the persistent and sometimes worsening situation. It has tended to focus primarily on longer-term factors such as differences between educational attainments of the Canadian labor force and that of the United States. More recently, increasing attention has been paid to the structural problems of industry. A comprehensive appraisal of the relative weakness of manufacturing industries of Canada and the United States was contained in a recent publication of the Canadian Trade Committee.[1] This showed that the output per unit of capital and per unit of labor was inferior to that in U.S. manufacturing, and that the record stood out clearly in contrast to that revealed in comparison of the Canadian and American economies more generally. The author concluded that, since the main distinguishing feature of the manufacturing sector was that it was for the most part operating under conditions of protection and lack of ready access to foreign markets, it would be desirable to explore ways of improving productivity performance through trade liberalization.

I. CANADA AND WORLD TRADE

During the first half of the twentieth century, the volume of world trade declined relative to total world output. However, since 1950, world trade has expanded at a faster rate than world production. In addition, the trade in manufactures, particularly among the industrialized nations, has increased relative to trade in primary products. Moreover, trade in manufactures has risen faster within the industrial continents (i.e., between Canada and the United States and among countries in western Europe) than between these continents. In contrast, exports of both primary products and manufactures from primary-producing countries have risen significantly less than exports of such goods from the industrial nations since the early 1950's. For the majority of the industrial nations in the non-Communist world, foreign trade is more important relative to their gross domestic product than it is for Canada.[2] Furthermore, there were more nations for which that was so in 1962–

1963 than in 1953. These facts are often overlooked by Canadians. Because of Canada's propinquity to the United States, where both exports and imports are less than 5 per cent of GDP, Canadians frequently tend to think that their dependence on trade is unusually great.

Openness tends to be a decreasing function of the size of a nation. For the smaller nations, foreign markets are often vital if economies of scale in production and distribution are to be achieved. Since they also do not have as broad a basis in technical know-how, heavy reliance on imports of capital equipment and of technology is essential to meet the needs of modern industry and society. These two facts are of great relevance in discussions of Canadian trade relationships.

In spite of the increasing proportion of world trade being conducted by the industrialized nations of the world, the Canadian share in world exports and imports has diminished since the mid-1950's; so has the Canadian share of exports of and imports of the industrial countries.

In the last few years, however, there has been an improvement in Canada's relative export performance. Whether this improvement is the beginning of a new long-run trend or a temporary phenomenon it is perhaps too early to say.

IMPORT AND EXPORT PATTERNS

The long-run decline in imports relative to GNE was attributable in the period 1900 to 1954–1956 to the slow growth of external purchases of agricultural and animal products and of fibres and textiles. Since 1956, animal and agricultural imports have ceased their relative decline, suggesting that import substitution has been achieved to the economically feasible maximum for this sector. What accounts for the more recent decline is the non-metallic minerals group, mainly because of the development of the petroleum and natural gas industry in western Canada (see Table 1). In addition, there has been outstanding growth in chemicals and miscellaneous commodities, where new products and materials abound. "The steady increases in the shares of these items extending over the decades strongly suggest the significance of new technology (defined

Table 1

MATERIAL-CONTENT CLASSIFICATION OF CANADA'S IMPORTS 1926–29, 1954–56, and 1963–65

Commodity Group	% of Total Imports Based on Current $ 1926–29	1954–56	1963–65	1963–65 as % of 1954–56 Based on Current $	Constant 1949 $
	(1)	(2)	(3)	(4)	(5)
Agriculture & vegetable products	19.8	12.0	11.8	153.9	144.9
Animals & animal products	5.5	2.1	2.0	155.5	
Fibres, textiles, & products	16.6	7.8	7.1	143.9	137.1
Wood, wood products, & paper	4.7	4.0	4.4	171.9	132.0
Iron & products	24.5	35.4	39.4	173.5	132.4
Nonferrous metals & products	5.9	8.7	8.7	160.8	130.8
Nonmetallic minerals & products	14.2	14.0	10.8	119.8	110.8
Chemicals & allied products	3.1	5.2	6.0	178.8	164.8
Miscellaneous commodities	5.7	10.8	9.6	138.9	162.1
Total Imports	100.0	100.0	100.0	161.0	134.8
Gross National Expenditure				172.9	144.9

Source: B. W. Wilkinson, *op. cit.*

broadly to include both new and improved processes of production and new and improved products) as a key determinant of international trade.[3] The other major change is the rise in consumer goods from 29 to 34 per cent of total imports—due to the increased significance of automobiles and parts, as well as other manufactured goods. The suggestion again is that technological change abroad, of a type that results in new products not produced in Canada, at least initially, may be an important factor influencing Canadian import patterns—insofar as these are not restricted by Canadian tariffs.

Since the early 1950's, manufactured imports, as a per cent of total imports, have enjoyed almost uninterrupted increase (see Table 2). This was entirely attributable to the growth of end products. Fabricated materials have actually diminished as a proportion of total imports. By far the fastest-growing group has been transportation equipment.

The tendency for manufactured imports to have a larger share relative to nonmanufactured imports is evident for other countries and for the world as a whole. However, most other nations and regional groups have experienced a decline in the proportion of raw material imports, while Canada has not. Food imports for the Western nations, both small and large, have diminished as a proportion of total imports, whereas Canadian food inflows have become of increasing relative importance. In this respect, the Canadian performance is similar to the performance of both the low-income countries and the Communist nations, some of which are also at little better than subsistence incomes.

Apart from the expansion of imports from the United States occasioned by the Canada-U.S. agreement affecting automobiles and parts, the trend in recent years has been for a diminished proportion of Canadian purchases abroad to be made in that country. The share of the United States has diminished not only in total, but also for every major commodity group other than agriculture and vegetable products. Nevertheless, the United States still supplies over 50 per cent of total imports in each major product group except for petroleum products and textiles.

End-product exports still comprise less than 20 per cent

Table 2

PERCENTAGES OF CANADA'S IMPORTS, BY STAGES OF FABRICATION, AND CHANGES IN IMPORT PRICE INDEXES, SELECTED YEARS

Import Groups by Stages of Fabrication	Percentages of Total					Price Index Change. 1965 Index as % of 1955 Index[a]
	Based on Current $			Based on Constant 1948 $		
	1954–56	1960–61	1963–65	1954–56	1963–65	
Crude materials	20.9	19.3	18.3	22.3	23.1	102.1
Manufactured goods[b]	79.1	80.7	81.6	77.7	76.9	
	(80.3)[c]					
Fabricated materials	29.2	27.1	27.3	29.9	27.7	127.4
End products	49.9	53.6	54.3	47.8	49.2	131.9
Total	100.0	100.0	100.0	100.0	100.0	

[a] More correctly, the price indexes for 1955 and 1965 are both based on 1948 = 100 and then the former was divided into the latter.
[b] Sum of fabricated materials and end products.
[c] This percentage is the total of partially manufactured plus fully or chiefly manufactured imports as defined in the DBS import classification now discontinued. It illustrates that using the sum of fabricated materials and end products gives a similar estimate of the significance of manufactured goods in total imports.

Source: B. W. Wilkinson, *op. cit.*

of all exports, but are growing steadily. Canada still compares quite unfavorably with the other industrialized nations of the Western world in terms of the share of its exports that are in this highly processed category. The unweighted average of the ratio of such manufactures to total exports for thirteen industrialized countries (other than Canada) was 60 per cent in 1963. For Canada, the comparable ratio was 19 per cent. Moreover, between 1954 and 1963, the portion of highly processed manufactured goods in Canadian exports rose only about 12 per cent, whereas for other relatively small (in population) industrial countries, the unweighted average increase was 37 per cent.

With imports, a large portion of the relative diminution of Canadian trade with the United States and the United Kingdom was compensated for by increased trade with the other industrialized nations of western Europe. But with exports, no similar relative rise in trade with western Europe has occurred.

In short, then, the major changes in import commodity patterns between the mid-1950's and the 1960's relative to earlier decades have been as follows: the relative decline in agricultural and animal products, which was prominent up to the 1950's, has eased off so that these imports are now holding their own; nonmetallic-mineral inflows have diminished greatly; chemicals, miscellaneous commodities, and automobiles and machinery from the iron and products category are all growing more rapidly than average imports—as they have done for several decades; and finished manufactured goods as a percentage of the total value of imports are becoming increasingly important.

The United States remains Canada's most important source of imports, but between 1954 and 1956, and 1963 and 1965, some decline in the proportion of imports from the United States has occurred—although a reversal in the trend is indicated for 1966. The percentage of imports from the United Kingdom has also diminished, whereas western Europe and Japan have become increasingly significant suppliers; so have some less-developed nations.

Canadian exports remain heavily concentrated on relatively few product lines. Most of these are raw materials—wheat, iron ore, nickel, and other metallic ores, and petroleum and natural gas—or materials which have received only a limited amount of processing—lumber, woodpulp and newsprint, flour, aluminum, copper and nickel alloys, and primary iron and steel. Finished products, however, particularly automobiles, trucks and parts, and machinery, have formed a larger part of total exports in recent years. Dependence upon the United States and the United Kingdom as markets for Canadian exports remains great for all products other than grains, but it has diminished considerably over the period under review, except for some possible reversal of this trend with respect to the United States in the last one or two years. Japan, Russia, and the less-developed nations of the world have become increasingly important markets—primarily for crude materials—whereas the developed nations of western Europe take about the same share of exports today as they did ten or twelve years ago. In general, Canada's exports have been concentrated in products enjoying less than average growth in world trade and on two countries, the United States and the United Kingdom, which have been growing more slowly than many—at least until the last few years, when American growth has frequently surpassed that of many European countries. These two factors account for some, but not all, of the poorer Canadian export performance relative to the rest of the world.

The foregoing discussion makes several trends clear. On the one hand, a steadily diminishing fraction of Canadian foreign trade is with the United Kingdom; and until the automobile agreement with the United States, the same held true for Canadian trade with that country. Trade with Japan, on the other hand, has been expanding rapidly. Imports from western Europe are also a growing portion of total imports, but there has been little alteration in the proportion of Canadian exports going to that area.

Processed and manufactured goods are still a much larger percentage of imports (81.6) than they are of exports (64.0). Moreover, the total of these two categories has risen as a proportion of imports but has declined as a proportion of exports. Perhaps more important is the continuing great discrepancy in the share of end products in total imports and exports—54.3 per cent and 17.4 per cent, respectively.

This disparity implies that Canada may have considerable difficulty in maintaining a surplus on merchandise account. The reason for this is simply that world trade in highly manufactured goods is rising more rapidly than trade in industrial materials and primary products. If Canadian trade follows this pattern (and it promises to do so), then total imports, which are heavily concentrated on highly processed commodities, will tend to rise more rapidly than will total exports, which are largely raw and crudely processed materials. Since about 1961, Canadian exports of highly manufactured goods have been expanding a little more rapidly than have imports of such goods. If this trend continues, it may ease the situation somewhat, but the small weight of these end products in total exports suggests that the problem will still exist. Moreover, the difficulty would be compounded if two or three poor wheat crops should occur in succession.

II. SHORT-RUN INFLUENCES ON CANADIAN TRADE PATTERNS

Imports

The decrease in domestic expenditures on furniture, home furnishings and appliances, clothing and personal furnishings, and construction appear to be at least partially responsible for the shift in the composition of total imports away from these goods. Also, the increased part of gross expenditure devoted to automobiles has been significant in raising the share of automobiles and parts in total imports. But the rising share of foodstuffs, tobacco, and beverages in total imports can only be accounted for by the increased import content of such expenditures. In general, there appears to have been a slight decline in imports as a per cent of outlays for investment goods and a rise in imports as a per cent of consumption outlays—which is in accord with the changing proportions of these items in total imports.

Changes in Canadian tariffs seem to have been of minor

importance in influencing the commodity composition and the national source of Canadian imports since the mid-1950's—although the surcharges in 1962 and early 1963 did have a greater impact on imports from the United Kingdom than on those from the United States or other nations as a group. This suggests that tariff reductions by Canada over this period consisted in removal of superfluous protection.

De facto import quotas on particular commodity groups, such as some clothing and textiles, radio and television tubes, and some hardwoods and veneers, have restricted the inflow of these goods, and quite likely of other commodities too, wherever suppliers in Japan or the less-developed nations may have felt unrestricted flooding of the Canadian market would cause the Canadian authorities to demand imposition of specific export restraints.

The depreciation of the Canadian dollar has improved the competitive position of import-competing industries in Canada, especially that of the iron and steel and textiles and clothing industries. The continuity of such benefits depends, however, upon the role of imported inputs and other price-raising considerations related to the consequences of devaluation.

Exports

Exports of highly processed goods have expanded much more rapidly than total exports over the period since 1961. The factors that, on occasion, have been mentioned in connection with this upsurge include (1) the 1961–1962 depreciation; (2) the Canadian-U.S. defense production sharing program; (3) the automotive export incentive program; (4) improved export credit and insurance provisions, etc. (5) the upswing in the U.S. business cycle which began about the end of the first quarter of 1961. An assessment of these forces has a bearing upon what future export patterns may be under present conditions and under conditions of substantially reduced tariffs between Canada and the United States and Canada and other nations of the North Atlantic region.

The effect of depreciation of the Canadian dollar can be

treated as a residual, but has clearly been of major support for the rapid expansion of highly manufactured exports in the past six years. This is worth emphasizing, since discussions of the several other export-encouraging forces which came into being about the same time tend to leave the impression that the depreciation by itself had an almost negligible impact upon exports. The improvement in Canadian exports of agricultural machinery since devaluation has helped to restore the relative importance of exports of these products to their position before the period of overvaluation of the Canadian dollar in the late 1950's.

Between 1958 and 1965, the defense-sharing program has resulted in expenditure in Canada by the United States of $1.2 billion. (Just to put this in a perspective of magnitude, the annual expenditure in 1965 was equivalent to 31 per cent of Canadian inedible end-product exports to the United States.)

An enormous stimulus was given to trade between 1962 and 1965 by the Canadian-U.S. automotive agreement; exports of automobiles and parts rose from 9 per cent of highly manufactured exports to 27 per cent.

III. LONGER-RUN TRADE DETERMINANTS

Some indications of the relative importance of exports and imports and their size relative to domestic production in each of the twenty major manufacturing industry groups is shown in Table 3. On the export side, pulp and paper products, wood products, primary metal, and machinery, export the largest proportion of their domestic production—in each industry in excess of 25 per cent. The first three of these also have exports as a per cent of total manufactured exports greater than for all other industry groups. Imports as a per cent of domestic production are greater than 25 per cent for six industries—machinery, miscellaneous manufacturing, transportation equipment, textiles, chemicals, and electrical products. Outstanding is machinery, with imports equaling 130 per cent of domestic production.

Table 3

MANUFACTURED IMPORTS AND EXPORTS, BY MAJOR INDUSTRY GROUPS, AS PERCENTAGES OF TOTAL MANUFACTURED IMPORTS AND EXPORTS AND AS PERCENTAGE OF DOMESTIC PRODUCTION, 1963

Major Manufacturing Industry Groups	Imports as % of Total Manufactured Imports	Exports as % of Total Manufactured Exports	Imports as % of Domestic Production	Exports as % of Domestic Production
	(1)	(2)	(3)	(4)
Food & beverages	7.3	11.7	6.4	9.3
Tobacco products	0.1	0.6	2.1	8.3
Rubber	0.9	0.3	11.5	4.1
Leather	0.7	0.3	11.5	4.6
Textiles	5.8	0.8	26.1	3.0
Knitting mills	0.5	0.1	10.4	2.0
Clothing	0.9	0.3	4.8	1.3
Wood	1.4	12.1	5.6	43.1
Furniture & fixtures	0.4	0.1	4.3	0.9
Paper & allied	1.6	26.8	3.3	50.0
Printing, publishing, & allied	2.4	0.2	12.3	1.0
Primary metal	4.6	19.3	7.5	28.3
Metal fabricating	7.6	2.7	20.2	6.4
Machinery (except electrical)	23.0	6.0	130.1	31.1
Transportation equipment	15.8	5.8	27.7	9.3
Elecrical products	7.7	3.1	25.0	9.3
Nonmetallic minerals	2.6	0.5	16.1	2.9
Petroleum & coal	2.0	0.2	7.4	0.6
Chemicals & chemical products	8.4	6.7	25.5	18.7
Miscellaneous manufacturing	6.4	2.3	42.7	14.0
	100.0	100.0	17.3	15.7

Source: B. W. Wilkinson, *op. cit.*

Factor Endowments

Traditionally, it has been thought that a nation's relative endowments of labor and capital would determine the products in which it had a comparative advantage and could therefore export. To illustrate, a nation having relatively abundant labor would tend to have cheaper wage rates and therefore a cost advantage in producing those products requiring a relatively large amount of labor. A nation with relatively large amounts of capital would tend to specialize in those goods needing relatively big amounts of capital.

Today there is much less confidence in this simple form of the theory. In the first place, the need to consider other factors besides homogeneous labor and capital has been recognized. Skill endowments and natural resources have been observed to be important. The abundance and quality of natural resources are undoubtedly significant in dictating Canadian raw material exports. They also appear to be of no small importance in Canadian exports of primary manufacturing; that is, manufacturing in which at least 50 per cent of the inputs are products of the Canadian primary sector.

In addition, for secondary manufactures (that is, for the more highly processed goods), the other considerations indicated above are now widely accepted as more important determinants of international trade than are relative factor endowments. It is to these that we now turn.

Economies of Scale and Tariffs

Economies of scale and tariffs must be examined together as they are intrinsically related. The crux of the argument is that it is difficult for firms to achieve all economies of scale in production within the confines of the Canadian market; that foreign tariffs (particularly those of the United States, our largest trading partner) inhibit the achievement of these economies through exports; and that the protection provided by the Canadian tariff seriously reduces incentives for firms in Canada to take steps to rationalize their production and achieve even those economies of scale attainable within the Canadian market. Domestic producers can price up to the foreign price plus the Canadian tariff. If one firm in an industry attempts to achieve economies of scale by reducing its price, it may precipitate a costly price war lasting until one or more firms are driven out of operation. The initiating firm could not be certain that it would be one of those remaining. Consequently, and inefficient structure of production activities can be perpetuated and Canadian exports of specialized product lines do not develop.

TECHNOLOGICAL ADVANCE

Technological advance as a result of research and development also appears to be an important determinant of international trade. The new products and processes developed provide the innovating country with the opportunity of exporting to its trading partners. Subsequently, the importing nation may commence production too. But the innovating country will be able to continue exporting until foreign production catches up with foreign demand. It may prolong its "technological-gap" trade by achieving economies of scale of larger output, or economies from "learning by doing," that is, from workers becoming increasingly familiar with the production process and developing short cuts or more efficient ways of carrying out their duties. Moreover, by the time foreign producers are able to produce the product competitively (perhaps because production is now standardized and entails use of mass-production equipment and a relatively large proportion of unskilled, low-priced labor), the original innovating nation may well have developed other new products. It therefore maintains or increases its total exports through new "technological-gap" trade.

Although the Canadian industrial research effort is minuscule compared with that of the United States and a number of the other developed nations, Canadian secondary manufacturing exports nevertheless tend to be greater in those industries where research and development is relatively more important. Imports of secondary manufactures also tend to be concentrated in lines where research and development are important. Clearly, new technology is a significant factor in Canadian trade in manufactures. It has received all too little attention in the past, perhaps because technology has often been readily available to Canadian manufacturers through the parent-subsidiary relationship.

Foreign Ownership

Foreign ownership of Canadian industry also may have an impact upon trade patterns. First, all other things being equal, imports will tend to be greater the more of an industry that is under foreign ownership. This follows because the foreign subsidiaries, owing to their close association with their foreign parents (and in turn with the suppliers of these parents), will tend to possess, or be able to obtain at lower cost of search, more information about foreign products and prices than their domestically owned competitors. The empirical evidence that has been gathered to date supports this contention.

Furthermore, in production activities in which assembly of final products and packaging can economically be separated from component or basic ingredient manufacture, the foreign company can readily establish a Canadian subsidiary, while an independent firm would have difficulty acquiring the same components or ingredients.

With respect to exports, the situation is more ambiguous. Empirical evidence suggests that non-resident owned firms do not, on the average, export more than their Canadian-owned competitors in the same industries. This comparison is of limited meaning, however, since in many important resource processing industries the foreign firms are much more important and initially developed the export market, especially in the United States, on the basis of their corporate connections. In the manufacturing sector, on the other hand, development of Canadian exports would be enhanced by the availability of marketing facilities, but cannot be realized given the present barriers to trade and consequent cost handicaps experienced by Canadian firms.

Aggressiveness

Another consideration which has been largely neglected in discussions of Canadian trade performance has been the degree of aggressiveness shown (or not shown, as the case may be) by Canadian manufacturers in winning world markets. To obtain a share of the market outside Canada requires a product that buyers want (or can be persuaded they want) and attention to buyers' wishes. This in turn implies original research and development or competent imitation. It also implies the need for vision and foresight to see the potential of new markets, the willingness to take risks, well-qualified salesmen, large-scale selling organizations, and for many buyers, liberal credit. Moreover, it requires the use of modern technology (e.g., computers) in inventory and other cost control, production scheduling, inspection, and so on. Variations in the extent to which aggressiveness, as here defined, is demonstrated by the firms in different industries may account for some of the divergence in export performance of these industries.

IV. IMPLICATIONS OF FREE TRADE FOR THE CANADIAN ECONOMY

Views on this subject have ranged from destruction to salvation, with extreme positions apparently innocent of the adjustment mechanism. Of course, it is difficult to specify what the aggregative implications will be, whether capital flows will increase or fall off, whether wages and prices will rise or possibly even fall,[4] whether payments pressures will require a new exchange rate before equilibrating factor market adjustments can occur. The relative importance of these features of the adjustment process must be evaluated to determine their probable significance for Canada and to determine the policy measures appropriate for the transition adjustments anticipated. But the crucial issue is whether the impact on Canadian industries and regions is likely to be positive or negative, whether the unrealized potential for internationally competitive production is sufficient to ensure that the benefits of trade liberalization will be derived through increased exports as well as lower-priced imports. Only when we have some idea of the direction and order of magnitude of these sectoral effects is it relevant to introduce a discussion of the adjustment mechanism.

Fortunately, in recent years a number of studies have focused on the effects of trade barriers on the Canadian economy, and the probable implications of their reduction or removal.[5] Of these, the most directly relevant is that by the Wonnacotts on the implications for Canadian manufacturing of free trade between Canada and the United States, in view of the dominant role of the United States in Canada's trade, especially in manufactured goods, and of the expectation that the major new opportunities and adjustments lie in this sector. In industrial materials at present produced in Canada, no one doubts that free trade would enable the maintenance and improvement of Canada's position in general and in most particular products. In agriculture, the problem is more complex, with climatic conditions clearly placing Canadian producers at a disadvantage relative to those in the southern states. But there are also a number of Canadian products which could effectively compete in the United States. It is anticipated by some experts on the comparative advantages of Canadian agriculture that free trade in livestock and livestock products would produce clear mutual benefits, but there is more doubt about the adjustment problems for certain specialized regions of the Canadian economy devoted to fruit and vegetable production. Even here, there is a difference in the relative position of particular products; however, apples, for example, are in a better competitive position than peaches. Of course, the major Canadian exports will continue to be grains and oilseeds, and here overseas markets are essential. Canada has come to rely on a diversification of these markets, with the Soviet Union and China being important customers in recent years. Some observers have pointed to the prospect for increased North American exports of grains to the developing countries. In any case, two points can be made: 1) Markets other than the United States will be important for Canadian agricultural products; and 2) arrangements for expansion of agricultural trade should probably be independent of those relating to industrial materials and manufactures. In view of the special protective treatment accorded to agriculture by the European countries and by Japan, even if the United States and Canada are prepared to reduce their more limited levels of protection for agriculture, they will probably find it much easier to attract the Europeans and Japanese into trading arrangements involving either or both the agricultural and the nonagricultural sector if they do not call for exactly the same all-encompassing approach to trade liberalization in both these sectors. In any event, the much more pervasive importance of nontariff barriers in agriculture would seem to make such separate treatment unavoidable.

Free Trade and Canadian Manufacturing

It is frequently, and fallaciously, assumed in discussing the potential impact of free trade on Canada's manufacturers, that present Canadian production costs are relevant. However, the great majority of firms that are now relatively inefficient because of tariff protection would become much more specialized and efficient when import duties were removed. This change, the result of lowered costs of imported materials and components, on the one hand, and increased scale of production for the newly opened Continental (or wider) market on the other, would alter the entire basis on which the competitive situation of Canada's industries must be judged. After a period of adjustment—which might involve significant temporary dislocations—many Canadian manufacturing plants should be rendered as potentially effective as comparable U.S. factories.

The appropriate question, then, is not how present Canadian cost levels compare with those of the United States, but rather how the costs of reorganized Canadian manufacturing industries would compare with the corresponding U.S. figures. The Wonnacotts, in their book *Free Trade Between the United States and Canada,* approach this issue as an examination of relative competitive advantages—in terms of such factors as raw materials costs, wages, proximity to markets, etc.—in the five main regions of Canada and thirteen regions of the United States, under circumstances of an integrated North American market of 220 million people.

Viewing the problem in this light, the Wonnacotts point out,

The industrial heartland of North America lies in a large triangle running roughly from Chicago to Boston to Baltimore. The southermost part of Ontario lies *within* this triangle, and the whole of the major Canadian manufacturing belt in southern Ontario and along the St. Lawrence valley is close to this industrial heartland. If economic forces are allowed to operate without the interference of tariff barriers, it is difficult to see why industry should stop abruptly at the Detroit River and Niagara Falls.

Wage Levels

The manufacturing wage level in the United States is 30 per cent higher than in Canada; however, wages in the adjacent northern areas of the United States are 36 per cent higher. Comparing regions within the United States, the Pacific Coast and Chicago-Cleveland areas are the high-wage areas, and New England and the South pay the lowest wages; within Canada, British Columbia and Ontario have the highest wages, and Quebec and the Maritimes the lowest. In comparing Canadian areas (except British Columbia) with U.S. areas, all Canadian regions have lower wages than all U.S. regions.

Market Proximity

Two location influences must be considered simultaneously: the desire of producers to locate close to major markets and their desire to avoid areas already heavily serviced by competitors. On the basis of these criteria, Ontario and, to a lesser degree, Quebec are the best situated regions in Canada by a substantial margin. Ontario is at a disadvantage in comparison with only a limited area in the United States—that is, the heavily industrialized area from Chicago to the east coast of the United States. Otherwise Ontario is to be perferred to all other regions of the United States.

In general, Ontario is favorably located for the production of goods that may be marketed widely over space because of its proximity to the richest North American markets along the

Chicago-New York axis. However, for manufactured goods which are economically produced only for a market of more than ten to twelve million people and can be marketed most effectively only for markets in excess of this size, the Windsor-Montreal strip would be at some disadvantage relative to the heart of the industrial triangle. The doubling of both the Canadian population and of per capita income since interwar years has played a major role in increasing the locational attractiveness of Central Canada for manufacturing.

Market Transportation Costs

Ontario is the best region in Canada in terms of minimizing transportation costs in shipping final output to the North American market. In comparison with the thirteen U.S. regions, Ontario ranks midway down the scale. However, a comparison of Ontario with any specific U.S. region is often not possible without specifying the spatial pattern of markets which must be serviced to achieve a competitive position.

If all North American markets are serviced equally by a producer in any location, Ontario is one of the five or six best locations on the North American continent, being clearly inferior only to the U.S. East Lake, West Lake, Lower Midwest, and Capital regions. If a producer services regional markets more heavily than those at a distance, Ontario becomes less favorably situated and the province ranks below the regions mentioned above (except the Lower Midwest) and below the Middle Atlantic, Pacific Southwest, and New England areas as well. Of course, if the regional market is limited to the size of the region itself or little more, this factor plays no significant role in a cost comparison.

Proximity to Resources

Canadian regions are well situated (with certain exceptions). There are two producing sectors—tobacco products and textiles—in which Canadian regions are apparently at a disadvantage since both cotton and raw tobacco production are concentrated in the southern United States. However, a substantial share of the tobacco used in the Canadian industry is supplied by domestic producers. Furthermore, these are resources with low transport costs; hence, any location disadvantages tend to lose significance. Petroleum production is also centered in the South. Unlike cotton and tobacco, required petroleum supplies are more expensive to transport; as a consequence, some Canadian (and U.S.) areas may be at a cost disadvantage vis-à-vis Texas, California, and the Canadian Prairies.

The eastern Canadian regions are in a relatively attractive position in terms of proximity to the newly developed major source of iron ore in Labrador.

Canadian areas are at least as well situated as comparable U.S. areas in terms of proximity to lumber supplies; British Columbia is an area of heavy lumber extraction for the wood products sector, and Quebec is the major source of wood for pulp and paper.

The only resources which may provide substantial competitive edge to the U.S. production locations are petroleum and coal; and even in these cases it should be noted that the Canadian Prairies have recently become a major source of petroleum supply, and the eastern industrial center of Canada is relatively close to North American coal concentration in Pennsylvania and West Virginia.

Not all aspects of relative raw material costs under free trade can be readily identified in advance. Especially under conditions of integrated, raw-material production and processing, the pricing of raw materials may have little relation to the cost of exploitation under free trade. Under the latter conditions, a lower return on the primary stage of production would be entirely compatible with more extensive development of Canadian rather than foreign resources if it can be accompanied by more efficient processing.

Proximity to Manufactured Supplies

An industry that is interested in its proximity to sources of immediate manufactured supplies will be attracted to those North American areas of heaviest industrial concentration along the Chicago-New York axis, which includes the West Lake, Capital, Middle Atlantic, and East Lake areas. These regions are well endowed with all lines of manufacturing and hence provide the best selection of available inputs. The heavy concentration of production in this central area in almost all industrial lines—along with the employment and income generated as a direct result—combined with the fact that this area is centrally located to the North American continent in purely spatial terms make this a preferred area in terms of proximity to intermediate manufactured supplies and in terms of a whole group of other location influences. The next best sources of intermediate supplies are those areas on the periphery of the central region—New England, Ontario, and Quebec. Almost without exception, they are superior to other U.S. regions in the south and west. The Canadian Maritimes and Prairies remain the least favored.

Capital Costs

Interest costs in Canada exceed those in the United States by just over one per cent. This is explained largely in terms of exchange-rate risk and other restraints on the free flow of capital between the two countries. They may remain substantially unchanged by tariff reductions. The Wonnacotts estimate that this higher interest carrying cost of debt could, under free trade, keep total costs for firms producing in Canada higher than in the United States by about one-tenth of one per cent.

If, in order to attract and hold equity in Canada, the rate of return on equity must be higher to the same degree as interest returns, then total Canadian manufacturing costs could as a consequence be raised by somewhat more than one per cent.

V. LOCATIONAL FORCES: A SUMMARY

In this study, we are not making precise predictions of where industry would go if there were free trade; we can only identify those regions in which growth conditions would be favorable.

Two sets of locational influences have been considered. The one set, summarized in Figure 1, consists of influences—such

Figure 1
A COMPARISON OF TOTAL COSTS, BY SELECTED INDUSTRY, 1958

Total Costs as Compared to Ontario %	Food & Beverages	Apparel & Related Products	Printing & Publishing	Electrical Machinery & Apparatus	Chemicals & Products	Metallic Products & Nonelectrical Machinery	Transportation Equipment
−10%							
−9							
−8							
−7							
−6							
−5							
−4							
−3			*Mar.*				
−2						*Que.*	*Que.*
			Prai.		Cap.		
				Que.	W.Lake		
−1	Cap.		*Que.*				
				Prai.	Mid.Ad.		
		Prai.			*Que.*		
ONTARIO	*Que.*			*Mar.*	N.Engl.		

Source: Ronald J. Wonnacott and Paul Wonnacott, *op. cit.*, p. 16.

as wage rates and transportation costs—which can be measured in terms of cost; these indicate that the major Canadian industrial region in Ontario and Quebec would have a noticeable advantage over adjacent U.S. regions representing the industrial heartland of that country. For example, Ontario has a cost advantage over the adjacent East Lake region of almost 2 per cent in food and beverages, about 5 per cent in printing, electrical machinery, nonelectrical machinery, and transportation equipment, and almost 10 per cent in apparel. (These percentages were calculated on the basis of an exchange rate of $1.00 Canadian = $1.00 U.S. The Canadian cost advantage would be even greater if the present exchange rate of $1.00 Canadian = 92.5 cents U.S. were retained into a period of free trade.)

On the other hand, it is just as clear from Figure 2 that the industrial triangle in the United States has a clear advantage over Ontario and Quebec in terms of proximity to markets, manufactured inputs, and competitors. In the event of free trade, then, we would expect this area of the United States to continue to be in a very good position to attract industries sensitive to these intangibles. In contrast, in industries where such intangibles are not important in the location decision, Ontario and Quebec should be attractive areas because of their favorable costs based on lower wages. But this is as far as a comparison of these two areas can be pushed. Because there is no way to trade off the nonquantifiable advantages of the U.S. heartland regions with the cost advantages of Ontario and Quebec, one cannot directly infer from this information alone how this area of Canada would fare in free trade competition. The question can only be answered by comparing Ontario and Quebec with the other U.S. regions outside the industrial triangle.

In such a comparison, Ontario and Quebec have an unambiguous advantage: they have an edge over these noncentral U.S. regions in terms of both quantifiable cost influences (Figure 1) and nonquantifiable influences (Figure 2). In short, they have more favorable quantifiable costs, based primarily on low wage rates, and they are closer to market, inputs, and competitors. Hence a conservative estimate of the free trade performance of these two Canadian provinces can be inferred from the past success of these nonheartland U.S. regions in the U.S. free trade area.

In summary, then, it would seem that the free trade prospects for Ontario and Quebec are better than the prospects of the U.S. regions outside the great industrial triangle. They may be better or worse than the prospects of the U.S. regions within the triangle, but the evidence on this issue is not clear.

So much for Ontario and Quebec. It may have been reason-

NONQUANTIFIABLE LOCATIONAL FORCES: THE STANDING OF COMPARISON AREAS RELATIVE TO ONTARIO IN TERMS OF PROXIMITY TO MARKETS, SUPPLIES, AND COMPETITORS; BY INDUSTRY, 1958

	Food & Beverages	Apparel & Related Products	Printing & Publishing	Electrical Machinery & Apparatus	Chemicals & Products	Metallic Products & Non-electrical Machinery	Transportation Equipment
Areas superior to Ontario in all 3 rankings	W.Lake Mid.Atl. E.Lake N.Engl.	W.Lake Mid.Atl. Cap. N.Engl.	W.Lake Mid.Atl. N.Engl.	W.Lake Mid.Atl. E.Lake	W.Lake Mid.Atl. Cap. E.Lake	W.Lake Cap. Mid.Atl. E.Lake N.Engl.	W.Lake E.Lake Cap. Mid.Atl.
Areas superior to Ontario in 2 rankings but inferior in 1	Cap.	P.S.W. *Que.* E.Lake	Cap. E.Lake P.S.W.	Cap. N.Engl. P.S.W.	N.Engl. P.S.W.	P.S.W.	N.Engl.
ONTARIO							
Areas inferior to Ontario in 2 rankings but superior in 1	*Que.* L.Mid.W. P.S.W. Up.Mid.W.	L.Mid.W. South *Br.Col.* P.N.W.	*Que.* *Br.Col.*	*Br.Col.*	L.Mid.W. South *Que.* S.West *Br.Col.*	L.M.W. Up.Mid.W. S.West *Br.Col.*	L.Mid.W. *Que.* P.S.W. South S. West P.N.W. Up.Mid.W.
Areas inferior to Ontario in all 3 rankings	South S.West *Br.Col.* Fla. Mount. P.N.W. *Prair.* *Mar.*	Up.Mid.W. S.West Fla. Mount. *Prair.* (*Mar.*) *	L.Mid.W. South Up.Mid.W. S.West P.N.W. Fla. Mount. *Mar.* *Prair.*	*Que.* L.Mid.W. South Up.Mid.W. P.N.W. S.West Fla. Mount. *Prair.* (*Mar.*) *	Up.Mid.W. Fla. Mount. P.N.W. *Prai.* *Mar.*	*Que.* South P.N.W. Fla. Mount. *Prair.* (*Mar.*) *	*Br.Col.* Fla. Mount. *Prair.* (*Mar.*) *

* No production statistics available.

Source: Wonnacotts, *op. cit.*, p. 24.

able to concentrate on them because Canadian industry is centered there: but what about the other provinces? Since they would not enjoy the advantage of Ontario and Quebec in lying so close to the North American industrial heartland, an evaluation of their free trade prospects is more difficult. From their standings in Figures 1 and 2, it is clear that they would not be favored locations for industry on the North American continent with free trade; but then with protection they are not either. The question is not whether free trade would bring them the kind of industry that better locations like New York (or Toronto) now enjoy, but whether free trade would improve their present situation.

There would be one major and obvious advantage of free trade to these regions: they would no longer have to pay such high prices for manufactured goods imported from central Canada. Whenever Ontario and Quebec manufacturers failed to meet U.S. competition, purchases could be made from U.S. sources.

British Columbia, an area of recent rapid growth, would seem to be in a good position to continue this expansion under free trade. Current growth is built on the wealth of resources in that province, and there is no reason to expect that resource extraction and processing would not prosper under free trade. Since there is not yet a substantial concentration of other industries in British Columbia, any losses to import competition that they might suffer would be unlikely to offset the advantages of lower import prices.

Most industry in the Prairies, as in British Columbia, is resource based, although in this case it is tied to agriculture or oil or other minerals. Prospects for these sectors depend heavily on how governmental policies in both areas might be modified. This question takes us a bit far afield, since such policies depend more on political than on economic considerations. As in British Columbia, the only other industries of any great significance are the service industries, which are largely immune to tariff changes. Since there is now no heavy concentration in this region of the sensitive industries being studied here, it is difficult to see how the damage caused by import competition in these areas could fail to be offset—indeed, outweighed—by the more widely distributed benefits of lower-priced imports.

The Maritimes would be in an ambiguous situation. The opening of the rich adjacent markets around Boston and New York might stimulate development of this area: these are more "natural" markets than many present Maritime markets in Montreal and points west in Canada. But the picture is not entirely clear, since Maritime industries serving Canadian markets would face much stiffer competition from U.S. industry.

The major hope for the Prairies and the Maritimes would be specialization. The best prospects are in industries in which transport costs are relatively low and labor costs high. Clearly, if the most attractive products for specialization are to be sought out, the analysis will have to search out subindustries in more detail than our broad industrial classifications allow. But even using our broad categories, low wages in the Maritimes and the Prairies more than offset high transport costs in several industries, including printing, electrical machinery, and rubber and plastic products. The first two create special problems, however, since it may be important for producers to be "in the center of things." However, there has been a tendency to separate publishing from the actual printing operation, with labor costs being the more important factor for printing and central location the more important for publishing. In electrical manufacturing, the Minneapolis-St. Paul area has enjoyed a conspicuous success, even though it faces much the same problem of geographical isolation as Winnipeg.

Tariffs

Costs of the two tariffs to Canada have been estimated at approximately 10.5 per cent of GNP. Of this, no more, and possibly much less, than 4.5 per cent can be attributed to the Canadian tariff. The balance can be attributed to the U.S. tariff; however, if this tariff is eliminated, it is likely that these losses would be recouped only after an extended time period—and even then perhaps not completely.

Adjustment to Free Trade

The foregoing suggests that the free trade adjustment is likely to occur within manufacturing rather than between manufacturing and nonmanufacturing. Moreover, Canadian specialization is likely to occur within broad industrial sectors, rather than between them. Thus, there is little danger of Canadians becoming "hewers of wood and drawers of water" in the event of reciprocal tariff elimination. This conclusion holds regardless of the direction of change in wage and exchange rates, though the form and the difficulty of adjustment will depend in part on the relative flexibility of the various elements in the system of prices.

Present high Canadian costs of manufacturing may be attributed largely to fragmented production lines, which are in turn a result of North American protection. Free trade would create pressures for reorganization and specialization of Canadian industry. With such reorganization, the Canadian capital-output ratio would decline towards the U.S. level, thus decreasing the gap between the Canadian demand for and supply of capital. In the longer-run, the Canadian import of capital would be diminished by a free trade arrangement. However, in the short-run, the need for additional capital to achieve the reorganization of industry might be substantial. Some have raised the question whether additional foreign financial resources would be readily available. Quite apart from U.S. balance-of-payments policies and the fact that a large inflow already takes place, there is the claim that many U.S. firms had previously established branches in Canada rather than to export to Canada, primarily because of the trade barriers. They, it is presumed, might stop supplying capital to their Canadian subsidiaries. This would appear to be possible for those who are abandoning their Canadian operations entirely. But for those who are forced by the tariff changes to rationalize their production, it seems most improbable that parent firms could not supply the required capital, at least through retained profits. This brings the argument back to the basic competitive position which these businesses could expect to enjoy at the end of the adjustment process.

The flexibility of wages and prices is clearly of great importance in assessing the form of the adjustment. There has been considerable concern about pressures for wage parity in industries in which productivity is not improving *pari passu.* Indeed, in the transitional phase of a Free Trade Association, there might be considerable advantage to a wage restraint which would enable the price and cost gap between Canadian and U.S. industries to close. Such a tendency would encourage the maintenance of capital flows, and partly as a consequence of this, deter any tendency for short-run downward pressures on the exchange rate which might otherwise occur. Given the kind of long-run prospect for competitive strength in Canadian manufacturing identified by the Wonnacotts, there would seem good reason for avoiding short-term distortions in the cost pattern arising out of any downward fluctuation of the exchange rate which was largely a consequence of the uncertainties affecting international capital flows or unusual wage or price pressures. One of the real advantages of a Free Trade Association should be the possibility of avoiding the distortion of costs which can arise in a sectoral scheme such as that applied to the automotive industries.

The foregoing comments have referred to the importance of the transition period. It must be recognized that while the opportunities and challenges facing Canadian industry will be heightened by the adoption of a liberal trade policy, the extent of adjustment will differ considerably from sector to sector and perhaps from firm to firm. Those firms which have developed a distinctive line of products and have access to technology and market facilities in other countries will be at a clear initial advantage. In general, the subsidiary firms associated with international corporations will find adjustment easier. Others who have tended to rely upon a protected domestic market have neither the experience, organization, nor even, perhaps, the attitudes required to reach aggressively into markets which may require substantial capital outlays and selling efforts to penetrate. The pattern of transitional policies must permit reorganization not only of production, but of marketing and research and development activity. Given the encouragement and assistance which appropriate public policies can supply, and the long-term commercial policy objectives of a Free Trade Association, businesses should find it possible to plan both the restructuring of production and investment programs meaningfully.

VI. THE RELATIVE MERITS FOR CANADA OF THE TRADITIONAL GATT APPROACH AND THE FREE TRADE ASSOCIATION APPROACH

From the Canadian viewpoint, the main problems associated with a further exploitation of the traditional multilateral approach to trade liberalization are two: 1) the fact that a clear commitment to free trade to be attained by a clearly defined route would provide Canadian producers with the motivation and confidence they require to undertake more specialized and, in some cases, larger scale production at internationally competitive cost levels; and 2) the probability that the traditional multilateral approach cannot bring about this kind of trade policy commitment, because it requires too general support for a commitment of that scope and because in the near future GATT countries as a group will be most unlikely to support substantial multilateral advances toward free trade.

Following the establishment of the two European communities and the Kennedy Round of GATT negotiations, the level of nominal tariffs between developed countries has been greatly reduced from the levels operative ten yars ago. There will soon be free trade in industrial goods within each of the two European groups, the EEC and EFTA, and the external tariffs of these groups and of the United States range for the most part between 5 and 10 per cent, after the Kennedy Round reductions have been affected through staged reductions ending in the early 1970's. Canada, Australia, and New Zealand will now be among those few with relatively higher tariffs and an assured tariff-free zone of less than 100 million people.

A number of conclusions about future trade policy have been drawn by GATT authorities and by spokesmen for the United States and the EEC:

1. No further general round of tariff reductions under GATT is likely, both because of the time it will take to effect

the Kennedy Round concessions and because the remaining tariffs are in many cases not high enough to generate much enthusiasm for the benefits their removal would provide.

2. Since tariffs of the larger trading partners are now low, any further negotiations would likely involve movements to free trade, and this would be meaningful only if such negotiations were also to include nontariff barriers.

3. Since multilateral across-the-board removal of remaining tariffs and nontariff barriers is too far reaching to contemplate, a sectoral approach is proposed, with the emphasis on the industrial materials sectors suggested as the first area for exploring the application of such an approach.

It is also generally acknowledged that the EEC will not be much interested in pressing ahead with this or any other GATT negotiations for several years. At this point, the common external tariff and common agricultural policy at present represent the main symbols of the Community's economic identity, and much of its substance.

Now it is quite clear that the above conclusions concerning GATT are not nearly so relevant for Canada as they are for the EEC and the United States (a fact which has not deterred some Canadian spokesmen from echoing them). There can be little doubt that Canada could benefit from free trade in industrial raw materials, but in fact many of her raw material exports already enjoy almost free access to important markets. And for other similar products, such as industrial chemicals, sectoral free trade could leave Canadian industry with significant negative effective protection unless materials and equipment used by the industry were also subject to sectoral free trade. And if all sectors except consumer goods were incorporated into sectoral free trade, the effective protection of such industries would be increased, an outcome which, as past Canadian experience suggests, could merely accentuate the present inefficient structuring of industry. Canada would be far better off economically with across-the-board free trade, assuming an appropriate transition period and adjustment policies.

Canada's trading interests are sufficiently diversified that she is likely to be interested in a number of alternative groupings which would provide the market opportunities required.

Clearly, the only partner essential to all really relevant groupings is the United States. At the same time, political considerations make it desirable from the Canadian viewpoint for other countries to be involved. Of course, if Canada were to join in a Free Trade Association with the United States alone, the nature of the Free Trade Association would permit Canadian participation in other free trade groupings even if the United States were not a member of such groups. But it would be more likely politically, and in some respects more desirable economically, if a larger grouping could be formed. The participation of one or more of Britain, the other EFTA countries, the EEC if interested, and Japan, Australia, and New Zealand would significantly alter the nature of the specific adjustments and opportunities in the Canadian economy. But it seems most unlikely that Canada will be faced in general with significantly more serious reorganizational difficulties under these circumstances than would occur in a purely Canada-U.S. Association.

One final point—there is little that Canada can do alone to provide scope for the exports of the developing industries of the countries of Latin America, Asia, and Africa. The wider the association of developed countries which can be formed, the better the prospect for important unilateral concessions to those nations. Canadian interest in meeting the trade as well as the aid requirements of these countries will continue to be a factor encouraging Canadian support for substantial and early progress toward free trade.

NOTES

1. N. H. Lithwick, *Prices, Productivity, and Canada's Competitive Position* (Montreal: Canadian Trade Committee, 1967).

2. B. W. Wilkinson, *Canada's International Trade: An Analysis of Recent Trends and Patterns* (Montreal: Canadian Trade Committee, 1968).

3. B. W. Wilkinson, *op. cit.*, p. 23.

4. Some have insisted that migration of people might prove to be an important means of adjustment.

5. H. E. English, *Industrial Structure in Canada's International Competitive Position* (Montreal: Canadian Trade Committee,

1964); Ronald J. Wonnacott and Paul Wonnacott, *Free Trade Between the United States and Canada: The Potential Economic Effects* (Cambridge: Harvard University Press, 1967); H. C. Eastman and S. Stykolt, *The Tariff and Competition in Canada*, (Toronto: Macmillan, 1967). Forthcoming is a series of studies on particular industries and regional sectors (Montreal: Canadian Trade Committee, forthcoming).

The Monetary Implications of a Free Trade Association

by Harry G. Johnson

I. INTRODUCTION

In the course of the movement since World War II toward the liberalization of international trade, in which the proposal for a Free Trade Association seems to many people the logical next step, ideas on the relation between cooperation in the reduction of trade barriers and cooperation in international monetary affairs have undergone substantial change. At the outset, the planners of Bretton Woods, who established the institutional framework that governs international economic relations to this day, envisaged that money and trade would each be governed by a separate new international institution—in the event, the International Monetary Fund and the General Agreement on Tariffs and Trade. These institutions were intended to operate largely independently, but with the monetary institution being the senior partner, in the sense that balance-of-payments disequilibria would justify the use of controls on short-term capital movements, the use of temporary quota restrictions on imports, and concerted trade discrimination against a country whose currency was declared "scarce," in temporary contravention of the general GATT principles of nondiscrimination among trading partners and protection by tariff only.

The immediate postwar problem, however, turned out to be to unravel the tangle of restrictions on European trade and payments that developed rapidly in response to the so-called "dollar shortage." This problem was tackled, not through the new international institutions, but on the basis of regional co-operation through the Organization for European Economic Co-operation, the European side of the Marshall Plan. In this first effort toward freeing trade on a regional basis, it was found essential to coordinate cooperation in the liberation of trade with cooperation in the restoration of transferability and convertibility of currencies. The agency established for this purpose, the European Payments Union, functioned successfully until its disappearance with the restoration of convertibility of the European currencies.

The successful experience with the EPU was at least partly responsible for the fact that the Treaty of Rome, which formally initiated the next major step toward the establishment of free trade on a regional basis—the formation of the European Economic Community—envisaged monetary cooperation among the members as an important part of the operations of the Community. The exact form of cooperation envisaged, however, was never precisely defined, and in any event, little has been accomplished in this area, though this may be merely a symptom of the more general failure of the Community to move on as expected from customs union and common agricultural policy to full economic integration. The second European regional free trade arrangement, the European Free Trade Association, made no provision for formal monetary co-operation.

In the meanwhile, with the successful completion of the Marshall Plan and general restoration of convertibility, and subsequently with the chronic weakness of sterling and the persistence of substantial United States balance-of-payments deficits since 1958, the IMF system of international monetary organization has encountered and weathered a series of potentially disruptive disturbances, culminating in the devaluation of sterling in November, 1967. In the course of this experience there has developed a high degree of consultation and cooperation among the treasury and central bank officials of the major countries, and between them and the officials of the International Monetary Fund. There remain, unfortunately, deep-seated and potentially dangerous differences of opinion and policy between France and some of her European partners on the one hand, and the United States, the United Kingdom, and a group of lesser countries on the other, which differences have been reflected in the four-year delay in arriving at the contingency plan for a new form of international reserve agreed upon at the September, 1967, Rio meetings of the World Bank and the Fund, and in the uncertainties that still surround the implementation of that agreement, and in the French tactics of rumor-mongering and noncooperation during the period of sterling devaluation and the gold speculation that followed. But the machinery of consultation, confrontation, cooperation, and collaboration has become reasonably firmly established, and constitutes a system for informed and immediate decision taking far more effective than anything that could have been imagined by the postwar planners at Bretton Woods.

In the light of this postwar experience of the freeing of trade on a regional basis and of international monetary cooperation, it would appear not to be necessary for a Free Trade Association arrangement to include formal arrangements for monetary cooperation among its members, for two reasons. First, both experience and theory indicate that regional free trade arrangements do not require formal monetary cooperation on a regional basis; this is especially true for a Free Trade Association, which does not contemplate eventual full economic integration. Second, effective machinery for consultation and cooperation in international monetary affairs already exists, and is geared into the international monetary system. Two other considerations support the same conclusion. One is a general point of principle. The intention of the NAFTA proposal is an open-ended arrangement, which other countries—including the EEC as a group—would subsequently be welcome to join, not an exclusive grouping designed to maximize the economic benefits derived by members as contrasted with nonmembers; consistency with this intention would indicate the desirability of minimizing formal arrangements differentiating members from nonmembers. The other is a practical consideration. Apart from an agreement to establish a single currency for the area to promote economic integration, which would be a further step beyond free trade which the prospective members of NAFTA would be very unlikely to consider, the logical purpose of formal arrangements for monetary cooperation would be to lend the financial support of the two largest members, the reserve currency countries, to each other, and especially to the smaller member countries when one of them got into serious balance-of-payments deficit; but with the pound and the dollar both in chronic deficit, and likely to remain under pressure for some years to come, the United Kingdom and the United States are not in a position to freely offer balance-of-payments support to each other and to smaller members.

While there is thus no argument for formal arrangements for monetary cooperation in a NAFTA, and several arguments against such arrangements, there are a variety of ways in which member countries might usefully cooperate to improve the international monetary system, and collaborate to smooth the operations of that system as it affects themselves. There is also the possibility that the system will break down in a crisis, in which case it would be highly desirable to have a contingency plan for maintaining orderly monetary relations among the members of NAFTA and minimizing the damaging effects of the crisis on their international trade and domestic economies. These aspects of monetary cooperation are discussed in detail below. As a preliminary to that discussion, however, it is necessary to describe briefly the present international monetary system and its problems.

II. THE INTERNATIONAL MONETARY SYSTEM

The present international monetary system is one of fixed rates of exchange between national currencies, based on the obligation of each country to maintain a fixed par value for its currency in terms of gold. In the case of the United States, this obligation is fulfilled by the legal obligation on the U.S. Treasury to buy gold from, or sell gold to, official monetary institutions in other countries at the official price. The other leading countries fulfill the obligation by buying or selling U.S. dollars or other major currencies in the foreign exchange markets so as to keep the value of their own currency within a narrow margin of its par value, holding reserves in the form of gold, sterling, or dollars to enable them to offset excesses of commercial demand for foreign exchange over the supplies forthcoming at the current exchange rate.

The system rests on gold as the ultimate international monetary reserve. Any such commodity-based monetary system is subject to the potential problem that the growth of the basic reserve through new production of the commodity will not match the growth of the demand for reserves, and especially that the stock of reserves will grow less rapidly than the demand for them. This has been a chronic problem of the gold standard in the twentieth century. It was responsible for the development in the 1920's of the gold exchange standard system, under which countries held their reserves in the form of other countries' gold-backed currencies, the system which crashed so disastrously during the early 1930's. It was a major objective of the architects of the International Monetary Fund to guard against a repetition of international financial crisis, by providing international liquidity on a credit basis in the form of rights to draw other countries' currencies against the deposit of one's own, up to a formally specified ceiling and subject to various conditions. But the problem reemerged after World War II. The rate of growth of monetary gold stocks—determined by the net outcome of new production, Russian gold sales, and private purchases for hoarding or for commercial use—has fallen far short of the rate of growth of demand for international reserves. The difference has been made good by the sustained U.S. deficit, which has enabled the demand to be satisfied partly by redistribution of the United States' originally large gold reserves to other countries and, more significantly, by the accumulation of holdings of reserves in the form of U.S. dollars.

This solution could only be a transitory one, however, for several reasons, of which the most important are its dependence on a continuing U.S. deficit and the continuing willingness of the other countries to finance that deficit by accumulating dollars, and its effect in steadily worsening the U.S. international liquidity position (the ratio of dollar liabilities to foreign monetary institutions to the U.S. gold reserves) and thereby undermining confidence in the maintenance of the gold value of the dollar. For the longer run, a more fundamental solution to the problem of providing an adequate rate of growth of international liquidity is required. The problem has been under discussion among academic experts since the late 1950's, and under official study since 1963, which study has produced the contingency plan for Special Drawing Rights agreed on at the September meeting in Rio de Janeiro of the Governors of the International Monetary Fund. Basically, there have been two alternative possible solutions to this problem of the system. One is to raise the price of gold, which besides increasing the monetary value of existing stocks would increase the current rate of production and draw gold back out of private hoards; this solution has been advocated in principle by a number of economists, especially Jacques Rueff, but, more important, many private citizens have been willing to speculate that the price of gold will be raised as a consequence of the system breaking down in a crisis. The other is to supplement gold—and sterling and the dollar—by the creation of a new international reserve asset based on credit. This is the purpose of the contingency plan for Special Drawing Rights approved at Rio. In principle, this plan marks a very long step ahead in official thinking about the international monetary system, since it proposes a pure credit asset based on acceptance of it in international settlements, with no lip service to the irrelevant commercial banking principle that liabilities must be backed by assets. It is therefore an important step toward the ultimate dethronement of gold as the basic reserve of the system, and the replacement of it by a rationally managed credit reserve money. On the other hand, the long delay in arriving at this point reflects a deep disagreement between the Americans (and the British) on the one hand, and the Europeans (led by the French) on the other. This disagreement, which has focused on the control of the supply of the new asset, reflects the views on each side of the U.S. deficit-European surplus situation that that side has been asked to bear an undue share of the burden of adjustment, and the associated European desire for a larger voice in the control of the International Monetary Fund. The fact that the implementation of the contingency plan has been made conditional on changes in the control of the INF to this end may foreshadow considerable delay in the actual inauguration of the plan for Special Drawing Rights.

Aside from the problem of providing adequate long-run growth of liquidity, the present international monetary system entails two other problems requiring solution.

The first is the problem of confidence, or more accurately, the problem that the development of distrust of a currency may lead to a flight of capital from it based on the expectation of a devaluation. The problem of confidence comes in two versions in the present system. First, there may be a flight out of (or onto) a particular currency other than the dollar, prompted by fear of impending devaluation (hope of impending appreciation). Where the currency in question is agreed by international officialdom to be sound and the exchange rate sustainable, such capital flights can be offset or absorbed without serious disturbance, through inter-central-bank lending of funds back to the country or countries from which the capital has moved, for the short period required for the situation to calm down. At an earlier stage of postwar experience, there were some grounds for fearing that the central bankers might lose their nerve on one of these occasions, and precipitate a crisis. The successful weathering of a series of potentially serious international monetary disturbances, and the machinery of close contact built up in the light of experience, however, provide grounds for regarding this as no longer a serious problem of the system. There does, however, remain a rather different problem: While current methods of cooperation among central banks are quite adequate for the provision of temporary finance in times of crises, the magnitude and duration of the deficits of the chief chronically deficit countries would seem to require international lending and borrowing on a larger scale and for longer periods than fit comfortably into traditional central banking operations and the IMF concept. It would therefore seem desirable to develop new machinery to provide larger and longer-term intergovernmental loans.

The second type of confidence problem arises when there is an expectation that the United States will not be able to hold the $35.00 per ounce price of gold. When this first happened, in the autumn of 1960, it manifested itself in a rise in the price of gold in the London market, because the Bank of England, which normally stabilizes that market, was unsure whether if it continued its stabilization operations it could replenish its gold supplies by use of its dollar reserves without violating the United States embargo on the sale of its gold reserves to private purchasers. This difficulty was resolved by the formation of the gold pool, by which the major central banks agreed to share in the Bank of England's stabilization operations, supplying gold for sale and dividing up gold purchased in fixed proportions. This arrangement worked satisfactorily until 1966–1967, because until then on balance the pool acquired substantial amounts of gold; but then various changes in demand and supply raised the prospect of growing net sales of gold from official reserves, and induced the expectation that the participants in the pool might lose their nerve and attempt to divorce the monetary and nonmonetary markets for gold, letting the London price rise. This was the climate of opinion on which French policy operated after the devaluation of sterling to encourage a raid on the dollar by speculators in gold, by leaking various rumors and the information that France had ceased to participate in the pool in June. Fortunately, the speculation was checked by a firm statement by the United States that the gold pool would continue to operate. However, the elementary economics of holding down the price of one commodity—and one which has potentially important industrial as well as decorative uses if its price is competitive—ensure that eventually in the future, gold will be drained out of official reserves into private hands through the gold pool, a process that might provoke an international monetary crisis but that one hopes would instead lead to the demonetization of gold as an international reserve.

The final major problem of the present international monetary system is the so-called "problem of adjustment." International imbalances must eventually be corrected; and if the international monetary system is to serve its ultimate purpose of facilitating freedom of trade and capital movements, the adjustments must be made primarily through movements of relative prices and interest rates. Relative price adjustments can be made in two ways: through domestic deflation in deficit countries and inflation in surplus countries, relative to world price trends, or through currency devaluation or appreciation.

It was the serious difficulty and social hardship of the deflationary method of the interwar gold standard that led to the inclusion in the Articles of Agreement of the IMF of provision for the agreed devaluation of a currency in the case of "fundamental disequilibrium." However, as a result of dissatisfaction with the experience of devaluation in 1949, the emergence of the dollar as an international reserve currency whose value in terms of gold, it was thought, could not be changed, and for various other reasons, the use of exchange rate change as a method of adjustment available to a major country was increasingly ruled out of consideration until the events of 1967 forced the devaluation of sterling. It is as yet too early to determine whether that devaluation will initiate a reversal of trend back toward the original IMF concept, or whether the bumbling way it was effected and the ensuing speculation against the dollar will reinforce the previously mounting aversion to any change in the major exchange rates. For the sake of the argument, however, it is necessary to make some assumption on this point, and the latter alternative seems more justifiable as well as more probable.

If a system of rigidly fixed exchange rates is to be maintained, payments imbalances must be corrected by the adjustment of the domestic currency to the international, by means of some sort of equivalent to the inflationary-deflationary mechanism of the gold standard. Yet countries have adopted other objectives than balance-of-payments equilibrium—commitments to the maintenance of full employment, the avoidance of price inflation, the achievement of a satisfactory rate of economic growth, and, in the case of the United States, the prosecution of the war in Vietnam—to which in practice they attach a higher priority. Consequently there has been considerable reluctance to use the classical gold-standard policies of deflation in deficit countries and inflation in surplus countries—especially as the United Kingdom and the United States, which have been the deficit countries, have special historical reasons for wanting to minimize unemployment, while the European surplus countries have special historical reasons for wanting to avoid inflation. In place of deflation of demand, the deficit countries have been attempting to develop the use of "incomes policy" or "wage-price guideposts policy"—the policy of inducing or coercing labor and management to keep prices stable and wage increases within the limits permitted by increases in productivity. This policy, which is in any case of very dubious effectiveness—particularly as regards prices, which are the ultimate object of control—presupposes a context of inflation in the surplus countries, and must necessarily operate very slowly and erratically to restore international competitiveness. The classical policies of deflation and inflation have, of course, been applied to some extent; but they have been applied reluctantly, under the pressures of deficit and surplus, and to the accompaniment of much mutual recrimination between deficit and surplus countries. As a result the process of international adjustment has been slow and erratic—a process of "reluctant adjustment" is bound to be uncertain and unsatisfactory.

In order to keep their deficits within manageable limits consistent with the priorities of other policy objectives, in the absence of an effective method of adjusting relative prices, deficit countries have resorted to various policies of intervention which have come to be regarded officially as adjustment policies, but are in fact policies for "financing" the deficit. These include the policies of preferring domestic over foreign suppliers in government procurement, the tying of foreign aid, tax changes designed to discourage overseas investment and/or encourage exports, the U.S. interest equalization tax, and the "voluntary" programs of restraint on direct and indirect foreign investment by U.S. manufacturing corporations and financial institutions. A number of these devices have their counterparts on the side of the surplus countries, for example, financial regulations designed to discourage capital inflows of various sorts. The general effect of these devices is to interfere, in the name of preserving the international monetary system, with the freedom of international trade and payments that the system is intended to facilitate.

The same is essentially true also of a policy method for mentioning full employment while offsetting any associated current account deficit with a capital inflow, or matching the current account surplus by a capital outflow of the same size, which has been much propounded—and applied—in recent years: the so-called "fiscal-monetary mix" policy. The basic theory calls for the government to select the mixture of monetary contraction and fiscal expansion required to set domestic interest rates at the level that will secure the required international capital movement. While this technique appears superficially to make use only of orthodox general techniques of overall economic control traditionally regarded as "liberal," in fact it works by tailoring the economy's rate of saving, and hence indirectly its economic growth, to what the current account surplus or deficit will permit—which may be very different from what the public would choose if it could choose subject to the current account constraint on the total capital movement permitted.

There is, therefore, a problem outstanding of improving the international adjustment mechanism so as to reduce the need for resort to these types of policies, which as already noted are inconsistent with the purposes which the international monetary system is intended to serve.

III. POSSIBILITIES OF INTERNATIONAL MONETARY COOPERATION IN AN FTA

For the reason given in Section I, the FTA proposal does not require formal arrangements for monetary cooperation among its members. There would be, however, a basis for informal cooperation among them, inasmuch as the key initial members, Canada, the United Kingdom, and the United States, are more alike in their fundamental thinking about economic policy questions and their general approach to policy problems than the advanced industrial nations as a group. In particular, their thinking may be described as Keynesian and their approach as pragmatic, in contrast to the pre-Keynesian thinking and dogmatism-cum-logic-chopping that at least occasionally governs the approach of some of the European countries to international monetary problems. It is also relevant that these three countries were primarily responsible for designing the International Monetary Fund, and that the United States and the United Kingdom have played dominating roles in the subsequent evolution of that institution.

The analysis of the present international monetary system in Section II indicates that there are many opportunities for informal cooperation of the type envisaged, both with respect to the improvement of the system and with respect to operations by members within the system.

As regards the improvement of the system, members could cooperate in pressing for the implementation of the contingency plan for Special Drawing Rights and for the steady expansion of the use of this new form of international reserve asset. In the early stages of the discussion of the liquidity problem, there was some tendency for the two reserve-currency countries to be reluctant to support the creation of a new form of international liquidity, rival to their currencies, because it was then widely believed that this use of their currencies as reserves by other countries yielded them important economic gains. Subsequent experience has made it clear that their overriding interest is in the establishment of a system that will supply additional genuinely international reserves on an adequate scale. The transition to the new SDR system will pose certain technical problems of "coexistence" of SDR's, reserve currencies, and gold, which may require special cooperative measures between the U.K. and the U.S. monetary authorities. If, as was suggested in Section II might happen, disagreement over control of the SDR's and of the IMF led to indefinite delay in the institution of SDR it might prove desirable for the FTA group to take the initiative of creating an SDR or similar credit-reserve facility for their own use, making it available to any nonmember countries that were willing to participate.

With respect to operations by FTA members within the present international monetary system, there are a variety of ways in which cooperation could prove helpful, if members were willing to cooperate.

In the first place, the establishment of free trade among the members might make it desirable to institute closer arrangements for consultation on and coordination of members' domestic and balance-of-payments policies. Free trade on a regional basis does not necessarily imply that members will be likely to encounter more serious balance-of-payments policies than heretofore, since while it would mean that disequilibrating charges in domestic effective demand and wage-price levels in individual members would be likely to show up more quickly in balance-of-payments deficits or surpluses, it would also mean more direct competitive pressures on national wage-price levels to keep them aligned with one another. But it would mean, most probably, that the effects of such disequilibrating developments as did occur, together with those of corrective or other policy changes, would be relatively more concentrated on the economies of fellow members. This would imply that the smooth working of the free trade arrangements would be facilitated by mutual understanding of the policy problems facing individual members and the reasons underlying their policy decisions; and by cooperation in attempting to prevent serious balance-of-payments disturbances from arising in the first place.

In the second place, while present arrangements for handling the two types of confidence problems that may arise in the present international monetary system are probably adequate to the purpose—at least they stood the test of the sterling devaluation and gold speculation of the end of 1967—and while the weak balance-of-payments positions of the dollar and the pound would seem to preclude any near-term special arrangements in FTA for mutual support against problems of this kind, it might in the longer run prove desirable to work out such special arrangements, especially if and when the U.S. balance of payments returns to a surplus or near-balanced position. Such arrangements could include formal arrangements for members automatically to accumulate holdings of the currencies of members temporarily in deficit, to assist such members to overcome speculation against their currencies; such arrangements would, of course, have to be geared into machinery for consultation on and coordination of general economic policies. The other members could also assist more positively in overcoming speculation against the dollar (speculation on a rise in the price of gold) through arrangements to put some of their own gold reserves at the disposal of the United States in case of need, according to some agreed sharing formula (Canada, for example, is not presently a member of the gold pool). To set up arrangements of this kind, however, would imply acceptance of the proposition that gold derives its value from the dollar and not vice versa, and of a formal commitment to support the present international role of the dollar, which the other members might not be willing to undertake, and which the potential value of the arrangements in helping to preserve the system might not justify.

In the third place, there is the possibility of special measures of cooperation in the administration of what are currently classed as methods of adjustment, though as pointed out in Section II they are mostly methods of financing balance-of-payments disequilibria. Thus, though considerable skepticism was expressed in Section II about the potentialities of incomes policy, it is possible that it would be made more effective by recognition of it as primarily a tool of international adjustment rather than of domestic anti-inflation policies, which recognition might be fostered by consultation and cooperation among FTA members. Similarly the adverse consequences on economic efficiency of the resort to tying of foreign aid, preferences for domestic producers in government procurement, and interventions in the export of private capital might be mitigated by implementing these policies on a FTA-wide basis. To attempt to do so, however, would raise two problems that might well be better avoided: first, such measures would have to be implemented by all members, not just those in deficit, and coordinated; and second, they involve discrimination in favor of other members as against outsiders going substantially beyond the original concept of an open-ended free trade area. It would probably be more satisfactory, therefore, to leave such arrangements to be determined by ad hoc agreement on particular problem cases, the method employed to deal with the impact of U.S. capital-export restrictions on the flow of U.S. capital to Canada.

While these three possible areas for cooperation with respect to international monetary affairs and balance-of-payments problems have been discussed separately, it is self-evident that measures of cooperation in them would necessarily be interrelated. For example, agreement to discriminate in favor of partner countries in the application of controls on trade and capital movements would most likely have to be conditional on a reciprocal agreement to help to finance any consequent deficits.

Finally, there is the possibility that the present international monetary system will break down in crisis, rather than—as is greatly to be hoped—gradually being transformed into a rational system based on international credit reserves and cut free of the link with gold. This possibility calls for contingency planning, if a repetition of the constriction of international trade and payments by new forms of control that followed on the international monetary collapse of the 1930's is to be prevented from breaking up the Free Trade Association arrangements. One possibility would be for other members to peg their currencies to the dollar, while the dollar itself was allowed to float against nonmember currencies. This would preserve whatever advantages in facilitating international trade and payments may be claimed for the fixed rate system, with regard to economic relations among the members, while enabling the latter to avoid the need to impose new interventions designed to discriminate against nonmembers. Alternatively, given the wide variations in the relative importance to the individual members of trade with other members and with nonmembers respectively, it might be preferable for members to move to exchange rates fluctuating freely in relation to the currencies of other members as well to the currencies of nonmembers. This system would be quite compatible with the maintenance of free trade among the members, and would even permit relaxation of the interventionist policies that currently form part of the so-called adjusted mechanism. But it would be necessary to rely on the sense of responsibility of individual members of the Group, and on the machinery of consultation and coordination, to restrain members from any temptation to use floating exchange rates for beggar-my-neighbor trade policies.